HOSEA

Readings: A New Biblical Commentary

General Editor
John Jarick

HOSEA

Second Edition

Francis Landy

SHEFFIELD PHOENIX PRESS

2011

Copyright © Sheffield Phoenix Press, 2011
First published by Sheffield Academic Press, 1995

Published by Sheffield Phoenix Press
Department of Biblical Studies, University of Sheffield
Sheffield S3 7QB England

www.sheffieldphoenix.com

All rights reserved.
No part of this publication may be reproduced or transmitted
in any form or by any means, electronic or mechanical,
including photocopying, recording or any information storage
or retrieval system, without the publisher's permission in
writing.

A CIP catalogue record for this book
is available from the British Library

Typeset by Vikatan Publishing Solutions, Chennai, India

Printed by
Lightning Source Inc.

ISBN 978-1-905048-98-4 (hardback)
ISBN 978-1-905048-99-1 (paperback)

Contents

Preface to the Second Edition and Acknowledgments	vii
List of Abbreviations	ix
Introduction	1
Hosea 1.1–2.3	13
Hosea 2.4–25	25
Hosea 3	47
Hosea 4	53
Hosea 5	71
Hosea 6	86
Hosea 7	97
Hosea 8	113
Hosea 9	126
Hosea 10	142
Hosea 11	157
Hosea 12	168
Hosea 13.1–14.1	181
Hosea 14.2–10	197
Select Bibliography	207
Index of Authors	213
Index of References	215

Preface to the Second Edition and Acknowledgments

This is a revised edition of my original commentary on Hosea, published in 1995. It differs from the first edition in a number of ways. I have provided a translation for each chapter. Translation of Hosea is an impossible task, since the meaning is dependent on multiple ambiguities, and much is totally obscure. I have avoided, insofar as is possible, representing the ambiguities in the translation, for instance by putting alternatives in brackets, and I have not attempted to communicate the power of the poetry. The translation is simply to enable the reader to follow how I am interpreting the text, without resorting to translations like the NRSV or the NJPS, which are very different.

Secondly, I have redivided the chapters so as to coincide with those of the Hebrew text. There was no literary justification for my original decision to make chs. 4-7 into three units, with demarcations at 5.7 and 6.6. The text can be read in many ways, and conventional chapter divisions are as good as any.

Thirdly, I have updated the commentary, so as to take into account recent scholarship. Since the commentary was originally published, several important literary studies have appeared, notably those by Sherwood, Keefe and Morris. Of recent commentaries, I have been most indebted to Ben Zvi and Macintosh. Ben Zvi's commentary in the Forms of Old Testament Literature (FOTL) series is unique for its very close attention to wordplays and allusions and its assumption of a sophisticated original readership. Ben Zvi also ascribes the entire composition to literati in 5th century Jerusalem, for whom the fate of the northern kingdom was a distant if instructive memory. This is not a view I have adopted in this commentary, in which I try to maintain both an 8th and a 5th century perspective. However, fundamentally I am not interested in original readerships. For me, the book is the work of a poet, trying to make sense of a world on the eve of destruction, in brilliant, jarring, and recondite language. This is not a work that could ever be understood, since its subject is both mysterious and mystical, the fateful encounter of God and humanity. Equally, like much of the greatest poetry, it is written in the face of death, a skirmish in the struggle between language and silence, meaning and non-meaning. To quote Hélène Cixous, "to begin (writing, living) we must have death... the writers I love above all are of the dying-clairvoyant kind" (*Three Steps on the Ladder of Writing* pp. 7, 63).

The Readings series is intended to liberate contributors from the constraints of conventional commentaries, such as engagement with the history of scholarship and from institutional interests. It encourages free interpretive play, acknowledging that all interpretations are partial and ideologically motivated. It thus has a certain postmodern aura, in that it is less interested in historical veracity and original meaning than in the imaginative possibilities the text opens up. I am not convinced, though, that this is the whole story. For as readers, we have a responsibility to the poet and the world for which the poet speaks. I am not sure I have been successful; recent studies have shown me many other possibilities. However, throughout I have tried to avoid the temptation of paraphrase. It is not my job to translate the poetry into language accessible to the modern reader and into simple and acceptable messages. Instead I wish to convey how problematic it is; its aesthetic power, its beauty and horror; how metaphors and other figures of speech complicate meaning, and how they become instruments for the subversion of one's implicit understandings of the world. And I have tried to write as well as I can.

Some of my assistants have departed this life. In particular, Frances is pursuing her literary career in a different feline world. Zilpah is still with us, but resting on her royalties. Our family has grown with the addition of our son, Joseph, and several pets, but, apart from Joseph, none shows any literary propensities. I remain grateful to the Social Sciences and Humanities Research Council of Canada, who helped to fund some of the work; to the Phoenix Press and to the series editor, John Jarick, for offering to republish this work and for assistance and advice; to my research assistant, Timothy Langille; to Linda Bridges, for retyping missing material; and, as ever, to my wife, Bennett Matthews, for making life worthwhile.

February 19th, 2008

List of Abbreviations

AB	Anchor Bible
AV	Authorised Version
BN	*Biblische Notizen*
BZ	*Biblische Zeitschrift*
BZAW	Beihefte zur *Zeitschrift für die alttestamentliche Wissenschaft*
CBQ	*Catholic Biblical Quarterly*
ETL	*Ephemerides theologicae lovanienses*
ETR	*Etudes théologiques et Religieuses*
FOTL	Forms of the Old Testament Literature
HAR	*Hebrew Annual Review*
HB	Hebrew Bible
HR	*History of Religions*
JANES	*Journal of the Near Eastern Society of Columbia University*
JBL	*Journal of Biblical Literature*
JNES	*Journal of Near Eastern Studies*
JNWSL	*Journal of Northwest Semitic Languages*
JSJ	*Journal of Jewish Studies*
JSOT	*Journal for the Study of the Old Testament*
NJPS	Tanakh: The Holy Scriptures. The New JPS Translation according to the Traditional Hebrew Text
NRSV	New Revised Standard Version
OTWSA	Die Ou Testamentiese Werkgemeenskap in Suid-Afrika
PEQ	*Palestine Exploration Quarterly*
RevExp	*Review and Expositor*
RevScRel	*Revue des sciences religieuses*
SBL	Society of Biblical Literature
SEÅ	*Svensk exegetisk årsbok*
SJOT	*Scandinavian Journal of the Old Testament*
TQ	*Theologische Quartalschrift*
VT	*Vetus Testamentum*
ZAW	*Zeitschrift für die alttestamentliche Wissenschaft*

Introduction

The Book and the Author

How are we to imagine Hosea, the person and the book? Does the person disappear into the book? Is he simply the creation, the projection of later scribal circles?[1] The book itself complicates the issue by supposing at least two levels of composition, that of the prophet/God himself—personae split in the book—and that of the transmitters who composed the first verse and, perhaps, the last.[2] The first chapter and the third suppose different authors, since the former is a third person narrative and the latter a first person one; thus disunity is already implicit in the text. In addition, ch. 3 presents itself as an excerpt from a longer autobiographical account. Our text is accordingly both a torso and a conglomerate.

Most critics regard the text as having grown by accretion, and distinguish between the words of the historical Hosea and those of his epigones. The discrimination of redactional levels will, however, disrupt poetic unity, and introduce presuppositions as to what the prophet might or might not have believed or written, which will themselves be used as the basis for determining his thought. For this reason, no attempt to ascertain the development of the text is made in this work. On the other hand, there

---

1. This position has been forcibly argued in relation to Jeremiah by R.P. Carroll in his *Jeremiah: A Commentary* (Old Testament Library; London: SCM, 1986) and Jeremiah (Old Testament Guides; Sheffield: JSOT Press, 1989).

2. Most critics ascribe the last verse to later Wisdom circles; if so, it would introduce a third level of explicit composition. However, H. Fisch ('Hosea: A Poetics of Violence', in *Poetry with a Purpose: Biblical Poetics and Interpretation* [Bloomington: Indiana University Press, 1988], pp. 137-58) treats it as a metapoetic comment by the poet/prophet (p. 148); one could equally well attribute it to the Judean framers of the first verse, or whichever person or community was responsible for its composition (Ehud Ben-Zvi, oral communication).

are some passages which do seem anachronistic; the reference to "David their king" in 3.5 is an outstanding example. To claim that these and these alone are supplements would be arbitrary. Consequently, I will work with a double focus, on the prophet and on the Judean tradents, on the eighth century in northern Israel, and on whatever period(s) may supply the context for its later reception and composition. Instead of authorship, we have a play of mirrors: the prophet speaks and/or writes for and about a future, including those listeners who write the script of the prophet who writes about them. Analogously, the book is set, extremely realistically, in a world that is about to disappear; but it speaks also of that world from the other side of the disappearance, from the perspective of the survivors.

The book, despite its inherent incompleteness and multiplicity of authorship, has a certain coherence. On the narrative plane, it begins with the commencement of Yhwh's word to Hosea, his marriage and the birth of his children, and ends with the fall of Samaria and the hope for future restoration. The chapters follow a rough chronological sequence; in the early chapters, for instance, the Assyrian peril is barely evident, while in the later ones it becomes ever more dominant. Numerous cross-references bind the chapters together; one might illustrate this by the fulfillment of the threat to abolish the Israelite monarchy at the beginning of the book (1.4) at its conclusion (13.11).

The book is generally divided into three parts: chs. 1–3, 4–11, and 12–14. Each of these parts has considerable internal integration and ends with a very similar vision of return; there are notable connections between them.[3] The narrative of ch. 1 is a prototype of that of the entire book, which ends with the death of mother and children; we will also consider ch. 2 as a *mise-en-abyme*, or microcosm, of the whole. Yet there is nothing to say that the three parts are by the same author, or that they

---

3. Some of these might be attributed to later redaction; for instance, 3.5 and 11.10-11 are among the passages most widely believed to be very late. Similarly, the beginning of the second part, 4.1-3, reverses the vision of the cosmic covenant in 2.20; both of these are frequently held to be additions. However, the more correlations one finds, the less convincing becomes the theory of supplementation. For example, the parallel between 3.5 and 11.10-11 depends on the convergence of the verbs 'dwell' and 'return,' which requires a linkage between 3.4 and 3.5. Without 3.4, the whole point of ch. 3 disappears.

share the same imagery and style. Differences are as great as similarities. For example, the discursive and fluid poetic idiom of ch. 2 contrasts markedly with the compression and fracture that characterize the style of succeeding chapters.[4]

Nevertheless, I still think of a poet. Primarily this is because the poetry is of a very high order, with an especial penchant for metaphor. If, as Fisch says, "Hosea's work of prophecy belongs to the greatest poetry",[5] it is improbable that there should be three such poets. But if chs. 1 and 3 are, at least ostensibly, from different authors, someone must have been responsible for putting them together, for creating the unity of chs. 1-3. Similarly, assuming that the prophecies of chs. 4-11 were composed throughout the prophet's real or fictive career, someone, if only the prophet himself, arranged them.

This raises the question of composition. Most critics hold that the book is a collection of brief oracles, delivered in public or private, subsequently perhaps polished for publication.[6] However, if Hosea was a great poet, it is inconceivable that our book should constitute his entire corpus. This in itself is an argument against reducing the prophet's oeuvre further by attributing parts to disciples and inventive scribes. Likewise, a brief oracle might well be rhetorically ineffective. What if someone were asleep or inattentive in the half-minute or so it took to recite it? The whole book would only require thirty or forty minutes. For a long time I played with the idea of a performance, analogous to Greek tragedy. If we think, for example, of a prophetic equivalent of the festival of Dionysus, our book would only be a tiny segment of the total prophetic production. There are, however, notable shifts of emphasis and focus as the prophecies progress, which tell against the thesis of a single composition. The theme of whoredom, for example, fades away.

---

4. For an excellent description of this style, see Fisch *Poetry with a Purpose*, pp. 138ff.' Two scholars have maintained that chs. 1–3 are the work of a different, ninth-century, prophet: Y. Kaufmann, *The Religion of Israel* (trans. M. Greenberg; London: Allen & Unwin; abridged edition, 1961), pp. 361-70; and H.L. Ginsberg, 'Hosea', in *Encyclopaedia Judaica* (New York: Macmillan, 1971), VIII, cols. 1010-1025.

5. Fisch *Poetry with a Purpose*, p. 149.

6. This, for instance, is the approach of J. Jeremias, *Der Prophet Hosea* (Das Alte Testament Deutsch, 24/1; Göttingen: Vandenhoeck & Ruprecht, 1983), pp. 18-19.

It is difficult to imagine a performance context for the work, given its subversiveness. Yet the book itself envisages a performance: it is addressed to Israel, princes, priests etc. It assumes a situation of conflict, which would only be apposite if the prophet's views were public. Otherwise, its rhetorical task of admonition and reformation would not be possible. We may be over-influenced by contemporary models of totalitarian societies. There is no reason to suppose that a king, priests etc., may not have believed in the power of prophets, especially in a time of crisis.[7]

How might a performance be conceived? Would it be after the completion of the work, less the framing sentences, which might situate it after the fall of Samaria, i.e., when it was too late? Would it have been published in instalments, like a Victorian novel or the Qu'ran, with different parts, e.g., chs. 4–11, performed separately? If so, what about the rest of the prophet's work? Would there have been several collections, with what we have but a small selection from the span of his career? What would be the status of the first three chapters? Would they have been a prologue, added after the main body of the text, or an autonomous composition?

It is easier to imagine a performance, in Judah or Samaria, after the completion of the text. One would begin with a distanced view, an introduction to the externals of the prophet's life, before embarking on its decoding in the allegory of ch. 2. But then there follows another version of the story, clearly parallel to the first, yet incompatible with it. Our assumption that we have been offered an authoritative narrative is thus rendered uncertain—nothing could be more reliable, we think, than the prophet's own words, but they are entirely frustrating. Chs. 4–11 are a topical application of the allegory to the daily life and political vicissitudes of Israel: the venal and ignorant priests and worship

---

7. For an illuminating model of the social setting of prophetic activity, see T.W. Overholt, *Channels of Prophecy: The Social Dynamic of Prophetic Activity* (Minneapolis: Fortress, 1989). K. Read ('Sacred Commoners: The Motion of Cosmic Powers in Mexican Rulership', *HR* 34 [1994] pp. 39-69) warns against assuming that ancient rulers were solely motivated by the desire to manipulate power, without having cosmological beliefs (p. 44). An extremely informative study of the interplay of shamanic and clerical religious modalities is G. Samuel, *Civilized Shamans* (Washington: Smithsonian, 1993), which focuses on Tibetan Buddhism.

Introduction 5

on the high places in ch. 4; the fratricidal conflict of Judah and Israel in chs. 5–6; the conspiratorial court in ch. 7; the Golden Calf in ch. 8. It is highly structured: ch. 4 divides into two equal and matching panels, as do chs. 9 and 10; ch. 7 is paralleled by ch. 8, which is coupled with ch. 10; ch. 9 is echoed in ch. 11. Going beyond the boundaries of the section, ch. 12 completes a set of wordplays from ch. 9 and 10. Yet the parallels are the base for a pattern of reversal and displacement: the calf that is to be shattered in ch. 8 is exiled in ch. 10; God's promise of strict retribution in 4.9 is retracted in the granting of immunity to promiscuous daughters and brides in 4.14. Two fates for Israel are posited: destruction in the land and exile from it. Correspondingly, the dominant pattern, whereby each section ends with a confirmation of the inevitability of doom, is counterpointed by the hope, always retracted, that exile will permit return. Neither plot is conclusive; each modifies or ironizes the other. The conflict between the two is apparently resolved at the end of ch. 11 in favour of restoration, only to be withdrawn at the beginning of ch. 12; we will find parallels between the transition from chs. 11 to 12 and that from chs. 6 to 7.

The centre of the book, then, is focused on contemporary events and problems, on the socio-political foreground. As it progresses, so does the scope of inquiry widen, so as to include all of Israel's experience. References to the past multiply and become more elaborate, culminating in the reflection on Jacob in ch. 12. The immediate circumstances acquire symbolic depth, as representative of the divine-human relation. Ch. 13 combines a summarizing reflection on Israel's history with the climactic juxtaposition of God and Death. Ch. 14 opens up an unparalleled future, in which the motif of paradisal return permits displacement into a different realm, the mythopoeic land of Lebanon.[8] The experience of the performance would thus focus in and out of the detailed exposition of daily life and its corruption in northern Israel, and evoke cathartic pity, fear and relief.

As well as a performance, we must suppose that the text was copied, edited, studied and repeated, from its very beginning, that it became Torah, or at least interpretation of Torah, for some groups of people. Learning fragments the text, appropriates it

8. For the mythic significance of Lebanon, see R. Haak, *Habakkuk* (Leiden: Brill, 1991), pp. 70ff., and G. Vermes, *Scripture and Tradition in Judaism* (Leiden: Brill, 1961), pp. 30, 32.

for its own agendas; the currency and significance of the words, certainly in a book as sophisticated as Hosea, greatly exceeds what could be understood on a first hearing. The compositional process is cumulative, aphoristic, and interweaves the personality of the poet with that which he perceives and the voices of the tradition to which he or she belongs. At every point we find unity and multiplicity, an individual claim that becomes generic—that of the prophet—self-conscious, and complicated by the number of authorial (and readerly) levels inherent in the text. These, however, serve to the focus our attention on the prophet: we see him from the outside, through the prefatory narrative, for instance, as well as from within. It is to this personality that I now turn: how it constructs itself, what impels it, how we may imagine the speaker in this dialogue.

The Prophet

Hosea sees himself as part of a succession of prophets, of which the prototypes are Samuel and Moses. The prophets are the guardians of Israel's passage from Egypt and faithfulness to Yhwh; they have had a history of chastising, appointing and dismissing rulers. They are thus the true leaders of Israel, even though their only source of power is Yhwh; through them, he kills with "the words of his mouth" and hews the forest of disloyalty and injustice (6.5). Their speech is performative, manifesting Yhwh's creative and destructive word. As critics of sacred and political authority, they are outside all systems of power, except for the power to persuade, recall and question, and the consciousness of being in touch with the power that ultimately controls events.

Prophets, like all dissidents, attract enmity; there is evidence for this in Hosea in 9.7-9. The prophet is a trap—a prophetic cliché[9]—since he articulates the fatality of the divine word. If Israel cannot but stray, by virtue of being human and different from Yhwh, the divine commission will be the occasion for perdition. The prophet, however, is also the exemplar of Israel, reminding it of its special responsibility and relationship with Yhwh. The prophet is parallel to Jacob in 12.13-14, and shares the metaphor of watchman with Ephraim (8.1, 9.7). Thus he is a microcosm, a mirror of Israel, which destroys it; God's house—the epitome of sacred order—is the scene of conflict, mined by pits into which the trappers and sappers (5.1, 6.9, 9.9) fall.

9. See below, p. 136.

Hosea, however, is a prophet with qualms; as we will see, he changes the implacable message, and can no longer fulfil his task as verbal executioner without second thoughts. Correspondingly, he cannot act, traditionally, as intercessor (9.14). His crisis of doubt reflects that of Yhwh, to produce the fundamental uncertainty of the book.

There is no biographical evidence for Hosea's social situation, which must consequently be inferred from the content of his prophecy. It is literature written about, if not exclusively for, an elite; especially surprising, in a prophetic context, is the total invisibility of the poor. The focus is on Samaria, on international politics and internal dissension, coupled with the royal shrine of Bethel. One or two references might locate the prophet in "the house of God," at Bethel or Gilgal, especially 9.7-9. One should beware, nevertheless, of extrapolating from these instances a regular performance context or social position (prophet-in-residence), especially since his attitude to sacred sites is so hostile. His education is evidenced by the range of reference and wide vocabulary of the work.[10] We may accordingly consider the prophet to be a member of the urban elite, probably close to royal circles, primarily concerned with the affairs of his class. That would not make his opposition more or less dangerous; that would depend on the social flux.[11] But it does mean that it would attract influential attention.

The image of the prophet projected by the first four chapters contrasts markedly with this construction. The setting is predominantly rural, the polemic directed at the worship at the high places and of the Baalim. The narratives, which should be most informative about the prophet's circumstances, take place in a social vacuum;[12] virtually the only significant detail is the

---

10. This is not conclusive evidence, since we cannot presuppose that literacy and erudition were the preserve of urban elites, especially given the ease with which alphabetic writing could be learned (cf. D.W. Jamieson-Drake, *Scribes and Schools in Monarchic Judah: A Socio-Archaeological Approach* [Sheffield: Almond, 1991], pp. 152-54).

11. For an excellent analysis of this flux in relation to Jeremiah, see B.O. Long, 'Social Dimensions of Prophetic Conflict', *Semeia* 21 (1981), pp. 31-53.

12. It is perhaps worth repeating that I am dealing with a fictive construct of the prophet, even if we accept the autobiographical claims of ch. 3, not with historical probity.

8   *Introduction*

payment in kind for the woman in 3.2, suggestive of agricultural economy. We know nothing of the prophet's reactions, only that he obeys God's strange commands implicitly. The character of the prophet in these narratives is reduced to mere sign; only in 3.3-5 is there perhaps some individual initiative. Even the sign, as we will see, is distinguished by its ordinariness.

How are the two portraits to be reconciled? We may conceive of them as being successive—Hosea was first a rural and then an urban prophet—or as belonging to two different genres of prophetic characterization. It may be that two authors should be posited, in line with the stylistic distinction I noted earlier; ch. 4, belonging to the main body of the work, would then be anomalous. One should not be too hasty in attempting a solution, to unify or separate these personae. Suppose the narratives and the prophecies coexisted, Hosea was busy cohabiting, having children, imposing isolation while commenting on his contemporary situation? The eerie suspension of the will and desire suggests dissociation, a compulsion to do strange acts attributed to some external imperative, that cannot be integrated with his self-reflexivity and elite status and preoccupations. Tension between normal and para-normal states of consciousness and behaviour is typical of prophetic and shamanic experience.[13] This tension may also be exhibited in the pressure on language in the poetry of the book, mediating between inspiration and control, the desire to articulate a fragmenting reality and the collapse of language which that articulation necessitates. According to 9.7, the prophet is mad, because of the antagonism he attracts and the evil he sees; the madness is related, in the same context, to entrapment by the word and impending destruction. The prophet's clairvoyance—his sanity—undoes the defences and repressions that maintain conventional reality. As a critique of normality, it courts insanity.

Schizoid states are characterized not only by a splitting of consciousness, but by a literalization of metaphor.[14] The prophet crosses the gap between the divine and the human by acting out the divine-human relationship; the poetic task of finding

---

13. G. Samuel defines shamanism as 'the regulation and transformation of human life and human society through the use...of alternate states of consciousness' (*Civilized Shamans*, pp. 8, 364).

14. S. Stewart, *Nonsense: Aspects of Intertextuality in Folklore and Literature* (Baltimore: Johns Hopkins University Press, 1979), pp. 31ff.

adequate metaphors is thus short-circuited, as the pathology is experienced in the human body, in the generative organs themselves. The narrative expresses a contradiction: a disclaimer of paternity that is nonetheless asserted, through the very act of naming.[15] This may correspond to the dissociation of his act from acknowledgement of desire; if the desire is illicit, a crossing of class and sexual boundaries, it suggests an involvement with the promiscuity it insistently condemns, that implicates God as well as his agent.

Metaphor, Mysticism, Misogyny

Finding metaphors for God is the business of prophets, according to Hosea (12.11); the multiplicity of visions and similes indicates their inadequacy. Unlike Amos and Isaiah, Hosea records no visions and has few doxologies. Through metaphor God may be accessible in human language; every metaphor establishes both a resemblance and difference. The metaphors for God are contradictory and unstable: destructive and redemptive lions, the moth, dew, cypress tree, lover and parent. The same image may change signification with different referents: dew may signify evanescence or ever-renewed fertility. The diversity of metaphor expresses an uncertainty of identity. Is God actually a parent, for example, or only adoptively so? Did he come across Israel by chance in the wilderness, or do they have an intrinsic connection? But it also communicates a preoccupation with God one may term mystical.[16] For Hosea what matters ultimately is knowledge of God, which will consummate the betrothal of God and Israel in 2.22. The absence of the knowledge of God has caused the dereliction of the earth according to 4.1; the perennial message of prophets is that knowledge of God is more desirable than sacrifices (6.6).

The knowledge is foundational to us; according to 11.9, God is an inner holiness, combining immanence with transcendence.

---

15. Cf. N. Jay, *Throughout your Generations Forever: Sacrifice, Religion, and Paternity* (Chicago: University of Chicago Press, 1992).

16. M. Verman (*The Books of Contemplation: Medieval Jewish Mystical Sources* [Albany: State University of New York Press, 1993]) argues against the conventional distinction between prophecy and mysticism, citing Aquinas's definition of mysticism as the *cognitio dei experimentalis*. Accordingly, he regards the biblical prophets as the first great Jewish mystics (pp. 6-10).

10   *Introduction*

God's difference from humanity ("For I am God and not human") is manifested by his presence in humanity ("in your midst holy"). Within us there is that which is not us, but which is the most intimate part of ourselves. God's immanence may be destructive; in 5.12 he is like rottenness in the bones. It may be as pervasive, invisible and undifferentiated as the dew (14.6). In 14.9, continuity between God and Ephraim is expressed through the metaphor of the fruit—a pun (*p^{e}ri*) on the name of Ephraim—and the tree.

Erotic union, the exchange of knowledge, kindness, love and faithfulness, is the goal of the book; 2.16-25, in particular, is an example of mystical love poetry. Eros, however, is achieved in spite of, or is subordinate to, Thanatos; the romance in the wilderness, we will see, is in part a mystification that conceals the reality of exile and death, and in part a conversion of death into life, silence into speech.[17] Hosea experiences preeminently the violence of God, and thus God as the agent of death; as recurrently in the mystical tradition, Hosea envisages a negativity in God, a reversion of his "I am" into "I am not," a dark ground from which God speaks. Whether death is the encompassing reality, or is non-existent, is entirely ambiguous (13.14).

Between his metaphors, his violence and his desire, there is no consistency; God's unity is as fissile and contingent as that of the human self. Fixity of purpose is only attainable, for example, at the cost of repression; he wills his disparate "compassions" to converge in 11.8, to dispel his destructive intent. The instability of language and metaphor especially disturbs that primary marker of identity, gender.

Hosea is undoubtedly patriarchal literature: its God is male, its world is governed by male authorities and conventions, and the prophet is male. Its use of female imagery is misogynistic; 2.4-15 is a fantasy of sadistic humiliation and bestial voracity; 4.13-14 exonerates women on grounds of their irresponsibility. However, gender identifications are constantly shifting, sometimes within the same verse (e.g., 4.16). A female image for Ephraim in one chapter will be complemented by an equally stereotypical male image in the next, as in the balanced portraits of dove and wild ass in chs. 7 and 8. The masculinity of God is apparently unvarying, and accounts for the female characteriza-

---

17. See below p. 38, and Fisch (*Poetry with a Purpose*, p. 143) for the consonantal identity of the words for 'wilderness' and 'speech.'

tion of male devotees in ch. 2.[18] Nevertheless, the phallic climax in 2.25 is suddenly transposed into a metaphor for sexual inversion. The seed which God sows is feminine; at the centre of the phallus, and hence of the divine creative potential, is the female matrix. The identity of the seed is uncertain. It could be Jezreel, evoked in the previous verse, despite its grammatical masculinity, or the earth itself. In either case, there is a paradox: the earth inseminates itself, the child is its own progenitor.

There is no partner for God, yet the metaphor of erotic union suggests that Israel is God's partner, his feminine complement. There is no goddess, but the book is haunted by images of ravaged maternity: the mother in ch. 2, the priest's mother in ch.4, the dessicated breasts and slit wombs of chs. 9, 10, and 14. In the rites of ch. 4, the men are attracted by a sexuality, a femininity, antonymic to God: the prostitutes and hierodules signify a sacrality, perhaps as devotees of Asherah, that is, at least for the moment, untouched. The goddess is on the margins of the work and its world, evoked metonymically and interstitially as a figure of exploited innocence that disappears for the rest of the book, and yet persists, uncannily, as an unmentioned, defiled (4.18-19) alterity.

Sexual nostalgia, desire and revulsion are the constituents of the prophet's libidinal dilemma; like much mystical literature, Hosea is profoundly ascetic. It (or he) is fascinated and appalled by promiscuity; the poetry itself is evidence of an intense erotic drive, a love of language and the world. The contradiction is apparent from the detached account of Hosea's marriage. He is drawn to the promiscuous woman, but refuses to acknowledge the desire or its offspring. Sexuality means death; in a world that is about to perish, every sign of life means its opposite. Again, however, gender is reciprocal; an image for female reproductive morbidity will be matched by a male one. In 9.14, for example, the prophet prays for a bereaving womb; in the same chapter, male sterility is represented by the image of the dry tree, and by a set of puns, interfusing the phallus with folly, greed, and grief.

18. Cf. H. Eilberg-Schwartz, *God's Phallus and Other Problems for Men and Monotheism* (Boston: Beacon Press, 1994), p. 99, who sees in this feminization a displacement of a 'homoerotic dilemma'.

By the end of the book the desire for sexual union has become entirely displaced and etherealized; only the conjunction of dew and lily in 14.6 hints at it. Nevertheless, there are indications that God seeks in Israel a matrix, a place in the world in which to be immanent. In 9.10 he is nourished by Israel in the wilderness; ch. 2 jarringly switches images of adult and infantile sexuality. According to one reading of 13.14, God emerges from death, from primal non-being. A reading of 2.25, as we have seen, is that the earth gives birth to itself, through God. None of this adds up to a mother, only to confused and negated counterfeits and felt absences of one. Likewise, Jacob/Israel suffers from inherent insecurity, since the womb, in which he fought with Esau (12.4), was never safe, and since he is an alien in his own land.

The Message

What is it to be human? To be human is to betray the covenant, to worship false gods, to finagle with the great powers, to practice the follies and iniquities and to be seduced by the distractions that Hosea ceaselessly satirizes. To be human is also to love, and to draw God into love (11.4). Hosea offers a way of liberation from our familiar constraints and surrogates, a way that he identifies as that of *ḥesed*[19] and justice, but also of patience, waiting for Yhwh in his own time (10.12; 12.7).

There is nothing surprising about this; Hosea repeats humanistic clichés. Yet the clichés bear repeating, for in the end only they survive. The human capacity for *ḥesed*, justice, and faith will sustain us, just as people will continue to plough fields, keep flocks, and maintain the cosmic covenant, though Samaria falls.

What will it be like, without kings, weapons, sacrifices, or altars?

Hosea is a poetry of despair, a vision of death, as well as of hope. It balances ambiguities, leaving itself open… always, elsewhere, perhaps.

---

19. 'Kindness' or 'loyalty'. Because of its pervasiveness and because it lacks any good English equivalent, I often leave this term untranslated.

Hosea 1.1–2.3*

(1) The word of Yhwh which came to Hosea ben Be'eri in the days of Uzziah, Jotham, Ahaz, Hezekiah, kings of Judah, and in the days of Jeroboam, son of Joash, king of Israel.
(2) Beginning of Yhwh spoke in Hosea:
And Yhwh said to Hosea:
'Go, take for yourself a wife of whoredoms,
and children of whoredoms,
For the land has, whoring, whored itself away from Yhwh'.
(3) And he went and took Gomer, daughter of Diblaim, and she conceived and bore him a son.
(4) And Yhwh said to him:
'Call his name Jezreel, for in yet a little while I will visit the blood of Jezreel on the house of Jehu, and I will cause the kingdom of the house of Israel to cease.
(5) And it shall be on that day that I will break the bow of Israel in the valley of Jezreel.'
(6) And she conceived again and bore a daughter, and he said to him:
'Call her name Lo-Ruhamah (*Uncompassioned*), for I will no longer have compassion on the house of Israel, for lifting, I will lift up for them.'
(7) But for the house of Judah I will have compassion,
And I will save them by Yhwh their God;
But I will not save them by bow, by sword, by war, by horses and riders.'
(8) And Lo-Ruhamah was weaned, and she conceived and bore a son.
(9) And he said. 'Call his name Lo-Ammi (*Not-my-people*), for you are not my people, and I will not be for you.
(2.1) And the number of the children of Israel shall be as the sand of the sea

---

* In most English Bibles 1.1–2.1.

14   *Hosea 1.1–2.3*

> Which can not be measured nor can it be counted,
> And in the place where it was said of them, "You are not my people",
> It will be said of them, "Children of the living God".
> (2) And the children of Judah and the children of Israel will be gathered together
> And they will appoint for themselves one head, and go up from the land,
> For great is the day of Jezreel.
> (3) Say to your brothers, "Ammi" (*My people*), and to your sisters "Ruhamah" (*Compassioned*).'

This happened long ago and in another country, so the superscription tells us, from the perspective of a Judean after the reign of Hezekiah, looking back to the long and glorious years of Jeroboam II, with the irony of hindsight. The distance in time and space, the location in a now vanished *alter ego*, makes of the narrative and prophecy a parable, an image of oneself as other, perceived timelessly and objectively. Whether recorded in the reign of bad king Manasseh or good king Josiah, or thereafter, the introductory note suggests the alternation of approval and disapproval, success and failure, in outer history, and the continuity of the divine word through them.

But the word begins: 'Beginning of Yhwh spoke in Hosea', a strange, broken phrase which takes us to a point of origin that is left discontinuous, as if the beginning has no connection with anything that follows (although translations generally try to make a connection by turning this first phrase into a subordinate clause, e.g. 'When the Lord first spoke to Hosea'). We then begin again, 'And Yhwh said to Hosea...', in the middle of a story, Hosea's, Israel's, God's. Across a white space—a paragraph division in the midst of the verse in the Hebrew text—this story is rooted in some beginning, yet separated from it.

The story, so adrift, is primordial: a man is told by God to take, in proper male fashion, a woman, just as in Exod. 2.1 a man from the house of Levi takes a daughter of Levi. As there, we expect great things from this union. But in fact it is only a shadow of a story: that the land has prostituted itself from Yhwh.

Why does the text have to go to such lengths to distance itself from the place, time, subject? Why the complex framing, that takes us through the details of outer history, through what appears to be the fragmentary introduction to a call narrative, to a continuing story set at two removes? Perhaps it is to impede a too rapid identification with the prophet, to present him as a whole and as a mystery. But why does God turn the prophet's life into an allegory of his own? Josipovici (1989: 181) writes, 'One senses in all these prophets a terrible longing to escape from the limited, contingency-bound use of words, to some absolute state where all will be visible and unambiguous'. However, this is not the prophet's desire here, but God's. Perhaps mime will succeed where words fail, through silence, imposing a trance. Perhaps in this trance an audience will perceive, beyond language, an image of themselves and an intimation of what it is to be God. For the parable/mime to work, we must know that it is a temporary reality. This is true for the prophets as well. We know that it is a charade, that after three years Isaiah will be able to put on clothes (Isaiah 20), after 390 days Ezekiel will get up (Ezek. 4.4ff.) and so on. With Hosea, on the other hand, it is reality, and that to which it refers, the prostitution of the land against God, is a metaphor. This is very disturbing. It is as if the player actually poured poison into the king's ear, and Claudius had done something else entirely. The question at this point is not so much of God as of Hosea: what happens when he consciously becomes a symbol? But it is a question of all of us as we enter the symbolic order, the order of culture.

What Hosea is meant to do is very ordinary; on the primary level it refers to the mess that most of us make of our lives. Is this what is meant by prostitution against Yhwh? If so, there is something yet more disturbing: the reality that Hosea is commanded to make visible is that of Yhwh. This differs from Isaiah, who acts out the captivity of the Egyptians, or Jeremiah, who places on himself the yoke of the Babylonians (Jeremiah 28-29). Only Hosea among the prophets 'plays' God. Yet, because of its ordinariness, the sign cannot but be invisible, unlike those of the other prophets. The attempt to escape from the contingency-boundedness of words results then in something totally secret, corresponding to the plenitude of inarticulate speech in Hosea's and the world's beginning. If Hosea's unhappiness—assuming it is that—matches the banal estrangement from life and from God of others in a similar predicament, and if he plays God, then God is implicated in this mess, this estrangement.

The land prostitutes itself against Yhwh: with the verb *znh*, 'to be licentious, fornicate, whore', repeated in the Hebrew four times in this verse, we come to the dominant metaphor of the first part of the book, corresponding to that of the lion at the beginning of Amos (1.2). (Keefe 2001: 16-18 argues that the primary meaning of *'ešet zĕnûnîm* is not prostitution but promiscuity. I retain the translation 'whoredoms' for the sake of its ambiguity.) Whereas in Amos the prophet turns the lion's roars into speech (3.8), and ultimately into his book, in Hosea the whorishness is a figure for a primary estrangement. The repetition, however, also suggests fixation. Fascination with the demimonde is pervasive, precisely because it is the other world. The whore offers a paradox of female freedom and subjugation; ever at the beck and call of male desire, she represents a world where sexuality is not repressed, not socialized. Hence the fantasy that, as Dworkin (1988: 9-12) says, women like it. Like the prophet, the whore is a symbol; hence the emphasis, in the Bible as in all cultures, on her distinctive clothing, which both advertises and hides her. In traditional patriarchal society, the whore succeeds through offering ultimate sexual pleasure, in contrast to the wife, with whom sex is unexciting and for whom it is a duty.

'The land' is ambiguous: it may refer to the people or the territory, to the nations or the world. The earth was God's partner in the creation of humanity; in Gen. 2.5 the earth is waiting to be fertilized by Yhwh's rain and human labour. Now, to combine both sets of meaning, the earth and its inhabitants seek other partners, and not only the earth as a whole, long since relinquished by God, but even the ideal microcosmic experiment, Israel.

Hosea is impelled always by a nostalgia for origins, such as God's love for Israel in the wilderness (2.16-17; 9.10; etc.). Perhaps the ideal beginning is a screen, so the multiple attempts at the beginning suggest. In the creation story, God and the earth are at one to form humanity; the sexual metaphor of estrangement in our text implies an initial coupling. A feminist interpretation might reverse the relationship; God would be a latecomer to the earth. But this raises a question suggested by the white space inserted in the verse: is there continuity between the voice and what it utters? What happens to the voice when it enters symbolic order, through the gap that it tries to fill with the discourse of the book? The overt messages of Hosea are those of a baffled deity, for whom the sensuality of the earth and its inhabitants is both the object of desire and profoundly threatening. Its perspective, as various feminist critics have pointed out, is exclusively masculine. The voice of the poet, however, its rhythm, timbre, the way in which sounds move together with other reflexes through the body, is intensely erotic, aligned with nature and the drives the book tries to repress.

Hosea takes a wife, Gomer bat-Diblaim, and she bears a son. We do not know, of course, whether she is promiscuous, or even whether Hosea is attempting to fulfil the divine command. At least his choice of a particular woman suggests a measure of individual initiative. If Gomer is a 'woman of whoredoms', her social status is intriguing. How did Diblaim accommodate himself to his miscreant daughter? In Deut. 22.21 the woman who 'fornicates' against her father's house is stoned at its entrance. Licentious women are marginalized, as are prophets. Sacred prostitution, ritual prenuptial initiation, orgies at Astarte's feasts have been suggested to explain Gomer's errant behaviour; poverty is equally likely, as is pleasure. On the other hand, Gomer may not have been promiscuous.

It must have been difficult to be married to Hosea. Gomer tries to keep the family together, while he insists on calling the children horrible names, on excoriating her as an example of Israel's infidelity, on provoking family quarrels. Perhaps she knows nothing of his fantasies; he sits in his room and writes at God's bidding—or listens—and she wonders *why* he is so brooding. Perhaps she admires him as a holy man, while he communicates only with his male disciples, who wink at her passing.

He (Hosea/God/narrator) calls the son a name: Jezreel. The nearest precedent is Solomon's reappellation as Yedidiah (Beloved-of-Yah) by the prophet Nathan in 2 Sam. 12.25, likewise at God's bidding. In the next quarter-century, Isaiah is divinely inspired to name his son Maher-shalal-hash-baz, and prophesies of a young woman who is to call her son Immanuel. One has to go back to Ishmael and Isaac for other instances of a God-given name. Whether the names with which Hosea graced his children were ever current (or even known) is doubtful; anthropological literature is full of sacred names that signify the mystery of the person, and that cannot be revealed publicly. Solomon is never subsequently called Yedidiah—and how unaccountable are God's affections! Maher-shalal-hash-baz is exhausting. As for Hosea and Gomer's next children, 'Uncompassioned' and 'Not-my-people', it is difficult to imagine such names being sustained. What did Gomer call them? Friends? What name is really real?

Buss (1984: 75) notes the paradox that while naming introduces a child into the family circle—it is an acknowledgment of relationship—these names disavow kinship and affection. Language incorporates the children into the human world as beings essentially alienated.

Jezreel, at least, sounds positive: literally it means 'God sows', just as he gives names, establishes the order of language. He is a comfortable, inseminatory God, reminiscent of Gen. 2.5, not to speak of Baal. But there are disturbing undertones (cf. Ben Zvi 2005: 47). The toponym perhaps associates the child with indigenous deities, figures of the earth, whose allegiance is in question (Keefe 2001: 67-69 questions the commonplace contrast of Yhwh's transcendence to the immanence of Canaanite deities. Nonetheless, the strangeness of Yhwh to the land is a persistent motif.)

The name is explicated by three parallel clauses, linking motive, the blood of Jezreel, to the result, the abolition of the monarchy, and the poetic justice that stages the decisive battle in the valley of Jezreel. The murder of Naboth of Jezreel, the nemesis of the house of Ahab (1 Kings 21; 2 Kings 9), envelopes ultimately the institution of the Israelite monarchy. The cessation of the Israelite monarchy, however, is not the logical consequence of the fall of the dynasty. The prediction of the latter is well within the tradition of northern Israel prophecy; the former is both new and unexplained. 'Breaking the bow of Israel' in v. 5 would seem to specify, to render dramatically and metaphorically, the destruction of the kingdom. But it is introduced by the formulaic 'On that day', the sign always of the intrusion of a new age. 'I will abolish' (*hišbattî*) parallels and alliterates closely with 'I will break' (*šābartî*); but does their equivalence conceal a slight modification? 'The monarchy of the house of Israel' is seemingly echoed in the 'bow of Israel', a symbol of broken power grounded in Jezreel, whose name (*yizrᵉ'ēl*) is a half-pun on that of (*yiśrā'ēl*). The imperfect homophony suggests an identification, but acts also as an irritant. Each term of this climactic dramatization of the prediction of doom opens the possibility of another nuance, presenting the issue of whether the metaphor of 'breaking the bow' is the same, more, or less, than the cessation of the kingdom.

The next child, a daughter, Lo-Ruhamah, 'Unloved' or 'Uncompassioned', signifies the fate of Israel, on whom God will no longer have compassion. Yet precisely contemporaneously, according to the word of Yhwh to Jonah in 2 Kgs 14.26-27, God did have compassion on the Israel of Jeroboam II, despite

Jeroboam's sinfulness, and made it into a substantial dominion. There is a double displacement and contradiction in the divine word. God commands Jehu, through Elijah, Elisha, and an anonymous 'son of the prophets' (2 Kgs 9), to wipe out the house of Ahab; this deed will only be avenged at four generations' remove, as God says comfortingly to Jehu (2 Kgs 10.30). Likewise, according to 1 Kgs 21.29, because he is repentant Ahab will not suffer directly for his sin, but retribution will be exacted from his son. Nemesis operates despite divine forgiveness or agency; there are thus two wills in God, that crime should be inexorably punished, and that punishment should be commuted. The gap between compassion and no compassion is that which the text attempts to cross.

God lays claim to 'No Compassion', makes himself the patron of nemesis. Nemesis, that blind force, is, however, antithetic to God. Nemesis demands that the blood of evil Ahab be avenged. However, since God has ordered that deed, a mystification suggests itself, that God is not actually its master, but its potential victim.

'I will no longer have compassion' matches God's words to Amos, 'I will no longer forgive him' (7.8; 8.2), uttered during his symbolic visions, referring to the same historical context. Together, they suggest a threshold between the era of compassion or forgiveness and that of implacability. But in our case this message is immediately subverted by its juxtaposition with the enigmatic phrase that follows, 'for lifting, I will lift up for them', and the promise of salvation to Judah in v. 7.

The verb $nś'$, 'lift up, carry', is frequently used in expressions of forgiveness, for example in the list of divine attributes in Exod. 34.6-7. But interpretation on these lines clearly contradicts the first clause: God cannot both forgive and have no compassion. It may be a reference to exile, whither God carries Israel away; it would then reverse the motif of God carrying Israel from Egypt, which we have, for example, in Exod. 19.4. This interpretation ill fits the indirect object 'for them'.

The point is not to solve the problem, but to recognize the puzzle. The unambiguous doom supposed by the name Lo-Ruhamah and its interpretation is thereby obscured. It offers the possibility of forgiveness as well as exile and the reversal of the Exodus. The doubling of the verb 'lift up' matches that of the verb znh, 'to be licentious', that characterizes the earth in v. 2. God is one who lifts up, both in the sense of sustaining through life and of absorbing sin. This combines with the quality of compassion that introduces the list of attributes in Exod. 34.6-7 and whose inextricability from God's nature is stressed by the first person construction of the verb in our verse. Thus it is God's identity that is in question, as we will see when we come to the last child (cf. the discussion in Sweeney 2000: 21).

From Israel we surprisingly switch in v. 7 to Judah, the home of the implied editor/author of v. 1. The distantiation achieved there boomerangs; the Judean narrator reports God, far away and long ago, speaking to Hosea of the narrator's world. Moreover, if the parabolic narrative raises the question of whether it concerns us, whether Israel's fate reflects Judah's, the answer is apparently negative. Divine compassion extends to Judah; the fall of the northern kingdom need not disturb us unduly. We read the text, perhaps out of commiseration, archival interest, or fascination for other people's disasters.

No reason is given for God's beneficence to Judah. It could be arbitrary, or dissimulate the contradiction between God's compassion and non-compassion by merging it with the binary opposition Israel/Judah. Judah then salves God's propensity for compassion while allowing his mercilessness full force.

The continuation of the verse couples compassion with salvation, by no less than Yhwh 'their God'; the impressiveness of the nomenclature combines with the insistence of the possessive to magnify the divine intervention and to contrast with God's severance from Israel in v. 9. It is followed by a long list of those things with which God will not save Israel: bow and sword, weapons of war, horses and riders. Hosea, at least in chs. 1–3, has a penchant for lists, whose main function is to suggest an accumulation of otiose objects. The list is unstructured, compared to the rhetorical flourish of 'by Yhwh their God'; the sentence accordingly becomes much too long and trails off into itemized military hardware. This accounts partially for the impression of stylistic crudity that critics often attribute to later redaction.

Clutter is powerfully anti-poetic; a God who saves with himself alone is less heavy-handed than one who mobilizes infantry and cavalry. We are in the realm of biblical cliché, which imposes a seductive ideological frame, setting transcendent word against material power, poetry against chaos. If God's non-compassion for Israel is manifested in the cessation of its kingdom and its broken bow in vv. 4-5, God's compassion for Judah renders bows superfluous. This could cast retrospective doubt on the finality of the catastrophe envisaged in those verses, a possibility already suggested by the imbalance of the parallelisms. *Bow* becomes a loaded term. Furthermore, it puts Judah beyond political and military common sense. The year of the fall of Samaria—722 BCE—and the boundary between north and south constitute the threshold between the normative and its supersession. If Israel, as the displaced 'other' kingdom, is the locus of conventional reality, the world of the narrator exists only through miracle. This reverses the familiar association of an alternative world with the fabulous, compared to our own mundane reality. It is the narrator's world that is estranged.

What can it mean to be saved 'by Yhwh their God'? The phrase lacks context or specificity; the presence or name of God, it would seem, spellbinds Judah's enemies and extricates Judah from peril. Judah is then abstracted from a world dependent on arms to an encompassing, protective magic. The abstraction from the world reverses the estrangement of the world from God in v. 2. Judah becomes other-worldly, transcendent.

Another child is born, another name is given, *lō' 'ammî*, 'Not-my-People'. As many commentators have noted, the explication 'I will not be' directly echoes God's revelation at the Burning Bush as 'I am that I am' (Exod. 3.14). It takes us back to the beginning of the narrative of Israel's liberation, which for Hosea is also its birth (cf. 9.10; 11.1), and to the intimacy of Moses' initiatory commission. Hosea then becomes an anti-Moses, speaking for a God who says 'I am not' to a people that is no longer his; the Exodus, and with it the entire prophetic vocation, is cancelled out.

'I am that I am' is not a very forthcoming name; in fact it does not seem to be name at all. Buber, in a celebrated discussion, argues that God thereby sets himself beyond linguistic control; if a name is held to be equivalent to essence, God's essence is inaccessible to conjuration and irreducible to any manifestation (Buber 1968: 59-60; cf. also Carroll 1994). This unconditionality, for Buber, is the prerequisite of dialogue. But it is also true of ourselves, that our identity is not ultimately determined by predicates or relationships. This disturbs the parallel with Hosea. God speaks to Moses about his incommunicability in a paradoxically intimate communication that comes as close as any in the Bible to the interiority of God. If this is reversed in

Hosea, then God's very existence, or at least self-consciousness, is at stake. This conclusion, however, is averted by the introduction of the indirect object 'for you'. The asymmetry salvages God's existence. God will cease to exist for the people, either in the sense that they will consider him to be a nonentity or that he will make himself a nonentity to them. He does, nevertheless, have the option of existing for a different people or planet or becoming a *deus absconditus*. Neither inspires confidence; a fresh start would be a confession of total failure, while withdrawing from the world would necessitate renouncing the power and authority that make divinity meaningful.

Like 1.7, 2.1-3 is a surprise. The boundary between non-compassion and compassion is that between present and a future marked, as in 1.5, by the formulaic 'And it shall be'; the ethnic divide is replaced by a temporal one. The more ominous the names and their attendant explanations, the more intense is their reversal, from the mere hint of a modification in 1.5, to the opposition of Israel and Judah in 1.7, and the salvation of the entire people in 2.1-3.

It is also a stylistic surprise; the niggardliness of 1.9 is relieved by lyrical expansiveness. The ingredients are very simple: syntactic convolution, insistent parallelism, undemanding but haunting vocabulary. The first results in a breakdown of structure; in 2.1, in particular, the two relative clauses, the two quoted speeches, and the simile overload and fragment the sentence. If biblical poetry is characterized by its elliptical density, this is not poetry. One may note also the prevalence of the prosaic conjunction 'and', and the irreducibility of the verse to any metrical balance.

It is, however, obtrusively parallelistic; parallelism is the hallmark of biblical poetry and, according to Roman Jakobson, the essence of poetry in general. Both sentences in v. 1 begin with 'And it shall be'; 'the children of Israel' at the beginning of v. 1 is matched by 'the children of Israel' at the beginning of v. 2, and 'the children of the living God' at the end of v. 1. Within each sentence, parallelism is exemplified by couplings such as 'cannot be measured nor can it be counted', and the closure of the first sentence (*yissāpēr*, 'counted') with an echo of its beginning (*mispār*, 'number'). The visibility of parallelism is compounded by its simplicity; for the most part, identical words are paralleled in identical positions. There are none of the transformations and modulations of parallelism wherewith biblical poetry renders itself complex and subtle.

The language of these verses presents no problems of poetic diction or compression. Instead its appeal is to the rhythms and imagery of the blessings to the Patriarchs. The speech is very familiar, since it constitutes us, and is correspondingly artless; if, as Blake says, 'bless relaxes', it does so through undoing the necessity of poetic work and through a return to origin, as the passive object of speech and enumeration.

The earth in 1.2 has prostituted itself from Yhwh; one expects this state of affairs to be resolved, just as the ominous names of the children change into their opposites, and the split kingdom is reunited. Instead we have a most enigmatic phrase: 'they shall go up from the land/earth.' It recalls Pharaoh's fear in Exod. 1.10 that the Israelites, multiplying exorbitantly, would 'go up from the land', a prediction that turns out to be self-fulfilling. Thus the reunion of Judah and Israel under one head will culminate in a new Exodus, reversing the implied retraction of the revelation at the Burning Bush in 1.9. But whence will this new Exodus be undertaken? 'The land' normally refers to the land of Israel and can only be transferred to a place of exile at the cost of some strain. And whither will the tribes ascend? It is unlikely that they will find a land less whoresome than Israel, quite apart from the divine breach of promise to the ancestors.

Utopia is the biblical destination as well as its matrix. Exodus is for the sake of its ever-receding realization in a land that is perpetually going astray. The distinctive dilemma of Hosea is an oscillation between the land and the wilderness, in which neither offers permanent rapprochement between Israel and God. That the land should be a figurative Egypt, with a Pharaoh-like king pondering impotently the prospect of mass defection, is plausible. Several commentators (e.g. Jeremias 1983: 35; Mays 1969: 32; Wolff 1974: 27) have deliberated whether the choice of a head instead of a king by the united tribes in this verse reflects an anti-royal or post-monarchic perspective.

One may consider it contextually. In 1.5 the bow of Israel is broken; in 1.7 Judah's deliverance does not depend on military prowess, and preserves a vestige of divine compassion. Now through the union of the two moieties Judah's salvation extends retroactively to Israel. But it is one beyond kingship, destroyed in 1.4, or political and military means, declared redundant in 1.7. The appointment of a 'head' indicates an unstructured polity, in which leaders are assigned no titles, characteristic of charismatic revolutionary movements as well as the original Exodus. Anti-structure is also antithesis, of the names of the children, of the self-negation of God. Across the threshold defined by the temporal marker 'And it shall be' ($w^e h\bar{a}y\hat{a}$) is a mirror image of our poetic and political realm. It is both liminal and otherworldly, like the survival of Judah under the divine protection. The 'other world', the anti-structure, carefully matches its counterpart in ch. 1, hence the abundance of structural inversions, and yet cannot be integrated with it.

What happens on 'the day of Jezreel'? Poetic justice: redress at the scene of crime and punishment. Wish-fulfilling grandiosity is a familiar gratification of apocalyptic poetry; the word becomes a vague triumphal gesture, an almost empty signifier, whose content is the divine advent and fulfillment of time. The day of Jezreel is both a new Passover, prefatory to the ascent from the land, and the completion of the historical process through disaster to restoration.

Jezreel, as we have seen, means 'God sows', associated with the fertility of the earth/land that has gone astray, and whose sinfulness is exemplified by the blood that is avenged on it. The great day of Jezreel suggests renewed insemination of the earth by God, and contrasts with the autonomous generation of 2.1, in which the unchecked proliferation of the divine seed is without territorial reference, and literally, in the Freudian sense, *unheimlich*, 'unhoused'; the simile 'as the sand of the seashore' confirms its marginality. Here, however, home is the point of departure. Thus the tension between structure and anti-structure, immanence and transcendence, is maintained throughout.

The breakdown of the duality of the sign in apocalyptic poetry suggests not only the structural disintegration characteristic of ecstatic speech but also a reversion from symbolic order—the meanings and constructions that constitute our world—to the semiotic processes wherewith language is articulated and sensually experienced. We return, across the white gap before anything is spoken (1.2), to the voice that can only uncertainly be accommodated in language and culture. If the object of the narrative is to free God and Israel from nemesis and death, and thus to grant them transcendence, that object is subverted through the very act of being spoken.

Hosea 2.4–25*

(2.4) Strive with your mother, strive, for she is not my wife, and I am not her husband,
that she may remove her harlotries from her face, and her adulteries from between her breasts,
(5) Lest I strip her bare, and expose her as on the day of her birth, and set her as a wilderness, and appoint her as a parched land, and make her die with thirst.
(6) And on her children I will have no pity, for they are children of harlotry.
(7) For their mother has played the whore, their parent acted shamefully, for she said, 'I will go after my lovers,
givers of my food and my water, my wool and my linen,
my oil and my drink.'
(8) Therefore I will hedge her way with thorns, and fence her in with a fence and she will not find her paths.
(9) And she will pursue her lovers and not reach them,
And seek them and not find;
And she will say, 'I will go and return to my first husband, for it was better for me then than now.'
(10) And she did not know that I gave her the corn, the new wine and the oil, And silver I multiplied for her, and gold—which they made for Baal.
(11) Therefore I will turn back and take my corn in its time, and my new wine in its season, and I will reclaim my wool and my linen, to cover her nakedness.
(12) And now I will expose her shame before her lovers, and no one will deliver her from my hand.
(13) And now I will make all her joy cease, her festivals, her new moons, her sabbaths and all her assemblies.
(14) And I will make desolate her vines and her fig trees, of which she said, 'They are my wages which my lovers

---

* 2.2-23 in most English versions.

gave me', and I will make them into a forest, and the wild beasts will devour them.

(15) And I will visit upon them the days of the Baalim, to which she would make offerings, and she would adorn herself with her nose rings and her jewellery, and go after her lovers, and me she would forget—says Yhwh.

The principal problems in ch. 2 are: (i) how to reconcile—if one may—the violence and obtrusiveness of the first part of the chapter with the blissful tour-de-force of the second; (ii) how it interacts with the framing parable in chs. 1 and 3; and (iii) how it functions as a microcosm, a *mise-en-abyme*, of the book as a whole. The feminist critique of the chapter is by now well-established: that it robs the woman of her voice and her point of view, that it objectifies and degrades her. We can build on this critique, not only by a detailed reading of the text, but by asking: where does the author stand? Is 'he'—distinguishing the biological gender of the presumably male author from his symbolic gender—the speaker or the addressee? What is the relationship in the text between mystification and discovery, desire and knowledge? The male control, undercut by uncertainty, revisions, and impossibility, may conceal a desire for surrender of power, knowledge and discourse. This will not breach the exclusivity of the male fantasy, but will make us aware that, as repeatedly in Hosea, it is also a fantasy of the transfer of gender, of slippage between male and female personae. This can be illustrated at the end of the chapter where the male child, Jezreel, is suddenly feminized; since Jezreel is etymologically correlated with the divine seed, God's insemination of the earth is also 'his' surrender to it.

The first part of the chapter (vv. 4-15) is a repeated fantasy of desolation and sexual exposure. The distancing parable frames the inner dynamic of God's jealousy, rage, and cruelty. But it is also framed by visions of reconciliation, marked by the transformation of the children's names in vv. 1-3 and vv. 24-25. The continuity between God's speeches in vv. 3 and 4, with their matching imperatives, 'Say...', 'Strive...', suggests that from the far future he turns to present alienation, that his acknowledgement of kinship and love for his children, reflected in their words to each other, is undercut by their immediate predicament, as agents of familial strife, and by doubts about their legitimacy. Inciting the children is, however, a displacement of his own quarrel. That it is transparently a delaying tactic, a mirror for his own contention, is evident from the silence; the only words we hear are his. Another form of displacement is that which renders the fantasy hypothetical, by introducing it with 'lest' (v. 5); only if the children's strife does not succeed, will it come into effect. Both displacements are rationalizations that distance the fantasy from himself; the children are screens or ventriloquists, whose intercession will avert punishment. In the next section (vv. 7-9), children and hypothesis disappear; instead God proposes to bring about the woman's return though preventive measures. Blocking her path with thorns may parallel the fantasy of exposure or preempt it, since it is justified as a means of rehabilitation. This line of thought is abandoned in the last section (vv. 10-15), in which the fantasy is unmediated by preventive measures or postponement.

Repetition is characteristic of obsession: the same scenario recurs, with greater or less aesthetic or ethical revision. In our section the masks are progressively stripped away; this may either be a Freudian 'working through', or typical of a sadistic process, in which the expenditure of violence leads to an access of love. Symptomatic of obsessiveness is its hypertrophic language: the long lists; the extended verses; the insistence of the repeated imperative 'Strive'; the punning focus on particular phonemes, whose elaboration suggests either a single underlying thought or the baroque pressure to generate as many permutations as possible. (T^{e}'$ēnātāh$, 'her fig tree', in v. 14 is compressed three words later into '$etnâ$, 'a [harlot's] hire' [Macintosh 1997: 63]; another example is the extraordinary concatenation of 'n's and 'p's in $w^{e}tāsēr\ z^{e}NûNeyhā\ miPPāNeyhā\ w^{e}Na^{a}PûPeyhā\ mibbên\ šādeyhā$, PeN '$aPšîteNNâ$, 'that she should remove her harlotries from her face and her adulteries from between her breasts, lest I strip her bare', in vv. 4-5.)

The fantasy is complex, overdetermined, and pornographic, in that, as Setel (1986) says, it depicts women's sexual shame. The infusion of violence into sexuality is not, however, primarily or only a means of excitation. Chapter 2 belongs to the literature of sexual disgust, in which desire appears only spectrally, as a revenant, and in reverse. Exposing the woman's nakedness to the gaze of her lovers is doubly voyeuristic. The viewer sees her through the eyes of others, and participates vicariously in their pleasure, except that the sight renders the lovers impotent: 'no one shall deliver her from my hand' (v. 12). The object of desire becomes undesirable, *nablût*, both 'contemptible' and 'foolish'. The jealous husband paradoxically acts as a pander, but only to nullify the jealous transaction, to divest the woman of cultural and social significance. She becomes a sign of the libidinal body; the word *nablût* 'folly' or 'shame', at least metonymically refers to her genitalia, and associates them with folly, contempt, and cosmic disorder. (The word *nablût* only occurs here in the Hebrew Bible, and is subject to extensive discussion: for *nablût* as a metonymy for genitalia, see Wolff 1974: 31, Stuart 1987: 51, and Keefe 2001: 215, though Macintosh 1997: 60 dissents; for the proposal that it is a term for cosmic disorder, see Murray 1992: 47. Sherwood [1996: 212] suggests a further meaning of 'degeneration', following Olyan [1992].) The body, imagined as anarchic and subversive, is nevertheless passive, subject to the look of the surrounding males. Vision is a means of appropriation of immense symbolic resonance, as the rhetoric of striptease and advertising shows. The underlying fantasy, then, is of gang-rape, the woman encircled by predators. The fantasy, however, is reversed; the sight turns back on the seers and taunts them with their incapacity to claim her. The husband, in exhibiting his wife, simultaneously discards her and asserts his prerogative over her.

The exposure of the woman is the prelude to her devastation, related in vv. 5 and 14. Predation is climactically embodied in the wild beasts, that consume 'them'—vine and fig tree, but also Israel—at the end of v. 14. The wild beasts are displaced figures of God, as executioners of his will; the identification becomes closer later in the book, when God adopts feral imagery for himself (5.14; 13.7-8). In 5.14 God, a metaphorical lion, boasts that 'none can deliver' from him, as does the husband in v. 12. Their rapacity converges with the desolation God brings in the first part of the verse. Verse 5 combines imagery of exposure with desiccation. There is a reversal both from adulthood to infancy, since the woman is naked 'as on the day of her birth', and from life to death. Death by thirst and drought negate her role as a source of life and sustenance, perceived through the prism of her breasts in v. 4. One may note a similar fantasy in the case of the woman suspected of adultery in Numbers 5, whose womb and thigh wither if she is guilty.

Verse 5 and 14 somewhat schematically match and oppose each other; God's threat in v. 5 to make Israel 'like a wilderness' is coupled in v. 14 with his intention to make it 'as a forest', two antithetical margins of culture (the parallel is perhaps clearer in

Hebrew than in English, since the verbal forms used are identical: $w^e\dot{s}amt\hat{\imath}h\bar{a}\ kammidb\bar{a}r$ and $w^e\dot{s}amt\hat{\imath}m\ l^eya\'ar$). The vision in v. 5 is passive, the woman abandoned and parched, while that in v. 14 is active, ravaging by wild beasts. In v. 5, moreover, there is a fantasy of infancy, immediately succeeded in v. 6 by Yhwh's rejection of his children. The baby is not merely helpless, but a precultural being; reducing her to its condition ejects the woman from the symbolic—social and linguistic—order to pure animality, as does the exposure of her body in v. 12. But it also infuses the fantasy of sexual exposure with the far more terrible one of the exposure of children. Lasciviousness and sexual disgust supervene on infanticide.

The husband is motivated by jealousy, which turns love into anti-love, rendered more intolerable by the memory of the love that has been defiled. Jealousy extenuates his vindictiveness, since the common wisdom is that he is not intrinsically full of hate, but driven to it by circumstances. Circumstances, however, license a pre-existing reservoir of repressed thoughts. Of these, the most important are the beliefs that women, archetypally the mother, will always let one down, that the present betrayal merely confirms this inherent unreliability, and that aggression, impelled by greed, hatred and envy, is therefore justified. That the woman, from being a source of succour, becomes a desert is the germinal fantasy in v. 5; that she is torn to pieces is that of v. 14. The transfer from breasts, in v. 4, to infant, in v. 5, suggests a projection, an exchange of identity between mother and child. This is amplified in v. 5, in which the abandoned child turns the mother into a figure of abandonment. One is reminded of those children who, according to Winnicott (1991: 112-13), are deprived of their mothers' presence for too long and, in despair, inwardly abandon them.

The two fantasies, of abandonment and aggression, are mutually dependent, in that the rage is provoked by frustration and in turn results in rejection. At the same time, they are incompatible, since the woman is both absent, dying of neglect, and available for laceration. For that reason, perhaps, they are separated by the span of the passage. Contradictory and complementary, they enact the metaphorical play of likeness and difference, the resistance of the imagination to a single construction. The satisfactions of violence breach, yet leave intact, the narcissistic space outlined by the presence/absence of the mourned mother/lover, in which the child fears death by exposure, a morbidity reflected in the sexual sphere by the cross-currents of sadism, isolation, and sterility.

Another element is introduced by the metaphor of blocking the woman's path with thorns in v. 8. This is a prelude to her subjection to her lovers' gaze in v. 12; as O'Connor (1987: 243) shows, a non-sequitur intervenes between prevention of access to them and humiliation before them. The logical obstacle is not only a sign of resistance to and rationalization of the underlying fantasy, but contributes an additional scenario of the woman suffering. At this point the passage comes closest to pornography, in the sense of the inscription of women's shame for the sake of male pleasure. It feeds off the woman's desperation and frustration, gratifying the man both with the vision of female desire and the assertion of his power. This may be combined, voyeuristically, with hatred and envy that the desire is not for himself. The thorns, in particular, suggest cruelty, and presage entrapment by the gaze of the lovers in v. 12. The sadistic fantasy relies on the pain of the woman, on imagining her consciousness; one notes the care with which God puts words in her mouth, projects himself into her speaking and acting. For this reason, the sadistic fantasy can never culminate in her destruction; it ritualistically exorcizes the hatred on which it draws, to which it alludes. The erotic cover is evoked only to be displaced. Underneath the hint of perversion (or diversion), toying with the woman, tormented by the memory of desire and the wish to punish, are the nullification of the sexual transaction through exposure and the complex metamorphoses suggested by the superimposed images of rape and bestial voracity. The one scene conceives of the woman stripped of her humanity, surrounded by hunters; the other turns the hunters into animals. Nothing suggests more clearly the contagion of destruction, that making the woman into a wilderness and consuming her reflects their own desolation and fear of dissolution.

The erotic substratum of the text, its reversal of the language of love, is more poignant because of its echoes of the Song of Songs. These are particularly evident in vv. 8-9 and contribute to the sexual suggestiveness of those verses. In the Song 3.1-4 the woman seeks her lover through the city at night, encountering watchmen before she eventually finds him; the phrase 'I sought him and did not find him' is repeated at the end of 3.1 and 2. In vv. 8-9 we find the same pair, 'seeking' and 'finding'; the phrase 'she will not find' likewise recurs at the end of clauses. In the

Song 5.2-7, a variant of the same passage, the phrase 'I sought him and did not find him' reappears (5.6). Here, however, the watchmen beat and strip the woman. In both texts the woman's search for her lover, contravening social propriety, is invested with erotic anticipation, intensified by frustration; she represents the amorous body. In both, she suffers humiliation. However, they are from opposite perspectives. Whereas in Hosea the voice is male and articulates a fantasy that passes from the sadistic game to voyeuristic exposure, in the Song it is female and expresses her outrage. We do not know what the watchmen feel, and the ordeal permits the celebration of her lover's beauty and thus of her own eros in Song 5.10-16.

Another difference is that in Hosea the woman's speech contradicts appearances; the pornographic gratification of witnessing her love-sickness is undercut by her confessedly economic motives. She will go after her lovers because they provide her with sustenance, according to v. 7, and she determines, in v. 9, to return to Yhwh because he was a better investment. As van Dijk-Hemmes shows (1989: 82), economic dependence is a powerful instrument of male control and rhetoric; women do not have libidos, or at least their libido does not count, but merely where their interest lies. Since they are not genuinely sexual beings, they can be subsumed by male fantasy. The woman then corroborates her whorishness by being mercenary, and is subject both to the man's resentment and his will. However, necessity provides a potential counter-argument against the passage's polemic: the woman is compelled by ignorance and destitution, not by lust. If she genuinely does not know that Yhwh is her benefactor (v. 10), and suffers from amnesia (v. 15), then her guilt is extenuated. The counter-argument is developed in ch. 4, where the people perish 'without knowledge' (4.5), because the priests have been negligent of their duty. On the other hand, daughters and brides are granted immunity, in a curious inversion of the double standard, because their sexual liaisons follow men's bad example.

The Song of Songs is a much more pervasive presence in this passage than has been previously recognized (the two previous studies are those of van Dijk-Hemmes and van Selms), not so much on the surface of the text as in its basic imagery. Whether one is dealing with the genre of love poetry, an early forerunner of the Song, or simple serendipity is impossible to determine, since the Song itself was probably composed much later. In any case, the invective in Hosea is directed against a valorization of love and the world represented most comprehensively by the Song. In the Song 1.13, the woman's lover lies between her breasts like a sachet of myrrh; in Hosea (v. 4) this is replaced by the signs of her adultery. In the Song, the birth of the lovers is an epiphany: the woman was 'splendid to the one who gave her birth' (6.9); the man is awakened to love and to life in a birth scene under an apple tree, full of cosmic significance (8.5). In Hosea, being reduced to one's birth state is evidence of utter dehumanization; nakedness is the subject of shame instead of celebration, as in the Song. The wilderness, in Hosea, is a sign of the woman's desolation and death by thirst; in the Song, it is the place of the lovers' tryst, associated with exotic spices and sights (1.14; 3.6; 8.5). In the Song 4.8, the woman is invited to come down from Lebanon, the home of the wild beasts; here they threaten devastation.

Like Hosea, the Song of Songs exposes the woman to the sight of others, the 'lovers' and 'friends' (sometimes obscured in translations, such as NRSV's 'with love' rather than 'lovers'), who are urged to 'eat' and 'drink' in the garden of love in 5.1, and in particular to the spectators who elicit her return in 7.1 (6.13 in English translations), that they may 'gaze' at her. In contrast to Hosea, however, their vision is positive; their voices must at least concur with that of the male lover in the descriptive catalogue of her beauty in 7.2-7. Like the woman in Hosea, she is metaphorically correlated with the land of Israel, as is particularly evident in this catalogue. The description fragments the body into part-objects, each one of which develops a life of its own and is complexly interconnected with the others; the metaphorical process *simultaneously* splits and recombines, resulting in a total vision of the world, integrated and transformed through love. In Hosea, sexual metaphor provides similar opportunities for the vision of recreation; fragmentation and integration are, however, projected *successively* into the text, rendering problematic its logical cohesion. Are they simply juxtaposed, or is the transformation an act of will? The denial of the sexual relationship at the beginning of the passage ('For she is not my wife and I am not her husband') implicitly cancels out all its associated couplings, the entire interaction of God and Israel. It thus becomes a metaphor for the failure of the metaphorical process, just as, in the Song of Songs, the union of lovers is the sign of its success; the work of the poem corresponds to their discourse. The failure of metaphor, however, can only be communicated through metaphor, which thus subverts itself. Further, the denial is countermanded by Yhwh's assumption of marital authority over the woman, by the woman's acknowledgement in v. 9, as well as by the framing narrative.

There is another contrast, another way in which the metaphor in Hosea is suspect. We know that the Song of Songs has its literal meaning, that it actually refers to the love of lovers. The reference of the metaphor in Hosea is quite opaque. It may refer to the exclusiveness of the cult, sacrificial communion as analogous to sexual communion, or to the transfer of moral qualities—loyalty, compassion and so on—as an equivalent to seminal fluids, as v. 22 might suggest, or to the fertilization of the earth, corresponding to the imagery of 'sowing' and 'answering' in vv. 23-25. If the passage accuses Israel of a category mistake—Yhwh is its husband, not Baal—it propagates the Baalization of Yhwh it denounces. The 'wife' may be land or people; the identification is alternatively assumed by the text and abandoned by it. The metaphor may accordingly be interpreted in various ways, none of which is decisive. (See the discussions in Jeremias 1983: 41-42; Fisch 1988: 147-48; Wolff 1974: 34; and Balz-Cochois 1982; Whitt 1992, at the cost of some radical textual excision, holds that the 'wife' is Asherah. Sherwood 1996: 214-35 systematically compares Hosea 2 to the Ras Shamra texts. Keefe 2001: 47-48 critiques the prevalent contrast of Yhwh and Baal.)

If the 'wife' is Israel, then it comprises both genders. The literal negation of the bond between 'my people' and 'I am' in 1.9 is transposed to the metaphorical one between 'husband' and 'wife' in v. 4. But this is hardly innocent. The supplementation, or mystification, is also a displacement: the male-dominated Israelite society is characterized as female. God is the supreme patriarch, before whom all men are women; the relation of male to female is that of God to humanity. The metaphor is, however, meaningless, since the shift in gender of the men corresponds to no social or sacred reality. Their classification as 'women' is not reflected in their behaviour or in their self-perception. Its sole function, indeed, is to activate the contrast between wife and whore as a metaphor for their faithlessness, to compound their vilification with misogyny, even if only in drag. However, the transfer from male to female serves also to foreground, to render visible, women as social actors. We catch glimpses of women's normal life, especially cultic life, in the indictment that fuels

Yhwh's fantasy, for instance in v. 15. It may be, as Bird (1989: 83) suggests, that women are especially implicated in the accusation of sacred and sexual perfidy, that while the polemic is ostensibly against Israel, male and female, and lacks overt sexual content on the level of denotation, in fact it connotes women as pre-eminent vehicles of estrangement, and thus a polemic against Israel easily becomes one against women.

In that case, the identification of the lovers is also in question. In v. 15 the lovers are parallel to the Baalim, whose days Yhwh will visit, and in v. 10 Yhwh's gifts of silver and gold are dedicated to Baal's image. The lovers whom Israel credits with her sustenance are likewise easily decoded as the indigenous gods, who are responsible for her fertility. There may be some reference to foreign powers, as elsewhere in the book (Kelle [2005: 119-22] thinks this is the exclusive reference; cf. also Keefe). But the transfer from metaphorical to real women, the focus on women as exemplars of Israel's cultic perversity, will also direct our attention to their real lovers, whose licentiousness at festivals is condemned in 4.12-14. If the lovers are not only Baalim but Israelite men, they participate in the scapegoating of women who, as Israel, represent themselves. The men are then ambiguous; as literally male and figuratively female, they are invited by Yhwh to a parody of male bonding whose victims they are. Literal and metaphorical domains mutually interact, in that the actual affairs of Israelite men and women give rise to, and are encouraged by, their metaphorical promiscuity. At the same time, the collapse of the metaphorical into the literal threatens the distinctions on which metaphor is based. The intensity and detail with which the passage is elaborated is proportionate to its tendency to fragment. The repetition of the argument is not only a sign of obsessiveness, but of a wish to integrate discordance, to achieve reconciliation.

(16) Therefore, behold I will allure her, and will lead her to the wilderness, and I will speak to her heart.
(17) And I will give her her vineyards thence, and I will turn the vale of Achor into an entrance of Hope, and she will answer there as in the days of her youth, as in the day of her going up from the land of Egypt.
(18) And it shall be on that day, says Yhwh, that you will call me 'my husband' and you will no longer call me 'my master'.

(19) And I will remove the names of the Baalim from her mouth, and they will no longer be remembered by their names.

(20) And I will make a covenant for them on that day, with the beasts of the field, and the birds of the heavens, and the creeping creatures of the ground, and I will break bow and sword and war from the earth, and I will make them lie down in safety.

(21) And I will betroth you to me for ever; and I will betroth you to me in equity and justice, and kindness and compassion.

(22) And I will betroth you to me in faithfulness, and you will know Yhwh.

(23) And it shall be on that day that I will answer, says Yhwh, I will answer the heavens, and they will answer the earth.

(24) And the earth will answer the corn, and the new wine, and oil, and they will answer Jezreel.

(25) And I will sow her for me in the earth, and I will have compassion on Uncompassioned, and I will say to Not-my-People 'You are my people', and he will say 'My God'.

Verse 16 is the turning-point, introduced by yet another 'Therefore'. As many commentators remark, the logical connection is surprising; nothing prepares us for the indictment to be followed by anything other than punishment. Clines (1978: 99) argues that the three 'therefores' represent alternatives, of which only the last is truly viable if Israel, and thus God's enterprise, is to survive. There is, however, a direct continuation from the previous section. Verse 15 ends, 'and me she forgot, says Yhwh'. Her forgetfulness annuls her history as the domain of memory, as well as providing potential extenuation. God, in turn, revokes history, takes her back to the beginning.

But is this possible? God supposes that through reversing time he can erase the memory of his violence, that he too can make a new beginning. However, in practice, return to the wilderness can only mean the end of Israel's political existence in the land, and hence the death and exile that the book portends (Rashi, Kimchi). It is coterminous with the deadly wilderness that Israel becomes in v. 5; the place of devastation and thirst is the scene of romantic fulfilment. The two aspects of the figure of the mother are divided: the land and the people. Only by leaving the land can Israel relinquish its identification with the land and its mésalliance with its indigenous gods. Only thus can it be exclusively Yhwh's. In the romance, the children disappear. The woman returns to a prenuptial condition, marked by freedom from social responsibility and prurience, beyond birth and conception, before the entrance into the land and history. The wilderness, as Leith (1989) has argued, is a liminal space, in between stages of life and geopolitical entities; she compares our chapter to a rite of initiation, in which the transition from one state to another is marked by symbolic death and the suspension of social norms. The wilderness is the place of barrenness and death, but also of a new birth and the passage from chaos to order (for the 'systemic' significance of the desert as a place of purification, especially in Achaemenid Judah, see Ben Zvi 2005: 72-73). The woman then passes through the fantasied death of v. 5 as a prelude to her initiation into her marriage and her affirmation as a sexual person.

Yhwh's desire may be construed in various ways: as an attempt at reparation, as the jealous person's desire for a lost love, as the sadist's longing for intimacy. Either the excitation of violence is transposed into that of sexuality, or the exhaustion of violence permits or provides an excuse for tenderness. Whereas in v. 5 the wilderness juxtaposed images of birth and death, in v. 17 birth, associated with the Exodus as well as the wilderness, is metaphorically aligned with sexual awakening, as in the Song of Songs. The two images of the wilderness are both discontinuous and concurrent, since the reality of exile is dissimulated by the romance. Nostalgic regress to the beginning coincides with the end of Israel's political history, with the death of the kingdom. If one of the principal problems of the chapter is how to reconcile its beginning and its end, the violence and obsessiveness of the first part with the blissful transformation of the second, its rhetoric and structure support both their integral connection and their disjunction. On the one hand, the second half reverses the first: the children, from being rejected as 'children of promiscuity', are acknowledged as 'My people'; compassion replaces lack of compassion; disavowal of marital status is redressed by betrothal; forgetfulness is transferred from Yhwh to the Baalim, and concomitantly ignorance of Yhwh's gifts becomes knowledge of Yhwh himself. Beasts are no longer destructive, since Yhwh establishes a covenant with them. On the other hand, the unexpectedness of the change, the incommensurability of the two parts, is marked by the threefold repetition of 'on that day' (vv. 18, 20, 23), corresponding to the threefold repetition of 'therefore' (vv. 8, 11, 16). In both cases, repetition imposes simultaneity on the sequence. 'On that day' suggests a radical transformation of reality, an entirely new temporal order; the collapse of so many events into one day both lengthens it indefinitely and separates it from everything that precedes it. 'On that day', in prophetic writings, is a formula for the new age the prophet heralds. Each event, moreover, accomplishes a resolution of narrative tension, the conclusion of the story which is also world history. The indefinitely long day verges on the infinity suggested by Yhwh's betrothal to Israel 'for ever' (v. 21). Each time 'on that day' recurs, it announces a new divine initiative, an unforeseen supervention in human affairs. That they all occur on the same day makes them coeval, so that they become variants of each other, different aspects of the same picture.

'Says the Lord' in v. 15 is followed by 'Therefore' at the beginning of v. 16. Together they function as a hinge that both separates and connects the two halves of the chapter (Ben Zvi 2005: 64). The two temporal planes then interlock; the transformative journey into the wilderness coincides, as we have seen, with death and dispossession. The phrase 'on that day' otherwise occurs in Hosea only in 1.5, in the context of the breach of Israel's military power. Whether it is identical with the day of ch. 2 is imponderable; at any rate, the formula associates the threshold of destruction with the advent of the new era. That it does not occur elsewhere broaches the question of whether ch. 2 is a microcosm of the rest of the book, which repeats the trajectory from destruction to restoration, the divine vacillation between condemnation and compassion. 'On that day' demarcates a time that is or is not coterminous with that of the conclusion in ch. 14; it potentially disrupts the integration of 2.16-25 into the book's structure.

In v. 16, Yhwh allures the woman and takes her into the wilderness; there he speaks to her heart. The word for 'allure' may refer to seduction (e.g. Exod. 2.20), to deception, and, in the case of Yhwh, to the entrapment of prophets and kings with misleading vaticination (cf. 1 Kgs 20–22; Jer. 20.7; Ezek. 14.9). Here, however, it loses the negative connotations familiar, for example, from Proverbs. Seduction may be an unusual pastime for Yhwh; nevertheless, it associates him not only with the paramours of the first part of the chapter, but with the lovers of the Song of Songs. As in the Song of Songs, the wilderness is the matrix of their speech, where the woman awakens her lover at the place where his mother bore him (8.5). Now it is the woman who is brought back to her beginning, to the 'days of her youth'. Yhwh persuades through speaking 'to her heart'; it is less the content of the speech that matters than its appeal to her sensory and affective faculties. As in the Song, language seduces indirectly, through imaginative and sensual richness. It seeks to lift the inhibitions that society imposes on young women; in other words, it counteracts the symbolic order that language itself constitutes. The words are a sign of the sexual male body, the nudity that society and its texts usually conceal; they elicit an equally expressive response. The word for 'allure' (*pth*) recurs in Hosea in 7.11, where Ephraim is a foolish (*pôtâ*) dove, courting the great powers; Yhwh thus takes advantage of its amorous susceptibility. In the Song, the woman is metaphorically a dove, whose voice her lover cultivates (2.14). The desire for the woman's speech is the first breach in the closed circle of male fantasy; it opens the possibility of a dialogue, albeit from within the fantasy, that will disrupt its exclusivity.

The word for 'wilderness' (*midbār*) puns on that for 'and I will speak' (*wᵉdibbartî*) that immediately follows it. The two are opposites: the wilderness is the land of silence, in which the speech of her lover is the only thing that is heard. The transformation of silence into speech is equivalent, on the sexual plane, to the poetic celebration of nakedness. The eeriness of the wilderness, its combination of dread and miracle, denaturalizes it; all that sustains Israel in this waste is the divine word. The matrix is paradoxically a hostile environment, where it is not at home. Intertextually, the speech would presumably correspond to the Torah that God gave to Israel in the wilderness, whose infringement he castigates. It is followed immediately by another transformation, of the wilderness into vineyards: 'I will give her thence her vineyards'. It is unclear whether the vineyards are conflated with the wilderness—so the detail 'thence' might suggest—or whether they contrast the desert and settled land, exile and return. At any rate, they are opposites; vineyards are associated with Dionysiac intoxication, and hence with the pleasures of the first half of the chapter. This leads in turn to another transformation, of the vale of Achor to the entrance of Hope. The vale of Achor was the site of the first sacrilege on Israel's entrance into the land (Joshua 7); the entrance of Hope promises a new beginning.

But there is another connection. The word for 'hope' (*tiquâ*) is identical to that for the 'thread' which Rahab, the prostitute who protected the Israelite spies, hung from the wall of Jericho to ensure her safety (Joshua 6). Achan, the victim of the vale of Achor, is the symbolic counterpart of Rahab: the one Israelite who pillaged the spoil of Jericho and was destroyed with it corresponds to the one Canaanite who survived. As a prostitute, moreover, Rahab symbolizes the land and its fecundity; her welcome to the spies is a displaced sexual transaction. She embodies the promiscuity attributed to the land and the worship of its deities, but also the possibility of renewal, of a union of Yhwh and Canaan, land and desert.

The promise of return to the wilderness is followed, in v. 18, by a further promise: 'On that day...you will call me "my man" (*'îšî*) and no longer "my master" (*ba'lî*)'. Both terms are synonyms for 'husband'; the second puns on the name of Baal. God is not equivalent to Baal; the worship of the one cannot be facilely transferred to the other. God differs from Baal apparently in being less abstract, less transcendent. The shock value of the expression may be gauged by comparison with v. 4, where God claims not to be the woman's man/husband, and 11.9, in which his inability to consummate his wrath is justified by his not being human. Moreover, it takes us back, beyond the wilderness, to an earlier point of origin. In the story of the Garden of Eden, the first human couple are differentiated as 'man' and 'woman' before the institution of male dominance in Gen. 3:16. The contrast between 'my man' and 'my master', as many critics note, suggests a relationship of complementarity and equality. In other words, within the male fantasy, patriarchy thinks beyond itself, just as in v. 17 the evocation of the woman's response turns seduction into dialogue.

At any rate, in v. 19 Yhwh reassumes control, removing the names of the Baalim from the woman's mouth. The Baalim are indigenous local deities, the numina of the landscape, responsible for its gifts. Through venerating the Baalim, the woman/Israel attaches herself to the divinity of the land, grants herself a retroactive autochthony, just as, according to Cooper and Goldstein (1993), accounts of altars raised and trees planted at sacred sites by the patriarchs serve to map them onto the landscape, to make the cult of the ancestors an assertion of patrimony. In contrast, the re-enactment of the initiatory compact in the wilderness dissociates Israel from any home; it is a stranger in the land. God is not a Baal in that he is not a local deity, and cannot even be identified as an overlord. If Baal, as 'master', guarantees hierarchies, God's desire to be called human deconstructs even the hierarchical difference of God and humanity (on the deconstructive critique of hierarchy, see Sherwood 1996: 207).

The verse systematically inverts the terms of vv. 14 and 15. In v. 15 the woman celebrates 'the days of the Baalim'; now she will no longer remember them. Conversely, the oblivion of which Yhwh complains in v. 15 is replaced by recollection. Memory in the Hebrew Bible is also a cultic resource; one remembers the name and acts of God at festivals (cf. for example Exod. 3.15, and Morris 1996: 128). Reciting the name of the deity conjures up its presence. Jeremias (1983: 49) points out that the epithet 'Name-of-Baal' was attributed also to the great goddesses, such as Anat and Astarte. Removal of the names of Baal is manifested in deprivation of their putative gifts of vine and fig in v. 14, since the word for names ($š^e mōt$) is mirrored in that for 'I will make desolate' ($w^e hašimmōtî$). The eradication of language is coordinated with the transformation of cultivated land into wilderness, especially since the following 'I will turn them ($w^e śamtîm$) into a forest' reproduces the same alliteration (a matter more evident in the Hebrew consonantal text than in transliteration, since 'sh' and 's' are represented by the same letter). What is undone ($w^e hašimmōtî$) through language are the names ($š^e mōt$), the visible signs, of Baal.

In v. 15, the woman is imagined adorned with rings and jewellery on the 'days of the Baalim', going after her lovers, who may be both human and divine. The scene permits access to an actuality in which women make themselves beautiful, take pleasure in themselves, experience value in terms of appearance, wealth, and social standing, conform to normal piety, and are embedded in the licit and illicit undercurrents that constitute society. Women have a certain autonomy within a highly structured, not particularly oppressive, social order. Yhwh's strategy is to destroy this autonomy through controlled aphasia; by eliminating all undesirable words, he will grant her unconditioned freedom, whose outcome is determined by himself. He wishes her to be a robot and not a robot at the same time. If she addresses him as 'my man', then she implicitly recognizes his intrinsic value, irrespective of his power. Behind this there is a desire, on his side, to be just a man, to relinquish or at least suspend power. The figure of the wilderness, which in v. 5 signified abandonment and death by thirst, now becomes one of possibility outside patriarchy. If the wilderness is the realm of desolation, the only thing that gives life to it is the love of the lovers. As in the Song of Songs, love and death are maximally contrasted. The wilderness will recur, and acquire additional significance, in the course of the book.

The next verse (v. 20) continues the process of inversion that we found in v. 19. Whereas wild beasts consumed the fruits of the land in v. 14, here God makes a covenant with them on Israel's behalf. Harmony between human beings and animals is another echo of the story of the Garden of Eden, before conflict between them introduced the discord of history. The threefold classification of animals is reproduced in God's original blessing to humanity and animals in Gen. 1.30 and its renewal after the Flood in Gen. 9.2. Our verse is paralleled in Lev. 26.6, in which God promises to give peace to the land, to cause noxious beasts to cease, and to remove the threat of the sword, and in Ezek. 34.25, which predicts 'a covenant of peace' with the animals, whereby they will remain undisturbed in their deserts and forests. Murray (1990: 31-32, 39) has seen in these texts and others evidence for a cosmic covenant, which God made with all creation, whose breach—archetypally denoted by the Flood—has ever to be repaired.

Verse 20 is central to the vision of restoration in vv. 16-25. Verses 16-17 correspond to vv. 23-25, in that both adumbrate the theme of 'answering', while the excision of Baalistic language in vv. 18-19 is reversed in the renewed knowledge of Yhwh in vv. 21-22. The dialogue in the outer pair, and the knowledge in the inner one, frame the utopian vision. If the cosmic covenant is the ultimate object of restoration, then it becomes an ideal for the rest of the book. The beginning of ch. 4 articulates its breach, which the succeeding chapters illustrate in detail. Whether the last chapter is a restatement of the cosmic vision, and whether the book therefore achieves closure, we shall consider in due course.

There are other cross-references. In 1.4-5 Yhwh, after explicating the name Jezreel, declares that he will cause the kingdom of Israel to cease and break the bow of Israel in the valley of Jezreel; in 1.7 Judah will be delivered, but not by 'bow and sword and war'. In our verse, the same sequence is repeated, as are the expressions 'I will break the bow' and 'on that day'. The end of sovereignty and the demilitarization of Israel—the death the book foreshadows—is the beginning of the new era.

'I will cause...to cease' in 1.5 recurs in v. 13, where, using the same verb, Yhwh threatens to end the woman's joy, festivals, new moons, and Sabbaths. 'I will cause to cease' (*hišbattî*) negates the word 'her sabbath' (*šabbattāh*); what Yhwh causes to cease is the day of cessation itself. If the Sabbath is Yhwh's sacred day, its abolition—together with festivals, new moons, and assemblies—withdraws God from his part in time. His disavowal is motivated or emphasized by its becoming 'her sabbath', 'her new moon', alienated from Yhwh; through annulling it, ironically he reclaims it. In Lev. 26.6 and Ezek. 34.25 the same expression, 'I will cause to cease', which could perhaps be interpreted as 'I will impose a sabbath', has 'evil beasts' as its object. One might expect it here, following or instead of 'I will make a covenant', especially given the parallelism between 'I will cause to cease' and 'I will break' in 1.4-5. The lacuna points us back to the presence of the verb in vv. 13-14, where the imposition of a sabbath on sabbaths and festivals is followed by the desolation of vine and fig tree, the turning of the land into a forest or wilderness, and the provision of food for the animals. These are characteristics of the sabbatical year, when the produce of the land was left for the beasts (Lev. 25.7). Once again, the two sabbaths, that of desolation and that of restoration, meet across the threshold marked by 'on that day'.

The sabbath immediately follows God's blessing of humans and animals in Gen. 1.26-30, and is identified with the cosmic or eternal covenant in Exod. 31.17. Since the word for 'land/earth' is ambiguous, it is not clear whether the peace predicted in v. 20 is universal, or only applies to the land of Israel; its association with the motif of the cosmic covenant at least suggests a cosmic dimension. If so, the ultimate horizon in Hosea is a world in which the abolition of war combines with an end to natural predation. That the universal perspective does not recur, at least not explicitly, in the rest of Hosea sketches an encompassing scheme into which the book fits. The overarching allegory lapses for a moment; the covenant is forged 'for them', Israel as a grammatically masculine collectivity. The phrase literally reads, 'I will cut a covenant for them'; it may be associated with the bow that God sets in the sky in Gen. 9.12-17, and hence with the bow that is broken in our verse, but more particularly with circumcision. Eilberg-Schwartz (1990: 169) claims that circumcision is an assertion of patrilineality, a phallic bond between father and son whose breach permits fertility, and Propp (1993) argues that it was originally a prenuptial rite. The allusion to the covenant in our verse precedes betrothal in vv. 21-22 and follows the removal of impure speech in v. 19, a surgical operation on language and memory that makes the new symbolic order possible. The suspension of the allegory exposes its patriarchal assumptions. It threatens to replace it, however, with an exclusive masculinity, in which only the beasts of the field and the broken weapons of war are, at least grammatically, feminine.

Verses 21-22 are among the most famous in the book, and are recited every morning by Jews putting on phylacteries. The threefold repetition of 'I will betroth you' suggests a binding formula, whose eternity is matched by faithfulness in v. 22, and guaranteed by the various attributes at the end of v. 21. Each occurrence is also metaphorically related to the others: the totality of 'for ever' splits into the paired terms equity and justice, kindness and compassion, which reunite in faithfulness. Eternity is constituted by these qualities. The formula, moreover, is ambiguous: Yhwh may infuse virtue into Israel as his brideprice, equivalent to his material benefits in v. 17, or equity, justice, kindness and compassion may be innate, shared qualities of God and humans, and hence the medium of divine-human communication. 'Faithfulness' may be a fifth attribute, parallel to the others, but climactically separated from them, or it may correspond to 'for ever,' as a divine guarantee. These possibilities are not exclusive and suggest both a transformation of Israel, given their lack of these qualities in the rest of the book, and a reciprocal relationship.

The betrothal ends in reversal: 'and you shall know Yhwh'. Knowledge is a frequent euphemism for sex in the Hebrew Bible, and this connotation is evident here in the context of romance. That the romance is metaphorical, instead of making knowledge a metaphor twice removed, literalizes it. Knowledge is the equivalent of sexual intimacy between humans and God (Macintosh 1997: 85). Throughout the book, knowledge of God is a goal that God desires (6.6), and whose absence he deplores. It is not clear that its acquisition is attained, even in ch. 14. Once again, ch. 2 projects an ultimate horizon, with correlates in the vision of universal peace and knowledge in Isaiah (2.2-4; 11.9), that both contributes to the overall frame and is separate from it.

To know God is to uncover his mystery, and conflicts with the insistence throughout the Hebrew Bible that God is concealed, that the cost of seeing his face is death. In a sexual context, uncovering discloses nakedness and is responsible for shame according to Gen. 3.7; it constitutes violation of incest taboos in Leviticus 18 and 20. The sexual union, likeness and difference of the divine and human are preoccupations throughout the early chapters of Genesis (cf. e.g. 4.1; 6.1-6). Moreover, this is the only time in the Hebrew Bible in which the woman is the subject of sexual knowledge, albeit through the man's eyes. If knowledge is power, then the attribution of knowledge to the woman undermines the patriarchal claim to benevolent authority (contrariwise, Ben Zvi [2005: 65] suggests that it may mean 'acknowledgement' of Yhwh's sovereignty). If the man is knowable by the woman, he is also controllable by her. Since this is still the man's fantasy, it must correspond to his desire. The desire for surrender and being intimately known reverses the fantasy of abandonment and rage that we found in v. 5, and, as we saw there, is its inner lining. God's fantasy of being known, of a complementary relationship, again reverses the story of the Garden of Eden, where the woman's desire for knowledge threatens his supremacy.

The prophet is the mediator of the betrothal, and the one who possesses knowledge of God; prophets are the guardians of the values of kindness and justice against their falsification (6.4-6; 12.7). The prophet then is a part of Israel that is already initiated into God's secret, in whom the prophecy is already fulfilled. As speaker and addressee, he is both subject and object, both masculine and feminine. In the prophet, the discourse is transferred to Israel. This raises the question of voice. The masculine fantasy is only heard and interpreted through Israel; it is always being appropriated, estranged from itself. The elaborate metaphysical union and sexual differentiation of God and Israel lapses momentarily in the embrace of the cosmic covenant, displacing masculine exclusivity with the vision of an end to the male game of war and of the hostility between humans and animals. The language of the poem speaks for God, humanity and the earth, and is accordingly ambiguated and riven. Poetic language is indirect, blurring the precise distinctions between words—an example is the chain 'righteousness and justice, kindness and compassion'—and substituting a continuum for the polarity of God and Israel, speaker and addressee.

The mantra-like repetition of 'I will betroth you' is proleptic; we do not know if the marriage will take place. It leaves us on the threshold of closure, a legal bond that just precedes consummation.

Betrothal marks the transition between the romance in the wilderness, with its Edenic connotations and its freedom from social constraints, and marital routine; it is a moment of heightened sexual expectation and social communion. Whether the last three verses represent fulfilment of these expectations is ambiguous. On the one hand, they direct attention away from the couple; on the other, the plethora of voices answering, the imagery of insemination, and the acknowledgement of legitimacy, indicate a healing of the breach between husband and wife that takes us back to the beginning of the relationship and the book.

In the last verses, the voice passes backwards and forwards, from God to the heavens, from the heavens to the earth, and then by way of Jezreel and the other two children, back to God. The poetic and spatial structure is concentric. In the centre, a focus on Jezreel is transformed, through word-play, into one on the proliferating divine seed, since Jezreel means 'God sows'; on either side, the earth both transmits the voice of Jezreel and is the receptacle for the seed. God, in the outer frame, is both responsible for and extraneous to the interaction of natural forces, the totality characteristic of the cosmic covenant. That he answers the heavens sets him outside them; likewise, that he says 'I will answer' at the beginning of v. 23, without any immediate object, isolated by the formulae 'says Yhwh' and 'It shall be on that day', unbalances the discourse.

There is a parallel ambiguity. I have already noted the transfer of gender, from Jezreel to the feminine object of 'I will sow' in v. 25, whose identity may be Israel, the woman in the allegory, or the earth, in v. 24. The terms are not altogether distinct; Israel is identified with the land, for instance in 1.2, and Jezreel is a metonymy for Israel (Sweeney 2000: 37 comments that Jezreel [$yizr^{e\varsigma}e\prime l$] sounds like Israel). The metaphor may mean that Israel will finally be implanted in the land and produce a crop for God (hence the detail, 'I will sow her for me'); nevertheless, the transfer from the woman to the seed is paradoxical—the earth, as it were, is sown in the earth, the woman is impregnated with herself. The phallic image recalls that of the covenant in v. 20; that God's seed is feminine demystifies the exclusive male community. Correspondingly, God's speech in vv. 21-22 can only be heard through becoming Israel's speech, and establishing the continuum of identity between them.

Israel oscillates between the poles of the land and the wilderness; it is both identical to the land and strange to it. If Israel only truly becomes itself and Yhwh's through leaving the land and going into exile, any return to the land risks entanglement with its indigenous deities and turning Yhwh into Baal. The counterpart of origination in the wilderness is the autochthonous source of Samaria in 13.15. Between the two matrices there is only alternation. Alongside the image of Israel's being sown in the land and the renewed fertility of Jezreel is God's recognition of Israel as 'My people'. The dialogue 'My people', 'My god', both corresponds to that of heaven and earth in v. 23, and goes beyond it.

Verses 23-25 are a counterpart to vv. 1-3; in both, the reversal of the names of the children is a sign of reconciliation with God and results in poetic closure. They use different materials, however; whereas vv. 1-3 describe a new Exodus, in vv. 23-25 Israel is implanted in the land, in a celebration of fertility that is not only reminiscent of a Baal text from Ugarit (Batto 1987: 199-201), but of human and divine responsibility for vegetation in Gen. 2.5. In v. 2 the day of Jezreel is the point of departure; in v. 24 it is the place of homecoming, where the echoing voices come to rest. In vv. 1-3 the transformation of names is one of human recognition: it is said of them, presumably from outside, 'children of the living God'; it is as a collectivity, brothers and sisters, Israel and Judah, that they call each other 'Compassioned' and 'My people'. God, through urging them to affection, hears his own emotions through them; in vv. 23-24 these voices are heard through those of nature. The two visions, though complementary, are irreconcilable. In one, the land is the recipient of blessing; in the other, it is metaphorically equivalent to Egypt. Each leads to the other: that is the persuasive effect, always undercut, of the narrative of ch. 2.

Hosea 3

(1) And Yhwh said to me, 'Go again, love a woman beloved of a friend and adulterous, just like the love of Yhwh for the Israelites, and they turn to other gods and are lovers of raisin-cakes.
(2) And I obtained her for myself with fifteen shekels of silver, and a *homer* of barley and a *letek* of barley.
(3) And I said to her, 'Many days stay with me; do not go a-whoring, do not be with a man, and also I to you.
(4) For many days the children of Israel shall remain, without king, without prince, without sacrifice, without sacred pillar, without ephod or teraphim.
(5) Afterwards the children of Israel shall return, and they shall seek Yhwh their God and David their king, and they will come fearfully to Yhwh and his goodness at the end of days.'

Chapter 3 parallels ch. 1 as a narrative concerning the prophet's relationship with a licentious woman. One of the perennial, but irresolvable, critical issues is whether or not it concerns the same woman, Gomer, and, if so, how the two stories intermesh. Unlike ch. 1, ch. 3 is not a complete story, and lacks clear correlations with ch. 2. We do not know what transpired, or what preceded the events recorded here. If Hosea did write his autobiography, why is only this snatch cited? Why does it intervene between the establishment of the cosmic covenant in ch. 2 and its reversal at the beginning of ch. 4? And why, above all, is it so clumsy? The story in ch. 1, if rudimentary, is clear, its attached oracles on the whole poetically well-constructed; ch. 3, with its interminable sentences, its repetitiveness, and its grammatical incoherence in v. 3, would scarcely seem to come from the same person. It is as if good writing comes from the editor, while the poet, when left to his own devices, produces a jarring, asyndetic narrative. Perhaps the breach of the frame, the temporal distance, allows us access to the mind of the poet, telling its own story, before it has aesthetically shaped itself, so that the dislocation is his. But it is also that of a narrative that bursts its own boundaries, in which the biography becomes a paradigm for another story—that of Israel—which in turn is displaced into another, that of the Davidic monarchy.

Equally disruptive of normal narrative coherence is the lack of relationship between the parties. God speaks, but the prophet does not respond except through tacit obedience; the command to love is transformed into an economic transaction; his address to the woman imposes a quarantine. His words to her are quite bizarre; the visions of a bereft Israel and a future deliverance have nothing to do with her as a person.

Verse 1 clearly recalls 1.2. As in the earlier verse, the command to associate with an adulterous woman is justified by Israel's unfaithfulness to Yhwh. It supplements 1.2 by making explicit the analogy with God's love for Israel and by specifying the nature of the latter's prostitution. One might note also that the word for 'from after (mē'ah^{a}rê) Yhwh' in 1.2 is echoed in that for 'other (^{a}ḥērîm) gods'. The parallel suggests a transfer, that Israel's infidelity is matched by God's love, which, as many critics note, implicitly conditions the entire passage.

The text is full of difficulties, which have taxed the minds of scholars. If the woman is his wife, his purchase of her is unnecessary. If she isn't, is he a would-be adulterer? If she is 'beloved of a friend', what would be his rapport with that 'friend'? (Andersen and Freedman 1980: 297, suggest attractively that the word 'friend' here does not mean 'paramour' so much as 'neighbour, fellow-citizen', as in Lev. 19.18.) The alternatives collude to marginalize the prophet. Either he is a cuckold, who even has to buy his wife back, or he is in the position of the unwise young man in Proverbs who falls for strange women (Ben Zvi 2005: 83, suggests a pun between rēa', 'friend,' and ra', 'disaster').

The other troublesome problem in the verse is the nature of the raisin cakes and their relation to the other gods. Most critics assume from the context that they were cultic foods; if so, apostasy in favour of other gods amounts to enjoying their festivities. If not, the conjunction of other gods and raisin cakes juxtaposes the sublime and the ridiculous (Ben-Zvi 2005: 82, 93). Again, both possibilities suggest a comic touch; God's love interacts with their desire for comfort food, as well as their continual straying away.

In v. 2, the details of the purchase of the woman introduce a reality effect: this is how sexual transactions were conducted in ancient Israel. As in Amos 7.1, where an aside dates Amos' first symbolic vision to the time of the late-sown crops and explains when this sowing takes place, the prosaic commonplace counterpoints God's strange command and Hosea's strange behaviour. The real is rendered unreal; the appearance of a prosperous and untroubled community, where women are routinely traded, belies the coming desolation and the urgency of God's speech. (The exact significance of the sums, and whether the price was high or paltry, has provoked massive scholarly discussion, which need not concern us here.)

Verses 3-5 are presented as a continuous speech to the woman, linked through catchwords such as 'many days' (vv. 3, 4) and 'stay, dwell, return' (vv. 3, 4, 5). In v. 3 Hosea's speech, translated literally, would read: 'Many days stay for me, do not go a-whoring, do not be with a man, and also I to you'. The problem is whether this imposes abstinence between Hosea and the woman, as well as between her and other men, and whether the same conditions apply to Hosea. If Hosea's symbolic act represents Yhwh's relation to his people, v. 5 would suppose his absence; correspondingly, in v. 3, 'and also I to you' would mean 'I will not be for you', as in 1.9. Nevertheless, the ellipsis is tantalizing, and holds open the possibility of a reversal.

In ch. 2 Israel prostitutes itself by consorting with the Baalim; this interpretation is confirmed by v. 1, where Israel's adultery is a metaphor for her turning to other gods. But in v. 4 prostitution is paralleled with the institutions of state and worship: king, prince, sacrifice, standing stone, ephod and teraphim. The other gods, then, would seem to be identified with a false mode of worship and human rulers. Without these institutions, Israel would become destitute; the dominant word in v. 4 is 'without'. But, as we have seen, this is also correlative with Yhwh's absence. None of the cult practices and objects mentioned are inherently anti-Yahwistic (Ben-Zvi 2005: 90-91). Political authority complements and underwrites sacred authority; kings are patrons of temples, officiants are also officials.

If the polemic against the Baalim and the other gods is in fact turned against all the familiar signs of Yhwh's presence, Yhwh and Baal/other gods become indistinguishable. True worship of Yhwh consists in the negation of everything one understands as such. Only by eliminating the traces of the divine presence can it be recovered. This may be because they have become irremediably corrupt: much of the rest of the book, indeed, unpacks the condemnation of the list in this verse. But it may be because Yhwh is resistant to icons, jealous of political structures and authorities. Douglas (1993: 30ff.) suggests that aniconic religions are characteristic of what she calls 'enclave societies', which are internally egalitarian and outwardly exclusive. Any figurations of Yhwh are liable to traduce him, to turn him into a Baal. The anti-metaphoricity of Yhwh undercuts the work, also taken by Yhwh, of finding metaphors that will make possible the relationship of God and Israel. Poetically, the moment is marked by simple aggregation; the loss of political and sacred order is reflected in language lacking all organization. The boredom of the many days' isolation and deprivation is aggravated by the repetitiousness and the retardation of the verse resulting from the succession of 'without's. The threshold between nullification and recuperation is then a poetic blank, characterized by what Kristeva (1989: 33) calls depressive asymbolia, the tendency for the language of people suffering from depression to be flat, monotonous, and incapable of expressing their pain. In depression, words lose their meaning. Here, the symbols are erased; in their place is simply the biological continuity of 'the children of Israel' subsisting in their land (Utzschneider 1980: 222).

But then there is a dramatic reversal: 'Afterwards the children of Israel shall return'. It turns on the coincidence of opposites in the almost identical verbs 'they shall remain/dwell' ($yēš^eḇû$) and 'they shall return' ($yāšuḇû$). In v. 4 it seems as if Israel remains in the land, in v. 5 that they come back from exile. The contradiction holds open the two possibilities and through the wordplay blurs their boundaries: dwelling in the land without autonomous governance or religious symbols could be construed as internal exile, or the word 'return' could refer to a conscious realignment with Yhwh, rather than a physical restoration, as in 14.2. At any rate, the combination of opposites conforms to the pattern that we found in ch. 2, where the eschatological retroversion 'on that day' is both rhetorically demarcated from the desolation that precedes it and paradoxically conflated with it.

The anomaly in the verse is the acceptance of the claims of David 'their king', the strangeness of which in the mouth of a northern Israelite and uniqueness in the book have induced most commentators to attribute the phrase to a Judean redactor (a noteworthy exception is Emmerson 1984: 101-13). In particular, there is no trace of such a future in the principal visions of eschatological hope in chs. 2 and 14. Indeed, in 11.5 Hosea asserts that Assyria is Israel's king. Whether or not 'the children of Israel' in our chapter refers to the collectivity of Israel and Judah, or simply to northern Israel, as in 2.2, is also ambiguous. If the former, then Judah too is subject to the kingless aporia, and the hope is not for the continuance of the Davidic dynasty but its restoration (Ben-Zvi 2005: 86, 93).

However, the reference, colourless as it is, is structurally integrated in the initial chapters. Its closest correlate is 1.7— also often attributed to a Judean redactor—in which the miraculous salvation of Judah occurs through the intervention of 'Yhwh their God', just as the children of Israel seek 'Yhwh their God' in our verse. 'David their king' would then rule, as a figurehead for God, without conventional weapons. As we have seen, 1.7 matches 2.20, in that both contain the sequence 'bow, sword, and war'. The vision of the cosmic covenant is thus accompanied by renewed loyalty to David. In contrast, there is the extinction of the Israelite monarchy and the condemnation of the house of Jehu in 1.4-5. The houses of Jehu and David are polar opposites at either end of the prefatory chapters.

Another contrast is between v. 5 and 2.1-3. In both, the fate of the children of Israel passes from non-relation with God to readoption and rapprochement; in both it is conceived as a reunion of the two kingdoms. Both model themselves on the ancient past. However, the models are different. In 2.1-3 the renewal of the blessing to Abraham combines with the motif of the Exodus and the appointment of a 'head' who will take them up from the land; it corresponds to the journey to the wilderness in 2.16. Here David represents return, sovereignty in the land. Moses and David are either simple alternatives, or the two are in some way correlated. Paradoxically, going up from the land—the new Exodus—is a precondition for or identical with return to the land.

David may be associated, as Emmerson suggests (1984: 103), with the succession to Saul, and thus with the legacy of the defunct northern kingdom. There may be some allusion to David's challenge to Goliath, that 'sword and spear and javelin' are useless against 'the name of Yhwh of Hosts' (1 Sam. 17.45). Essentially, the reference conforms to the pattern of displacement we have found throughout: the ideal king is elsewhere, in the far future and the distant past. It also takes us back to the first verse of the book, the list of Davidic kings with which the prophecy was supposedly contemporaneous, and thus to the writer(s), recording the words of someone in another kingdom writing of themselves, in an endless play of mirrors. The David who is sought, progenitor and progeny of the Davidic kings under whose auspices it was written, is an other, an ideal projection, with which identification must be deferred, if the book is to be written. In this play of mirrors, moreover, the true king is an anti-king, whose individuality and power is subsumed in Yhwh's glory.

But where is Yhwh? The end of the verse, 'they will come fearfully to Yhwh and his goodness at the end of days', is paralleled at the end of the next section of the book, in ch. 11, where Israel comes trembling like birds from exile and Yhwh settles them in their houses or cotes. The two passages are equivalent, but opposed, in that whereas here they return to Yhwh, in 11.10-11 they follow Yhwh, who leads them roaring like a lion. Yhwh then goes with them into the exile; the restoration the book seeks to accomplish is an integration of Yhwh with himself.

Hosea 4

(1) Hear the word of Yhwh, O children of Israel, for Yhwh has a dispute with the inhabitants of the earth, for there is no truth, and no kindness, and no knowledge of God in the earth.
(2) Cursing, lying, murder, theft, adultery burst forth and blood touches blood.
(3) Therefore the earth mourns, and all who dwell on it languish, the beasts of the field and the birds of the heavens, and also the fish of the sea are gathered up.
(4) Let no one dispute or reprove anyone; and your people are like contentious priests.
(5) And you shall stumble by day, and also the prophet shall stumble with you by night, and I will destroy your mother.
(6) My people are destroyed for lack of knowledge, for you have rejected knowledge, and I will reject you from serving as a priest to me; and you have forgotten the Torah of your God, and I will forget your children likewise.
(7) As they increased, so they sinned against me; I will exchange their glory for shame.
(8) They feed on the sin of my people; to their iniquity they lift up its soul.
(9) And it shall be like people, like priest; and I shall visit upon him its ways, and I will repay its deeds.
(10) And they shall eat and not be satisfied; they shall fornicate and not burst forth; for they have forsaken guarding Yhwh.
(11) Promiscuity, wine and new wine take away the heart.
(12) My people inquires of its wood, and its staff shall tell it, for the wind of adultery has caused it to go astray, and they have prostituted themselves from under their God.
(13) They sacrifice on the tops of the mountains, and they make offerings on the hills, under oak, and poplar, and terebinth, for their shade is good; for that reason your daughters fornicate and your brides commit adultery.

(14) I will not visit your daughters when they whore, or your brides when they commit adultery, for they separate themselves with whores, and sacrifice with prostitutes, and a people that does not understand will be crippled.
(15) If you play the whore, O Israel, let not Judah be rendered guilty; do not come to Gilgal, do not go up to Beth-Awen, do not swear 'As Yhwh lives'.
(16) For as a refractory cow Israel has gone astray; now Yhwh would graze them as a lamb in a broad meadow.
(17) Ephraim is yoked to idolatry; let him be.
(18) Their liquor has turned away; they have fornicated; their love they have spent; contemptible are her defences.
(19) The wind has bound her up in her skirts; and they will be confounded because of their sacrifices.

Chapter 4 introduces the main corpus of Hoseanic prophecies: there are no more narratives, and instead of the allegory in ch. 2, the comments are pertinent to particular situations, which are now obscure. The Hebrew text is often difficult, resulting in a large number of competing interpretations. The difficulty is compounded by our ignorance of the context the prophet is addressing, and by rapid and jarring switches of focus. Chapters 4–11 are generally considered to be the central collection, rounded off by the formulaic 'says Yhwh' at the end of ch. 11; chs. 12–14 comprise a climactic conclusion. The opening 'Hear the word of Yhwh, O children of Israel' in v. 1, and the announcement of a dispute with all the inhabitants of the earth, includes in its purview either chs. 4-11 or the entire book. Similarly, according to Jeremias (1983: 59-60), the listing of deficiencies and offences in vv. 1-2 functions as a table of contents, highlighting the themes that will be elaborated in the subsequent chapters.

Chapter 4 is frequently divided into two at the end of v. 10, to form two carefully constructed complementary poems or poetic units (for a different view, see Sweeney 2000: 46). The first poetic unit focuses on the priests, while the second is unified by the 'wind' or 'spirit' of fornication that impels the people. The theme of the chapter is the cultic disarray of Israel; it lacks altogether the foreign tensions and the sense of political crisis that dominates most of the rest of the book. This lack has led critics to date it early in Hosea's career.

God's dispute is motivated by the absence of kindness (*ḥesed*), truth, and the knowledge of God on the earth (v. 1). Their place is taken by a register of crimes—swearing, lying, murder, theft, adultery—in which critics have seen evidence for an early version of the Ten Commandments (v. 2). *Ḥesed* suggests the network of supererogatory affection and commitment on which society is founded; 'truth' is not merely propositional truth, but reliability, truthfulness, between people. At stake, then, in this world that Yhwh addresses, is the possibility of object relations; these are summed up in the knowledge of the ultimate object, Yhwh, who is the guarantor of *ḥesed* and truth. A world devoid of kindness, loyalty, truth, and knowledge of God is one of confusion, in which Yhwh's charge can only go unheard. Of course, it is self-contradictory in that at least one person does possess knowledge of God, namely the prophet himself. The disintegration of the social and cognitive worlds permits the proliferation of crimes, each one of which is isolated: in Hebrew there is merely a list of infinitives, without syntactic connections, without subject or object. They caricature proper relations; for example, swearing (*'ālōh*) invokes and presumably desecrates the name of God. The word echoes later in the chapter as the name of a tree (*'ēlâ*) that replaces God (v. 13). Murder, theft, and adultery cross the boundaries of life, property, and sex, and thus illustrate the non-recognition of boundaries. Lying imitates truth; where there is no truth, however, there is no discourse that does not falsify. The only connection is that of 'blood to blood' at the end of the verse, evoking not only the consequence of the explosion of violence, but the vengeance for which blood cries throughout the Hebrew Bible. The communion of blood recalls apocalyptic versions of the Flood Story in which the earth itself, weltering in blood, calls for retribution. The reference is supported by the next verse, in which universal annihilation follows. To the intimation of the Flood and hence the reversal of Creation adduced by DeRoche (1981), we may add another motif: the breaking of the covenant. In 2.20 God makes a covenant for Israel with all creatures, as a sign of Edenic harmony; here they are gathered up in its dissolution. They both mourn, as innocent bystanders, for human dereliction, and are its victims. In pointed contrast with the Flood, the fish, tagged on by the word 'also', are metonymic for the whole of creation. God's charge meets with a chorus of grief, of which human beings, so the succeeding passages suggest, remain oblivious.

In the face of the charge, humans are to be silent: 'Let no one dispute, or reprove anyone' (v. 4). If there is no truth, *ḥesed*, or knowledge of God, then all disputes are false, mere logomachy. The paradoxical force of the injunction arises from a comparison with Lev. 19.17: 'Do not hate your brother in your heart; you shall surely reprove your fellow...'. Yhwh's dispute takes the form of a revocation of the moral responsibility for one another on which the ideal priestly community of Leviticus is based. The cessation of disputation corresponds to the abolition of cultic and political institutions in 3.4-5. Instead, there is contention as travesty, exemplified by the continuation, 'and your people are like contentious priests' (I should note that the translation itself is extremely contentious; I follow Lundbom 1986). Quarrelsome priests, impelled by pettiness, greed or power, turn sacred order into cacophony; the analogy suggests that the recriminations of the people are as self-interested and as sacrilegious. God's interdict on dissension, so that his charge be heard in silence, is against a background of animosity that threatens the divine message with inaudibility. At this point, as innocent readers who have not read any further in the text, we may identify the 'your' of 'your people' with the prophet, the addressee of the message. By v. 6 the addressee is clearly the chief priest. Priest and prophet, each of whom bears responsibility as God's representative to the people, are functionally opposed and equivalent. Their tense and ambivalent relationship will permeate the text, as the prophet speaks in the language of and against hieratic institutions.

The people may not 'contend', yet in 2.4 they are urged to contend against their mother. On the one hand, the contradiction exposes the unreality of the allegory in ch. 2, in which the children are the mother. On the other hand, if the mother's whorishness manifests itself, in the widest sense, in contentiousness, as part of the malfeasance of which Israel is accused, then the contention is for the sake of non-contention.

The scene begins with the entirely conventional metaphor of 'stumbling' for downfall; it is rendered interesting by the recurrence of the metaphor, likewise repeated, in relation to Israel and Judah in 5.5. Day and night, priest and prophet, are opposed, and subject to the same vicissitude. The prophet who stumbles may be a 'false' prophet, whose interests are inextricable from those of the priesthood; he may be a 'true' prophet, horror-struck by what he envisions. If the prophet is associated with Hosea himself, this would reflect an ambivalence towards prophecy that we find developed later in the book, as well as in prophetic literature generally. At any rate, the intrusion of the prophet into the scene represents a nocturnal and shamanistic aspect of the sacred of which the hierarchy, in its daily activities, remains blissfully unaware.

The stumbling of priest and prophet is counter-balanced by a threat against the priest's mother. We do not know who she is. Analogously with the king's mother (e.g. 1 Kgs 16.7), she may be a sacred functionary, and thus represent a matriarchal origin of the priesthood that would demystify its masculine exclusiveness. She would then be correlative to the mother of chs. 1-2 as a symbol of the land in its resistance to God (cf. Sweeney 2000: 47). Primarily, however, she is a figure for the return to origins, the desire to reverse time and eradicate evil before its inception, that frequently recurs in Hosea (cf. 9.10-17). The destruction of the mother adumbrates a wish that the priest had never been born.

The verb for 'to destroy' used here (dmh) is very similar to that for 'to be silent' (dmm); a second meaning of dmh is 'to imagine, compare'. In 12.11, where the prophets are entrusted with transmitting similitudes of God, the same verb dmh is employed; the stumbling of the prophet would suggest an interruption of the communication. Correspondingly, the demise of the mother presages that of the priestly lineage. It is coupled with the statement that 'my people are destroyed' in v. 6. Clearly, this cannot be meant literally, since 'my people' are evoked in vv. 8 and 12, alive and well; the destruction is consequent on a 'lack of knowledge'.

The priest has rejected knowledge, and thus God rejects him from being priest (v. 6); the people perish for lack of knowledge, and concomitantly the mother perishes; the prophet stumbles in the night of visionary dreams and hence of the unconscious dynamic of the situation, linked both to conception and to the people's unawareness. Everything focuses on the priest, who bears the entire responsibility for the lack of knowledge of God in v. 1.

Rejection of knowledge is a paradoxical condition, since it implies a refusal to acknowledge what one actually knows. The priest, like the prophet, is an exception to the generalization that there is no knowledge of God on earth. Rejection implies division, separating the priest from his propensity to know, as well as from his office of 'teaching' (Lev. 10.11). Suppression of knowledge may be because it is fearful, as in Genesis 3, but also because forgetfulness and the creation of an unconscious are necessary for human autonomy.

God rejects him from being a priest. As DeRoche (1983: 191) has pointed out, the analogy between priest and people implicates also their function in the world, since the priest is the exemplar of Israel's responsibility as a kingdom of priests (Exod. 19.6). The high priest in the Pentateuch is the symbolic representative of the people; he bears their guilt (Exod. 28.30, 39). Here he is perceived in relation to God, as an attendant or steward of his sacred place but also of his presence in the world. The priest, through his possession of knowledge, is an intimate of God, and communicates that knowledge to the people, whereby it becomes '*my* people'. Being chosen by God, according to the Bible, constitutes Israel as a people. Knowledge, in v. 6, is paralleled by 'the Torah of your God'. The parallel suggests correspondence between cognition and practice: the knowledge of God is the essence of Torah and, concomitantly, the rejection of intimacy leads to the neglect of its outer expression. There may also be an allusion to the Wisdom tradition, in which Torah, a feminine noun, is conventionally inherited from the mother (Prov. 1.8; 6.20; cf. 31.1-9). Counterpoised to the priest's mother is the matrix of the Torah; they oppose human and divine origins, natural and symbolic orders. His mother, his natural parent, is the antithesis of God, who transforms him into a sacred functionary; she represents the claims of family, and the priest's genetic and cultural inheritance as a venial human (various critics have pointed out that since the priesthood was hereditary, the priest's father would have died, and his mother would be head of the household). If, as the succeeding verses suggest, the priest rejects God for the sake of being a self-interested, political human being, who uses the sacred office as a means of exploitation, then the matriarch imparts the authority of lineage and the kinship network, and thus an alternative—according to the prophets a subversive—tradition.

In recompense, God threatens to 'forget' his children. God is characterized by implacable memory, as indeed Israel complains in 7.2, and as is celebrated in 12.6; the promise that he will visit their ways and repay their deeds in v. 9 suggests an exact tally. As retribution for forgetting the Torah, forgetfulness does not seem ominous: indeed, sinners might welcome divine oversight. The passage is dominated by the rhetoric of retaliation that here apparently becomes merely petulant. In fact, the forgetfulness ironically dissembles and postpones the vindictive memory, which is activated in v. 10. If memory is the vehicle for God's providence and for his narrative, then by erasing it he removes the priests from his concern, from meaningful history. Severing the bond of memory, of the covenantal past, renders the priests otiose as contact points between God and the world. The loss of memory puts at risk the continuity of relationship between God and Israel, the tradition of which the priests are the guardians.

The immediate effect, however, is to encapsulate the ensuing description of the priests' activities. Indifferent to the impending divine amnesia, priests seem free to feather their nest. The aura of irresponsibility makes this passage functionally equivalent to the carefree pleasures of the festivities of vv. 13-14, and the immunity from punishment of the young women (daughters/brides) who participate in them.

The account satirizes and inverts the priestly functions. Priests, according to the Pentateuch, were decontaminants. Priests ritually consumed the people's impurity and thereby protected the holy from pollution and maintained the channels of communication between the human and the divine. In our passage, they merely live off sin, as it were immoral earnings; the figure of ingestion combines with that of diffusion to suggest an economy entirely based on impurity rather than sanctity. Sins are expended in the generation of more priests, who increase the production and consumption of sins. (In the Pentateuch, sin offerings were brought primarily for inadvertent sins and for defilement, while reparation offerings could be brought for deliberate offences, although, as Milgrom [1991a: 373-78] has pointed out, these were anomalous; in Hosea, however, 'sin' generally refers to intentional violations, but our text links the two meanings together.)

There may be an underlying critique of the impoverishment of people through priestly exploitation. The satire is intensified and summarized by the final clause, 'and to their iniquity they lift up its soul'. The expression 'lift up its soul' is multiply ambiguous. The word for 'soul' may mean 'life' or 'appetite'; 'lift up' is an idiom for forgiveness, while 'its' may refer either to people or priests. The diverse possibilities interplay impressionistically, so that the stimulation of the priests' greed by sin combines with their cultivation of sin among the people, in a context in which the risking of life is superimposed on the supposed granting of absolution. In Exodus, as we have seen, the priest 'bears'—the same verb as 'lift up'—the judgment of the people. The image of the priest has been transformed, using almost identical expressions.

Verse 7 is problematic, since there is evidence (for example, from the early Aramaic translation or Targum) for the euphemistic replacement of an original 'They have exchanged their glory for shame' by 'I will exchange...'. In either case, there is a play on the prohibition of $t^e m\hat{u}r\hat{a}$, the substitution of a devoted or tithed beast, whether for better or worse (Lev. 27.10, 33), crossing the boundaries between sacred and profane, glory and shame. 'Their glory' recurs as an attribute of which Ephraim is divested in 9.11, where its conventional reference to political glory is immediately supplanted by the sequence, 'from conception, pregnancy, birth', when we realize that it means the glory of life itself. Here 'their glory' presumably refers to their sacred office, their representation of the glory of God. They have replaced this with their own, self-serving glory, which God either will convert to shame or describes as shame. It should be noted that 'as they increased' at the beginning of v. 7 conjoins prosperity and progeny, thus opening up both lines of thought in the passage.

'Shame' is mirrored at the end of the chapter (v. 18), linking its two panels together. Its context in v. 18 is Ephraim's defencelessness, the sober sequel to its cultic excess, and is accompanied by a wholesale transformation of images. The exchange perpetrated by or on the priests, and their inversion of sacerdotal values, is transferred onto the nation as a whole.

The concluding verses of the first part of the chapter (vv. 9-10) summarize judgment against the priests, and include in it the people, who are to suffer the same fate. The equivalence of people and priest encloses the peculative priests in a frame (vv. 4, 9) as the innermost of the circles that provoke God's disputation. The problem is that the people are apparently not equally culpable, if indeed they are at all. The second part, with its description of popular festivals, might function as a metaphor for the first, to demonstrate the similarity of people and priest, except for the insistence that they can plead ignorance (vv. 6, 14). The problem is recurrent in prophetic literature (cf. Jer. 5.4-5), and is compounded by the haul of the innocent creatures in v. 3.

The coupling, however, also implies similarity: not only are the priests part of the people, but the people share their sanctity. While the primary reference of v. 10, then, is to the priests, the people are also implicated. If the priests are sustained by the people's sin in v. 8, their voracity will not be satisfying; the escalating demand suggests that this is not true nourishment. The next phrase, 'they fornicate but do not burst forth', links the beginning of the chapter to its end. Fornication—the word in Hebrew covers prostitution and promiscuity—introduces the theme of the second part of the chapter. Fornication is profoundly subversive of priestly distinctiveness. A priest's daughter who commits fornication is to be burnt (Lev. 21.9); priests may not marry prostitutes (Lev. 21.7); the word for sexual violation (*hallal*) is the same as that for sacrilege. Sexual and sacred boundaries are indistinguishable. Prostitution, of course, as throughout Hosea, is also a metaphor, in this case not directly for Baal-worship, but for trafficking in the sacred. Sexual and alimentary desire and fantasy aggregate around the mother and her displacements in later life. Prostitution, always associated with infantile fantasy, fosters illusions of omnipotence, limitlessness, and ideality. The divine animus against the mother clears imaginative as well as genealogical space in which the desire cannot be fulfilled. If sexual pleasure culminates in expenditure, then the priests are threatened with unremitting frustration. Conversely, the figure of the bottomless stomach suggests a vacuity that cannot be filled, and a rhythm of incorporation and discharge whose intensity is proportionate to its obstruction.

The priests 'fornicate, but do not burst forth'; in v. 2 the catalogue of sins, culminating in 'adultery', is capped by the single verb, 'they burst forth', expressing both the breach of boundaries and unchecked proliferation. Here the explosion of virulent energies has exhausted itself, and thus induces poetic closure.

The priests have failed in 'guarding Yhwh'; the passage opens with Yhwh's contention and the word Israel is summoned to hear. In between the two occurrences of Yhwh develops the entire interpersonal space of the poem, an exposition of what it is to guard Yhwh and how it has been forsaken. Preserving the sacred enclosure, and hence the divine order in the world, is one of the priests' pre-eminent responsibilities (Lev. 22.9). Our passage witnesses the breakup of this order (v. 2), but also the negation of the disintegration. The priests desire dissemination, a promiscuous relation with the multitudinous other; they are arrested in the act. Similarly, the vehemence and busyness of the description, and its rhetorical intensity, are neutralized by images of silence, forgetfulness, and unconsciousness. People may not strive (v. 4); the priest's mother is destroyed; her silencing is reflected in that of the people, which itself is the result of their lack of knowledge; the priestly excesses are prospectively nullified in God's lapse of memory.

The formulaic 'And I will visit upon it its ways, and its deeds I will return upon it' (v. 9) recurs in 12.3, as part of a general recapitulation of the beginning of ch. 4. In ch. 12 it refers to Jacob, as the prototype of Israel's history; it is problematic, in that Jacob's deeds are ambivalent. Here the promise of poetic retribution lacks specificity. We do not know whether it is people or priest who are the target, and what constitutes the people's sin. This facilitates the transition to the second half of the chapter. The reciprocity of 'its deeds I will return on it', and the scrupulousness conveyed by 'I will visit'—the verb is used for military roll-calls and temporal cycles—defines a poetic stance that will continue to be operative through the book. As the people's sins are evidenced, so will its retribution be elaborated. For the moment, it remains ominously open.

In the immediate context, it plays against its surprising reversal in the second half of the chapter: 'I will not visit your daughters when they whore, nor your brides/daughters-in-law when they commit adultery' (v. 14). Their immunity is justified as a protest against the double standard: if men are licentious, why should women not be so? Hosea's apparent egalitarianism, of course, masks paternalism, since men are assumed to have responsibility for women's behaviour. More significantly, however, it opens a female space free of divine judgment and male control, and transfers the founding fantasy of Hosea's marriage to the entire people. Divine indulgence contradicts the condemnation and isolation of the woman in chs. 1-3; it colludes with human weakness, and perhaps expresses or acknowledges God's original attraction to the woman in 1.3 and 2.16. At any rate, God appears to sanction, perhaps ironically, the carnival on the mountains, thus duplicating or authorizing the carnival's own function of accommodating unacceptable desire within the social order. The relaxation of poetic style in vv. 13-14 and of the unmitigated condemnation that dominates the book hints at complaisance, a hidden sympathy, as an underlying motivation. Moreover, the parallel with v. 9 points out the problem of culpability; the daughters, like the people, are the victims of wayward mentors. If they are blameless, so are the people. If the purpose of the book of Hosea is to justify the destruction of Samaria, then that process is incipiently destabilized. Suggestions that any group of miscreants can plead ignorance or be left unpunished disappear after ch. 4. Nevertheless, the carefully delimited zone of toleration, invested with Edenic innocence and pleasure, provides an ultimate asylum for unconscious resistance to God. God will not 'visit' the daughters and brides; historically they will survive the destruction of Israel and continue to be promiscuous and participate in arborial festivals—hence popular religion will outlast the divine programme—while rhetorically a point of reference is provided, an alternative ideal, from which to criticize the rest of the book.

The cultic vision unfolds between two aphorisms (vv. 11, 14), either taken from or alluding to the 'wisdom' or proverbial tradition (cf. Seow; for wordplay between the two aphorisms, see Morris 1996: 72). Proverbs are impersonal, detached, often amused, as the sage observes human folly, invested with the authority of tradition and the status quo. Adopting the persona of a sage invests the prophet with an ironic distance, a complaisance equivalent to that of God. The tableau that is inserted between the aphorisms breaks open the stance of detachment. The 'heart' that is taken away in v. 11 repairs to the hills and mountains in v. 13; the vision of the heart succumbing to wine and harlotry is the lens through which one perceives the fantasy delights of a society, with whose values and images the heart is filled. The tight aphoristic form, a medium of control and repression, is sundered by the expansiveness of the intervening verses, whose long rhythmic phrasing, capped or permeated by rhyme or assonance in Hebrew, metaphorically conforms to the energy of the 'wind/spirit of harlotry' (v. 12).

'Prostitution, wine, and new wine' in v. 11 is unbalanced, since wine and new wine are near synonyms. (It should be noted that many critics add 'prostitution', or indeed the whole sequence [Macintosh 1997: 148] to the previous verse, to yield 'forsake Yhwh to foster prostitution'; this is unjustified, in my view. Ben Zvi 2005: 105 suggests that vv. 10-11 are syntactically ambiguous.) Jeremias (1983: 69) holds that 'new wine' serves to date the festivities; the term recurs periodically in Hosea. Thus the supplement extracts the saying from sapiential timelessness, and integrates it in the language of the book. While prostitution is foregrounded as the theme of the second part of the chapter, wine drops out until v. 18. Wine and harlotry are metaphorically as well as contextually associated, especially in the ambiance of the festival.

The second aphorism, in v. 14, is incomprehensible, since we do not know the meaning of the last word (*yillābēṭ* in Hebrew). It occurs twice in Proverbs (10.8, 10); in each case its subject is 'one foolish of lips', and in neither can its meaning be determined (translations such as 'will be destroyed' are just guesses).

The tableau itself is comprised of multiple ironies: the wood to which the people speak, for lack of a heart, is associated with the trees that substitute for God; their whoring from underneath their God consists of their whoring under trees; the staff on which they rely is that which deprives them of support. The *wood* in v. 12 has generally been interpreted as an oracle, like Aaron's staff in Num. 17.25. Its connotations, however, are much more diffuse. It could refer to idols, and thus confirm Ephraim's attachment to idols in v. 17; the word for wood/ tree (*'ēṣ*) alliterates with that for idols (*'aṣabbîm*). It may be an institution on which they rely, such as the priesthood, of which the staff of office could be a metonymy. '*Ēṣô*, 'its wood/tree', is almost homonymic with '*ēṣâ*, 'counsel', which presumably they seek to obtain, and is thus suggestive of the inanity of their deliberations. There may be a very distant echo of the tree of knowledge (Ben Zvi, 2005: 106, suggests there may also be a phallic connotation). At any rate, the absurdity of the people's discourse with inanimate objects has a proverbial cast to it; those who talk to their sticks are sure to stumble. It suggests ventriloquism, hearing what one wishes.

Pre-emptive prestidigitation is the effect of the wind/spirit that makes the people turn astray. It is not only the people who programme their predictions, but they themselves are manipulated by some outside agency. The wind/spirit of promiscuity, of course, contrasts with the wind/spirit of prophecy, with the 'man of spirit' in 9.7. Equally, however, it is associated with Israel as the 'wife' and 'children' of promiscuity (1.2; 2.4, 6), since the same relatively rare word is used (*zᵉnûnîm*). Libidinal energy is directed against God; it is innate and it replaces the heart, the animating spirit of the prostitution that takes it away in v. 11. Under the impact of the wind, the people are estranged, both from themselves and from their constitutive relationship with God. The word for 'to go astray' (*t'h*) can also mean 'to totter' (e.g. in Isa. 28.7), and hence resonates with the drunkenness of the previous verse. From underneath God they go to the hills and mountains, seeking the shelter of the great trees; the irony is compounded because the word for 'under' can also mean 'instead'. The divine overarching of humans implies protection, but also, in the light of the global sexual metaphor for God's relation to Israel, intimacy; it is while they are still underneath God that they go a-whoring. The bizarre juxtaposition of God's embrace and Israel's dissoluteness—do they steal away, or just think lewd thoughts, during the erotic encounter?—represents succinctly the incompatibility of the two parties, especially if the wind/spirit of promiscuity, in its widest sense, denotes all human vagaries, the entire range of erotic attachment.

In the immediate context, the promiscuity refers both to the sacrifices and the profligacy that accompanied them. Sacrifice and offering incense are the regular forms of communion between God and humanity, and hence the equivalent, in the sacred sphere, of intercourse. The actual referent of the metaphor, the exchange of Yhwh for other deities, is reflected in the human domain by its literal counterpart. Mountains are associated with theophany throughout the Hebrew Bible; great trees are pervasive components of sacred sites; complaints about illicit practices on every high hill and under every leafy tree are a prophetic and Deuteronomistic cliché. The mountains and trees, natural objects of great power and longevity, replace God; the substitution is reinforced, in the case of the trees, by the wordplay between the names for the oak (*'allôn*) and terebinth (*'ēlâ*) and the word for God (*'elōhîm*). However, there is no direct reference to Baal-worship, none to the goddess Asherah and the ritual objects associated with her, and no evidence that the sexual acts, at least as engaged in by the daughters and brides, were of cultic significance. We do not know if Hosea objected to the worship on the summits in itself, whether he had an intrinsic objection to popular religion, or whether he simply described its degeneration, comparable to that of the priesthood. This is exemplified by the fornication of daughters and adultery of brides, 'because its shade is good'. Shade is a familiar metaphor for God's protection, here reduced to the natural phenomenon. It promises ease, langour, and a relaxation of vigilance suitable for amorous suggestion. What is important is the carefree triviality of the motive, that evokes the festivity as an escape from culture and its dictates and hence from the everyday ethical demands the book predominantly projects. The celebration would induce an experience of *communitas*, to introduce a concept popularized by

Victor Turner: the harmony of the human and natural community, marked by the breach of social and sexual boundaries, in liminal space. On the fringe of tilled land, love-making takes place under the shadow of trees, combining phallic potency with divine intimations; according to Ackerman (1988: 188ff.), sacred groves were associated with Asherah.

In the following verse, clemency for the daughters is justified by the perfidy of the men, who presumably have responsibility for them. The latter 'separate themselves with whores, and sacrifice with prostitutes'. Either they separate themselves from their daughters and brides, leaving them to their own devices, or from God; disintegration of the family is aligned with sacred disorder. From being places of communion with God, isolated from the everyday world, altars become opportunities for divertissements, offering an interlude from conventional constraints. The polarization of brothel and the shrine, as symbolically seductive social institutions, collapses. If in v. 10 prostitution is a sign of the priests' breach of their office and is an archetypal sacrilege, here the process is reversed: the prostitutes are brought to the sacred site itself. The presence of the $q^e d\bar{e}\check{s}\hat{o}t$—literally, 'holy women' as well as prostitutes—as counterparts to the priests in the first part of the chapter completes the feminization of the sacred (the existence of sacred prostitutes in ancient Israel or elsewhere in the ancient Near East is much disputed; cf. Kelle 2005: 122-37, and the balanced discussion of Macintosh 1997: 157-59, who translates 'cult-women').

The last section of the chapter transposes the thematics of the first two sections or tableaux onto the collective responsibility of twinned political entities: Israel and Judah in v. 15, Israel and Ephraim in vv. 16-19. It is characterized by an intensification of the ambiguities of gender we have discerned, by rapidly shifting images, and by a combination of regress—one reality being exposed to uncover another—with an effect of finality, as various motifs from across the chapter come home to roost.

Verse 15, often regarded as a later insertion, punctuates the sequence, rupturing the pastoral carefreeness of vv. 11-14, and demarcating the summary conclusion of vv. 16-19; it alerts us to elements that will be activated in the following chapter. Judah is the always ambiguous correlate of Israel. Its guiltless condition associates it with the daughters and brides in vv. 11-14, and perhaps with the people of vv. 4-9, who are dupes of the priests. The relation of people and priest is transferred then to the political realm. In the following chapter, Judah will be found to be guilty (5.6, 15); the exhortation will have been in vain. As well as being anticipatory, the verse recalls v. 4, with its injunctions not to contend with or reprove anyone. The two negatives of v. 4 are matched by four in v. 15. The silence imposed on people and priests is extended both to the dialogue between political entities and that between Israel and God. Gilgal and Bethel, sacred sites near the border of the northern and southern kingdoms and thus linking them, were pilgrimage sites, to which people would go to renew contact with God and to experience *communitas*. Disruption of the thrice yearly pilgrimage festivals—Passover, Pentecost, and Tabernacles—would mean rupture of sacred time and the relation between the sacred centre and the land as a whole. The concluding injunction, not to swear 'as the Lord lives', recapitulates the first of the offences in v. 2; thereby the binding verbal link between God and humanity is broken. Presumably these activities court sacrilege. Whether they exemplify Israel's whoremongering, so that sacerdotal and cultic corruption are concentrated at the shrines and in declarations of faith, or whether the holiness of God's presence and life has to be preserved from Israel's polluting and uncontained sexuality, is indeterminate. The two possibilities are not mutually exclusive. Hosea's habitual substitution of the name Bethel ('House of God') by Beth-Awen ('House of Folly') is indicative of this, since its true name and divine status remain implicit, as well as explicit in 10.15 and 12.5, despite its traducement.

Verse 16 introduces us to a set of wordplays on the names Israel and Ephraim: the word for 'refractory' (*srr*), which actually means to 'turn away', alliterates on that for Israel (*yiśrā'ēl*), while that for cow (*pārâ*) evokes the designation Ephraim (*'eprayim*) that appears in the next verse (Macintosh 1997: 166; cf. the extensive discussion in Morris 1996: 122-26). Israel is the people that turns away from God. The similes of cow and lamb alternate in gender, corresponding to the opposition of Israel as male lecher (*zōneh*) in v. 15 to its promiscuous female persona in chs. 1–3, and to that of male and female aggregates in vv. 13-14. Similarly, the contrast of the female image of the refractory cow with its masculine referent, 'Israel is refractory', sustains the ambiguity of gender. Israel behaves like a female, according to this verse, but is not; the prominence of women in the chapter not only reminds us of demographic facts, but destabilizes this bland assumption of identity. If Israel is grammatically masculine, but metaphorically feminine, the rhetoric of the chapter insistently inverts the relationship, for example, through directing animosity against the priest's mother, and thus his human origin.

The disjunction between the similes suggests one between reality and the divine programme. God mistakes a cow for a lamb, the one stereotypically characterized by wilfulness as well as richness, the other by docility. The familiar and comforting metaphor of the divine shepherd becomes disorienting because of this misapprehension, and because of its uncertain meaning: either it refers to the security God had intended for Israel ('now he would graze them') or its actuality ('now he grazes them'), contrasting their prosperity with their deserts. In either case, it communicates pathos and unreality, an island of indulgence in the midst of condemnation. It is linked with the enigmatic reprieve 'Let him be' in the next verse, as well as the exculpation of the daughters and brides in v. 14.

On the one hand, the animal images are reductive, expressing God's desire for a sheep-like Israel, or the human desire to be submissive to a pastoral God, and Israel's uncomprehending self-willedness. On the other hand, both images participate in large symbolic complexes in the book, focussing on the golden calf in the case of the cow, and on the conflict, in that of the lamb, between Israel's fortune and its forgetfulness (13.6), its attribution of dependence to the land and its products (cf. 9.2).

The cow, in its desire to be free to go its own way, fetters itself: 'Ephraim is bound to idols' (v. 17). The word for 'bound' ($h^ab\hat{u}r$) is a metathesis of that for 'a broad meadow' ($merh\bar{a}b$) that immediately precedes it. The generous pasture that Yhwh opens is suddenly constricted. Similarly, the cow is weighted down with images. Multiple wordplays imbue the phrase. The word for 'idols' ($^a\d{s}abb\hat{i}m$), as previously mentioned, alliterates with that for 'tree' or 'wood' ($^c\bar{e}\d{s}$) in v. 12, and consequently with the whole festive scene under the trees in vv. 12-14. The people, consulting with its wood for lack of a heart, substitute trees for God; these, in turn, are compressed into the lifeless figures with which they are encumbered. Moreover, $^a\d{s}abb\hat{i}m$ is virtually homonymous with the word for pains ($^a\d{s}\bar{a}b\hat{i}m$): Ephraim is attached to that which will cause it suffering. 'Bound' ($h^ab\hat{u}r$) frequently refers to the bond of friendship; in v. 16 $yir^c\bar{e}m$, 'will shepherd', may also mean 'befriend'. Israel replaces its true 'friend' and 'neighbour' ($r\bar{e}a^c$), Yhwh, with the false comradeship of idols. The polysemy brings immense pressure to bear on the last very short verses, as if the necessity to end makes urgent the desire to say everything, to tie together the threads of the entire chapter. If one image replaces the other, so that under the appearance of the headstrong cow, and alongside God's fantasy or misapprehension of a lamb, is the reality of a state wedded to idols, then the superimposition of multiple meanings is both a strategy of diffusion, so that we do not know what precisely is being said, and of intensification. The rapidity of change converges with the simultaneity of coexistent meanings.

The trisyllabic—in Hebrew as well as English—'Let him be' (*hannaḥ lô*) illustrates the potency of this compression. At first sight it is contradictory, since God would be unlikely to be permissive over such opprobrium, and Ephraim can hardly avail itself of the excuse of the daughters in v. 14. In any case, who is speaking: God to himself, to Hosea, or Hosea to God? This last fleeting reference to the motif of indulgence—this last impulse of resistance to judgment—is rendered otiose because it is so transitory, since in the last verses Ephraim collapses under its own disillusion. Divine neutrality will accordingly not prevent disintegration. (On the other hand, it could be seen as breaking off divine-human communication; cf. Macintosh 1997: 168.)

What 'turns away' (*sar*) is drunkenness (v. 18); Israel's fractiousness (*sārar*) in v. 16 is self-invalidating. Drunkenness corresponds to the 'wine and new vintage' that take away the heart in v. 11, and thus encompasses the entire passage. There is a possible connection with the description of the 'stubborn and rebellious son' in Deut. 21.20, where the two words, 'liquor' and 'refractory', occur in conjunction. Israel is then the archetype of that son, destined to be stoned. The intoxication is illustrated by fornication; in Hebrew the verb is doubled (*haznēh hiznû*, literally 'whoring they have whored'), which is both a sign of intensity and of finality. The orgy is over, and Israel wakes to cold sobriety. The verb recalls the frustrated promiscuity of the priests in v. 10. Priest and people are mirror images of each other, as in v. 9; in the wake of sexual excitement and alcoholic euphoria there is shame, defencelessness and exposure, just as in the first part of the chapter the bustle of the priests conceals silence and ignorance. The doubled verb for whoring is augmented by one for loving, which combines the motifs of desire, expenditure and sexual transaction, since the second verb in the phrase in Hebrew (*'āhᵃbû hēbû*) may mean 'give' as well as intensifying that for 'love' (cf. Ben Zvi 2005: 109). A similar pun is to be found in 8.13, also in connection with sacrifices. The consequence, that 'contemptible are her defences' (the Hebrew is difficult, and provokes a wide variety of translations), recalls v. 7, linking the tableaux of people and priests in the chapter; each exchange grandiosity and glory for corruption. The phrase completes the metaphorical transfer from the sexual and cultic domain to the national and political one. As in ch. 2 and later in the book, the figure of prostitution designates international relations, addiction to which leads to and is a symptom of Israel's bankruptcy, its lack of a true relation, 'whoring from under their God'.

This is confirmed by the last verse, in which the wind of v. 12 returns; instead of causing the people to go astray, taking them to the hills and mountains, it binds and exposes. Jeremias (1983: 73) associates the wind here with the Assyrians, as in 12.2 and 13.15, since they are pre-eminently the object of diplomatic solicitation; the carefree licentious wind/spirit reveals itself as that which will destroy them, as Thanatos, not Eros. The play on the word *sārar*, 'to turn away', recoils, since the word for 'to bind' or 'to war' (*ṣārar*) almost exactly echoes it. Israel's straying is recompensed by its constriction. Parallel to this is the merging of connotations of being trammeled with idols and being attached to them in the word $ḥ^abûr$, in v. 17.

Verse 19, at least in the traditional Masoretic text, exhibits some insoluble difficulties, which need not concern us here. What is important is the change of gender. The subject of both 'her defences' in v. 18 and 'her skirts' in v. 19 is female. Beneath, or in the aftermath of, insistence on male promiscuity and exploitation is a violated female persona.

Hosea 5

(1) Hear this, O priests, and listen, O house of Israel, and, house of the king, give ear, for to you belongs justice; for you have been a trap to Mizpah, and a net spread out upon Tabor.
(2) And in slaughter the perverse ones have delved deep; and I am the chastisement of them all.
(3) I know Ephraim; and Israel is not hid from me; for now you have gone whoring, Ephraim, and Israel is defiled.
(4) Their deeds do not allow them to return them to their God, for a spirit of promiscuity is in their midst, and they do not know Yhwh.
(5) And the pride of Israel answers in its face, and Israel and Ephraim stumble in their sin; Judah also stumbles with them.
(6) With their flocks and their herds they go to seek Yhwh, and they do not find him; he has vanished from them.
(7) Against Yhwh they have dealt treacherously, for they have born alien children; now he will consume them on the new moon with their fields.

5.1-7 is a transitional section, that serves both to introduce the concerns and imagery of 5.8-6.6 and to conclude those of ch. 4. The opening 'Hear this' marks it as a new speech unit, parallel to 'Hear the word of the Lord' at the beginning of ch. 4, and the imperative, 'Blow a shofar in Gibeah, a trumpet in Ramah' in 5.8. The different groups addressed—priests, the house of Israel, the house of the king—link the passage to the previous chapter, with its focus on the priesthood, and widen its scope. The relations of king and priest, political and sacred authority, will continue to preoccupy the book. One wonders about the relationship of the house of Israel and the king's house, and whether 'house of Israel' has a specific juridical sense here (for example, a body of elders), as some commentators suggest. The vagueness, however, is an effect of a greater uncertainty, for the passage as a whole has little to do with either monarchy or priests. We do not know how they have been a trap at Mizpah or a net on Tabor; the grandiose summons is unanswered, raises unfulfilled expectations of indictment, and in its place there is a divine soliloquy (vv. 3-4), and a dialogue of Israel with itself (v. 5). The voice, for all its insistence on attention, is finally rendered pointless by the withdrawal of its speaker (v. 6); at the centre is divine absence. The rhetoric of the passage progressively hollows itself out: God's knowledge is of Israel's lack of knowledge, and thus the impossibility of reciprocity, of response to the convocation; Israel's self-congratulation belies its stumbling; its search for God, in contradiction to its supposed imperviousness, is fruitless.

Mizpah and Tabor may refer to contemporary events, as many critics suggest. Nevertheless, their poetic significance, for us who are remote from these affairs, derives from their historical associations and from related passages in the book. Mizpah means lookout point; a trap laid at a lookout point snags the watchman, who surveys everything except his feet. The reference may be to the prophet; to Ephraim (cf. 9.8); to the judges, who lay a trap for themselves, as well as for unwary litigants. (The metaphor of the prophet as a watchman only occurs in Ezekiel [3.17; 33.2, 6, 7] and Isaiah [21.6-10]; however, in Hosea the archetypal prophet is the guardian of Israel [12.14], and the word 'watchman' occurs in a discussion of prophecy [9.7-9] that, by describing Ephraim as 'a watchman with my God', confers on the nation a prophetic status.)

In the Bible there are two Mizpahs, one in Benjamin, in Cisjordan, the other in Gilead, in Transjordan. The first is the place at which the kingdom was established (1 Sam. 10.17-27), and thus is reminiscent of the foundational conflict between prophet and king, Samuel and Saul. There Samuel deposited a book of the rule of the kingdom (1 Sam. 10.25), by which it is presumably judged. The second marks the boundary between Israel and Aram, and testifies to God's role as the one who keeps watch over Laban's daughters, Rachel and Leah, that Jacob not maltreat them (Gen. 31.49); their descendants, the tribes of Israel, are now victims of avaricious justice. Mizpah is also Jephthah's domicile and shrine, and hence recalls the paradigmatic case of a person trapped by a word. Tabor is the site of Deborah's victory, and consequently the classic instance of tribal solidarity; now the net trawls in the people to their destruction.

The vindication of the rule of judges (Judges 4-5) becomes its downfall. The motif of tribal assembly recurs in 5.9, where it is the occasion for the divine pronouncement of the doom of Ephraim; this attracts to itself the import of the other major tribal convocation in Judges, that which destroyed Benjamin (Judges 20–21), and hence the stigma of the sin of Gibeah (Judges 19). This is a leitmotif in Hosea (9.9; 10.9), already heralded in the previous verse (5.8), since it is in Gibeah that the shofar is urged to sound. The two passages are still more closely interconnected by a quotation from the Song of Deborah (Judg. 5.14), 'After you, O Benjamin' (5.8), which alludes to Benjamin's participation in the tribal confederacy. But Mizpah also associates the destruction of Ephraim with Jephthah and another verbal trap, since it was in Mizpah that Ephraim threatened to burn Jephthah's house (Judg. 12.1), and were subsequently defeated by the Gileadites and betrayed by their inability to pronounce 'Shibboleth' (Judg. 12.6). The complex network of allusions links the two Mizpahs together. The tribal assembly that establishes kingship but also encodes its failure is congruent with the witness that sets the boundaries of Israel, and watches to ensure that family relationships (husbands, wives, children) do not become predatory.

The next phrase, at the beginning of v. 2, is wholly obscure. There have been various attempts to resolve its difficulties, for instance by reading the rare and grammatically awkward *šēṭîm* ('rebels') as the place name Shittim, and the equally strange *šaḥᵃṭâ* ('slaughter'?) as 'they have dug deep' (*šāḥᵃṭû*). I will not concern myself with these problems, since smoothing out the text may preclude recognition of its resistance to interpretation. Fisch considers the incoherence of Hosea to be the consequence of the compression of its poetic message and the violence of its vision (see Fisch's comment on the 'spluttered alliteration' of this passage [1988: 139], and Morris's discussion of its complex punning [1996: 71]); whatever the 'original' text may have been, it leaves us with an impression of ever-deepening slaughter and insurrection. The failure to make sense is then an expression, a mimesis, of anarchy, in which there is one corrective: 'And I am the chastisement of them all.' 'Chastisement' (*mûsār*) completes the set of plays on the word *sarar* which we found towards the end of the last chapter. Yhwh restrains the straying cow of 4.16, operates through the receding (*sār*) of drunkenness in 4.18, and the inimical wind of 4.19. *Mûsār* is a term associated with sages, teachers, parents as well as God; in other words, with representatives of ethical order in the world. The totality subject to chastisement in our verse includes the groups addressed in v. 1 and their activities: Yhwh is the trap for the trappers, pulls the strings on the net, and, as in Amos 9.3, none can dig too deeply for him. This is confirmed by various cross-references. In 7.12 the imagery of our passage is transferred to the political arena: Yhwh spreads his net to bring down Ephraim in its flight, 'like a silly dove', between Assyria and Egypt. In 9.8 the prophet is a trap, presumably for those who lay traps, while in the immediately succeeding verse, 9.9, 'they have dug deep' recurs, in conjunction with 'they have destroyed' (šiḥētû) and the sin of Gibeah.

Verses 3-4 have a circular structure, as Jeremias points out (1983: 75). At their extremes, God's knowledge of Ephraim is matched by its ignorance of God; in the inner ring, the fornication and pollution of v. 3 is explicated by the spirit of promiscuity, leaving at the centre, 'Their deeds do not allow them to return to their God'. This is an evident inversion of 4.9, in which Yhwh declares, 'Its deeds I will return upon it'. If the latter suggests a principle of implacable retribution, whether or not the people are deliberately culpable, our verse presupposes that repentance is efficacious, but unattainable. Putting the two verses together, the deeds that Yhwh requites are those that prevent the people from returning. What may they be? The explanation, 'for a spirit of promiscuity is in their midst', would link them with the licentiousness on the high places in 4.12-14. The women who partake in these follies meet with Yhwh's indulgence, apparently because of the bad example of the men. The deeds that render reconciliation impossible are those of a spirit of promiscuity ($z^e nûnîm$ personified, from a male perspective, in the harlots [$zōnôt$] who haunt the sacred site, and embody a sanctity, through the parallel term $q^e dēšôt$, 'prostitutes', antithetic to monotheistic exclusiveness [cf. Deut. 23.18-19]). But the whores and prostitutes with whom the fathers and husbands consort in 4. 14 are not altogether distinct from their errant daughters and brides in 4. 13-14, since they are presumably the daughters and brides of someone. There thus seems to be a reversal of the double standard: God punishes the men and spares the women. But this conflicts with the ambiguity of gender of Ephraim that we found at the end of the last chapter. If Ephraim alternates male and female personae, it is alternately culpable and immune to censure.

More disturbingly, the book assumes, at least from time to time, that return is possible: otherwise its last chapter would be redundant. The last chapter, moreover, is rhetorically crucial, since it concludes the argument. If the thesis that return is abortive is maintained, then the book loses any rhetorical point, except the most negative—to persuade people to despair, or to entice them to repent, knowing that it is futile. In the parallel passage in ch. 12, the assertion that God will requite Jacob's deeds (12.3) is followed by an exhortation to return (12.7), and by the paradigmatic if enigmatic example of Jacob as one who did return, and who did have a transformative encounter with God. Jeremias (1983: 77) solves the problem diachronically, by dating 4.1–5.7 to an early stage in Hosea's career, and thus in the evolution of his thought. While not denying the possibility of dramatic and sequential development in the book, I would also regard it synchronically, as the presentation of one line of thought in a continuing dialectic. The question then is, what are the deeds that prevent one from returning? Licentiousness and the patronage of the high places would scarcely seem to be beyond renunciation. One may associate it with the corruption of the priests and their cultivation of the sins of the people, given the context of 4.9; indicative of this may be the reference to the pollution of Israel in v. 3. From being a land and people receptive to God, maintained in its purity by the priestly rites, it becomes one that defiles through those very rites, and thus repels him. More generally, the phrase may encompass the tangle of commitments, interests, and conventions that make actions irretrievable, of which the venality of the priests is but an example. The text, however, shifts the blame for the inability to return from the deeds themselves to an inner disposition ('the spirit of promiscuity in their midst') and thence to ignorance of God. We thus turn back to the absence of the knowledge of God at the beginning of ch. 4 and the priestly dereliction of responsibility for transmitting it to the people, with the attendant problem of culpability. If the clarity of God's knowledge exposes Israel's impurity, it associates him with the wind of 4.19 that reveals its shame. But the wind/spirit is also what is revealed. If the wind/spirit of promiscuity in 4.12 is an external agent of estrangement that takes away the heart, here it is internalized. The wind from outside (e.g. the Assyrians) and that from within are intricately interconnected, if not identical. In contrast is the non-reciprocity of

God's knowledge and Israel's lack of knowledge, that there is even anything to hide. If the wind/spirit of promiscuity is ultimately that of sexuality, experienced as external to and threatening the ego (the 'heart' of 4.11), and yet central to it, then it is at odds with another inner persona, God himself, described as 'in your midst holy' in 11.9.

Israel's ignorance is manifested in pride, which, in proverbial fashion, talks to itself and does not notice what is at its feet. The pride is equivalent to the glory that is exchanged for shame in 4.7 and 18, and hence Israel's military and cultic intoxication. The parallelism 'Israel and Ephraim will stumble in their iniquity; Judah also will stumble with them' matches that of priest and prophet in 4.5. If priest and prophet are complementary sacred functionaries, their duality is transferred, as in 4.15-19, to Israel and Judah. In 4.15 Judah's guilt remains undetermined; now it is evident. They go together to seek the Lord; their journey with their flocks and herds suggests participation in the prohibited pilgrimages of 4.15, and, as several commentators note, a rehearsal of the Exodus. Israel has become once more a nomad people, as in 2.16, with a nostalgia that conflicts with their sedentary complacency, with the rivalry between Israel and Judah in the next section, and with their actual courtship of the king of Assyria. It introduces the figure of seeking, withdrawal, the desire to be sought, and God's despair over Israel's unawareness of what it means to seek him that pervades 5.8–6.6. The flocks and herds the people bring in our verse become the sacrifices God rejects in 6.6 in favour of knowledge and kindness, and are thus a sign of their false construction of the quest, its thrice yearly institutionalization, and their mistaking the priestly economy for sacred order in 4.7-8. But perhaps they are truly seeking the Lord; the fleeting echo of Amos's vision of the future drought for the word of the Lord (8.11-14) is not entirely a contrast. Then God's withdrawal becomes paradoxical, terrifying. The verb used, *ḥālaṣ*, has two associations in the Hebrew Bible. The first is the *ḥāliṣâ* ceremony, performed when a man refuses to fulfil his obligation to wed his deceased brother's wife (Deut. 25.5-10; cf. Sweeney 2000: 57-58). As a sign of his derogation, she strips (*ḥᵃlaṣ*) his sandal from his foot and spits in his face. The second is with the crossing into Canaan and, in particular, the eager participation in it of the two and a half Transjordanian tribes—Reuben, Gad, and half of Manasseh—as shock troops (*ḥᵃlûṣîm*) before the Lord (Numbers 32 *passim*;

Deut. 3.18; Josh. 4.13). God's withdrawal thus reneges on the Conquest, as well as induces a breach in familial relations.

'The pride of Israel answers to its face' recurs in 7.10, in the context of Israel's unconsciousness that it is moribund; from not knowing God they come not to know themselves. There, in contrast to our verse, they do not seek Yhwh. Instead, as in 5.13, they cultivate Assyria and Egypt, and, in an echo of 5.1, are trapped in Yhwh's net. The transposition of terms raises questions of our passage. If, in 7.10, they *still* did not seek Yhwh, were they truly seeking him here? (For the interrelation of the two passages, see Morris 1996: 58-59.)

Verse 7 summarily adumbrates the theme of promiscuity: they have dealt treacherously with Yhwh and born strange children. 'They' may refer to the women of 4.13-14 or to the transfer of cultic allegiances their activities represent. But it may also allude to the priest's children in 4.6 and their strange, treacherous, and harlotrous activities. This may be supported by the conclusion of the verse, admittedly textually difficult—NJPS and NRSV take *ḥōdeš*, 'new moon', to be the subject of the sentence, but I regard it as adverbial (cf. Andersen and Freedman 1980: 396). The image of a God who devours 'them' with 'their fields' or 'portions' anticipates that of God as a moth in 5.12 (the Septuagint, indeed, has 'grasshopper' [Heb. *ḥāsîl*] here instead of the Masoretic *ḥōdeš*). God's withdrawal has reversed itself into, or taken the form of, incorporation. But it also reverses 4.8. There the priests batten on the sins of the people; now God feeds on them. The word *ḥelqêhem*, 'their fields' or 'portions', would lend further credence, since it denotes priestly cuts. The new moon, as a sacred day, would normally be a profitable one; it is turned into an eclipse, the end of the old order (Macintosh [1997: 188], following ibn Janah, takes it more generally to refer to a new period). Similar insistence that the old festival rhythms of new moons and festivals will cease is found in 2.13 and Amos 8.5. It is especially portentous, since the lunar cycle is short; disaster apparently is imminent.

There is another parallel passage. In 6.7, being treacherous to God is related to a breach of covenant; in 6.10 his appalled vision of Israel is expressed in a formula almost identical to 5.3: 'Ephraim's whoredom is there, Israel is defiled' (NRSV). As in 7.9-12, the effect is one of greater specificity: the treachery is illustrated by events in Gilead, on the road to Shechem, etc. At the same time, it reintroduces the possible distinction between Judah

78 *Hosea 5*

and Israel in the next phrase ('Also, O Judah, a harvest is appointed for you') and an even more tentative possibility of restoration ('When I would return the captivity of my people', 6.11).

(8) Blow the shofar in Gibeah, the trumpet in Ramah; sound the alarm, Beth-Awen; after you, O Benjamin.
(9) Ephraim shall be a desolation on the day of rebuke; among the tribes of Israel I have faithfully made it known.
(10) The princes of Judah are like those who move boundary stones; upon them I will pour my wrath like water.
(11) Ephraim is oppressed, shattered in judgment; for he insisted on going after futility.
(12) And I am like a moth to Ephraim, like rottenness to the house of Judah.
(13) And Ephraim saw his sickness, and Judah his sore, and Ephraim went to Assyria, and he sent to King Contentious, but he cannot heal you and he cannot bandage your sore.
(14) For I am like a lion to Ephraim, a young lion to the house of Judah: I, I will tear and I will go, and carry away, and none will deliver.
(15) I will go, I will return to my place, until they acknowledge their guilt and seek my face; in their trouble they will seek me out.

Verse 8 is the beginning of a new section, apparently discontinuous with the previous one. It is parallel to the imperatives that summon attention in 4.1 and 5.1. Now, however, the call is non-verbal, reaching below the level of conscious articulation; it portends the conclusion of the argument in 4.1, and the fulfilment of the chastisement in 5.2. The prohibition of reproof in 4.4 is a prelude to the day of reproof in 5.9; the lack of knowledge of God in 4.1, and God's unimpeded knowledge in 5.3, leads to his devastating communication of knowledge in 5.9. The same cluster recurs, but with its terms reversed, at the beginning of another section, ch. 8. There, recourse to the shofar—the ram's horn, ceremoniously sounded on festivals as well as an alarm or summons to war—is transferred to the prophet, in the context of Israel's claim to knowledge and God's profession of ignorance (8.2-3).

Commentators have by and large related this passage to the Syro-Ephraimite War of 733–32 BCE (for biblical accounts of this war, see 2 Kings 15.29, 37; 16.5-9; Isa. 7.1-2; and for a convincing critique of standard reconstructions, see Tomes). Hos. 5.10 is often seen as evidence for a Judean counter-attack, and 5.13 recounts embassies to the Assyrian monarch. The pressure of events increasingly dominates the flow of the book; my task, however, is not to use the text for historical reconstruction, but to examine how the necessarily vague allusions become symbols, and are integrated into its metaphoric structure (cf. Ben Zvi 2005: 140-41).

Gibeah, Ramah and Bethel are situated consecutively north of Jerusalem, and thus, according to most critics, mark the progress of the anticipated Judean counter-thrust. However, as Jeremias (1983: 80-81) points out, they are on opposite sides of the border; accordingly, he holds that the verse represents preparations for war by both parties. Benjamin, as the central tribe, mediates between Ephraim and Judah; conflict there is emblematic of the disunity of Israel, as in Judges, where Benjamin is the symbol for its coherence and weakness. The climax of Judges is the annihilation of Benjamin at Gibeah; on the ashes the Benjaminite Saul founds the capital of his abortive kingdom. Saul is important, not only as the first king, but as the only one who does not represent factional interests of north or south, who genuinely mediates between them. Two miles from Gibeah is Ramah, where Saul was anointed and where Samuel had his seat; the juxtaposition of Gibeah and Ramah recalls the tensions and affinity of Saul and Samuel, as determinative of the relations of prophet and king. Coupled with the reference to Mizpah in 5.1, it establishes a primal scene on which the latter-day prophet draws; he is the successor, the ghost of Samuel, proclaiming the abolition of the kingdom that Samuel so reluctantly endorsed. Bethel is an ambiguous and tenebrous figure, not least because of its by-name Beth-Awen, 'House of Wickedness/Folly', which nullifies any divine significance it might have. The prohibition on pilgrimage to Beth-Awen in 4.15 suggests that any assembly there will be of no account. This is supported by the verbs in the verse that belong to the language of festive celebration. In particular, 'Blow the shofar at Gibeah' recalls 'Blow the shofar at the new moon' in Ps. 81.4, and serves to link the beginning of this section to the end of the previous one. The imminent new moon is the one in which God will consume the fields or priestly portions.

In v. 8 Bethel is ambiguously Benjaminite, depending on whether one follows Josh. 18.13 or 23. If it is, the divisions of Israel are replicated within the central tribe itself. The quotation from the Song of Deborah, 'After you, O Benjamin' (Judg. 5.14), is recursive; the two parts of Benjamin are summoned against each other. In Judges 20 Bethel opposes Gibeah as the Israelite sacred headquarters; the enormity of God's oracle furthering the destruction of one of his tribes—adduced by its bizarre behaviour (20.18-26) and the people's contrition (21.3)—is transferred to the present situation, in which Bethel is a travesty of itself. There are other associations, however. In Judges 4, Deborah judges between Bethel and Ramah, while in 1 Sam. 10.3, as one of the signs of his election, Samuel tells Saul that he will encounter three men going to Bethel at 'the oak of Tabor', somewhere in the same vicinity. There are thus connections between Deborah's victory at Mt Tabor, the borders between Ephraim and Benjamin, northern and southern Israel, and Saul's election. It may be that Deborah is another prophetic persona for Hosea, a 'mother of Israel' (Judg. 5.7), representing the unity of the body politic at the point of its fragmentation. The echo of her Song, combined with the arboreal refiguration of the scene of her victory, establishes a poignant dissonance as a condition of his belated prophecy. Saul may read his 'sign' as evidence that he is to be a new Barak or Deborah, and so his early years promise. We, however, know that the signs are poisoned, that his election will lead to his downfall. From Hosea's perspective, this is a portent of the history of the entire kingdom.

In 6.6, there is another allusion to the conflict of Samuel and Saul. 'For I delight in lovingkindness (*ḥesed*) and not sacrifice, the knowledge of God more than burnt offerings' echoes Samuel's rejection of Saul on his return from defeating the Amalekites: 'Does Yhwh delight in burnt offerings and sacrifices more than hearing the voice of Yhwh? Behold, hearing is better than sacrifice, listening than the fat of rams' (1 Sam. 15.22). But the allusion exposes differences. The address in Hosea is to the people, not the king; the injunction is not to obedience, but to lovingkindness and the knowledge of God. As Andersen and Freedman point out (1980: 431), the verbs for 'hearing' and 'listening' occur in 5.1, again linking the two sections together; lovingkindness and the knowledge of God, together with truth, are the qualities whose absence provokes the divine disputation in 4.1. 6.6 could be seen as the summation of the divine message, especially since the summons to 'hear' and to 'listen' in 5.1 is not followed up by any conclusion. Saul, however, is charged with a failure of blind obedience; any knowledge he might obtain is of God at his most vindictive. Indeed, he sins in that he does show kindness in sparing Agag, king of the Amalekites. An interesting parallel is 1 Kgs 20.31, in which the servants of the king of Aram advise him, as a last resort, to throw himself on the mercy of the king of Israel, 'for the kings of Israel are kings of kindness (*ḥesed*)'.

The greatest difference, however, arises from the context. 6.6 is immediately preceded by 'Therefore I hewed with prophets, I slew them with the words of my mouth'. The history of prophecy is one of castigation; prophets are God's hewers of wood, clearing divine space through uttering performative words of death. Of such a prophet Samuel is an exemplar, and indeed the confrontation between Samuel and Saul ends with him hacking Agag to pieces (1 Sam. 15.33). The retrospective contrasts with God's perplexity in 6.4: 'What shall I do with you, Ephraim? What shall I do with you, Judah?' Hosea wears the cloak of Samuel to express God's vacillation. This may be simply the result of belatedness, the poet at the end of a tradition worrying about its value and his or her place in it. In particular, it raises the question of the meaning of the lovingkindness and knowledge God prefers. What is God's lovingkindness? A gap is opened between the uncompromising and heroic role of the succession of prophets and the inability to affirm it. Hosea is a Samuel suddenly unsure of himself.

This is manifest through the alternation of Ephraim and Judah, condemnation and reprieve, the coupling of images, and the prevalence of wordplays that continually change their significance. Ephraim is condemned on the day of reproof (v. 9), taking the place of Benjamin; in the next verse (v. 10), Judah is subject to divine wrath. The image of moving a border, and thus stealing territory, evokes, as most commentators note, the covenant curse in Deut. 27.17; like the tribal assembly in v. 9, the context is the ritual assent of the entire people, stationed on Mt Ebal and Mt Gerizim, to a set of curses. The word of assent, 'Amen', echoes Yhwh's decreeing faithfully (*ne'emānâ*) the desolation of Ephraim. Commentators interpret the image literally, as referring to Judah's territorial aggrandizement, but it is clearly also a metaphor for pride and greed, corresponding, for instance, to the depiction of the priests in 4.7 (Ben Zvi 2005: 140 notes that it is a common ancient Near Eastern topos). God's reaction, however, is one that will obliterate all boundaries: 'Upon them I will pour out my wrath like water'. The image is suggestive of bad temper, like God's casting his shoe at Edom and using Moab as his washing pot in Ps. 60.10 = 108.10. The dissonance between the petulance of the image and the divine pretensions to grandeur induces an intimation of the comic, combining the absurdity of the deflation of human conceit with the blasphemy of attributing infantile behaviour to God. Metaphor and humour are correlative experiences, both dependent on the recognition of unexpected conjunctions; a poor metaphor may well be unintentionally comic. In this instance, the dissonance, together with the alternation between Ephraim and Judah, is resolved by the intrusion of another emotion in the next verse, and introduces the key problem: whether God's wrath is compatible with God's desire and transcendence.

The focus switches to Ephraim, 'oppressed' and 'shattered with judgment'. Those who practised justice in v. 1 and used it as a trap are now judged. The immediate reference to the day of reproof in v. 9, however, leads to another inversion: we pass from the external condemnation to the experience of the victim, communicated through passive verbs, from judgment to sympathy. The passage from the preparations for war to their lamentable result is marked by a wordplay, linking the word for 'trumpet' ($h^a\bar{s}\bar{o}\bar{s}r\hat{a}$) with that for 'shattered' ($r^e\bar{s}\hat{u}\bar{s}$). The trumpets lie broken, their calls fragmented. The oppression and shattering of Ephraim results, however, from their untoward liberty: 'for he insisted on going after a command' (rendering the very uncertain last word as 'command'). On the one hand, this substantiates the metaphor of Ephraim as a wayward cow in 4.16; on the other, it anticipates Ephraim's courtship of the king of Assyria in v.13. If the last word of our verse does mean 'command', it would suggest that Ephraim is at the beck and call of Assyria, rather than God; it could, however, refer to excrement or nonsense (cf. Ben Zvi 2005: 143; NRSV 'vanity'; NJPS 'futility', with footnotes). These possibilities are evidently not exclusive, connoting the worthlessness of Assyria and linking it with the idols to which Ephraim is attached in 4.17. This is supported by the structural parallel between the two verses: 'Bound to idols is Ephraim' matches 'Oppressed is Ephraim'.

The oppression is immediately countered by another image: 'I am like a moth ($'\bar{a}\bar{s}$) to Ephraim, and like rottenness ($r\bar{a}q\bar{a}b$) to the house of Judah'. (Many commentators propose a second meaning of 'larvae' or 'pus' for the word $'\bar{a}\bar{s}$ here, to fit in with the context; this alleged second meaning, however, does not occur elsewhere and should be discarded.) The moth invisibly eats away at the social fabric, while rottenness refers most frequently to bone disease. From being an external judge, God becomes a destructive immanence, and thus subverts the focus on the pathos of the interiority of Ephraim in v. 11. The word for 'moth' (*'āš*) abbreviates that for 'oppressed' (*'āšûq*); at the centre of the people crushed from without is that which consumes it from within. Concomitantly, the word for 'rottenness' (*rāqāb*) inverts that for 'midst' (*qereb*) in v. 4. If the word *qereb* refers to the vital centre of the organism, *rāqāb* is that which dissolves it. In v. 4 the centrifugal wind/spirit of fornication occupies and hollows out the 'midst' of the people; the rottenness in its bones—equivalent in Hebrew idiom to its essence and its permanent structure—or its vital organs has a similar function. On the other side of licentiousness we find disintegration.

The nugatory narrative that follows in v. 13 affords a glimpse into a different imaginative domain, the quest for a cure. A doctor, especially one for whom one travels thousands of miles and who is also a king, promises a solution to the anguish of the body and hence, at least temporarily, an arrest of mortality. Medicine, especially in ancient times, is inextricable from magic, attunement with the mystery of the body and the powers that control it. A physician-king combines political and therapeutic power, responsibility for the physical body as well as its social counterpart. As a healer, he is construed as benevolent, relieving the world's miseries, in contrast to the perennial history of kings. The fantasy contradicts, of course, the actual historical referent: the submission of the two kingdoms to Assyria and the payment of tribute. We may suspect also that whatever God's ultimate responsibility, Assyria is the immediate cause of the wounds from which they seek healing. The title Hosea accords him alludes to his official title of 'The Great King' (*melek rab*), but it actually means 'the contentious king' (*melek yārēb*). As such, it recalls Yhwh's dispute with the earth in 4.1, and his prohibition of contention in 4.4. The king is either the one who acts as the ventriloquist's dummy for Yhwh's dispute, or is the prime disturber of the silence he imposes. In 4.19 the wind that binds or wars against Ephraim may be identified, as we have seen, both with the east wind of Yhwh in 13.15 and with the Assyrians; it correlates with the wind/spirit of promiscuity in 4.12 and 5.4 that both shifts the people from outside and is lodged in their midst. On the other side of this destructive nexus between inside and outside, Assyria and Israel, is Yhwh's erosion from within. The placement of the interlude of v. 13 between two opposed images of Yhwh contrasts the king of Assyria to Yhwh and exposes his impotence. If the original Samuel admonished Saul that the kingdom would be given to one who was better than himself (1 Sam. 15.28), his latter-day successor acknowledges the transfer of sovereignty to Assyria. Whether behind the power of Assyria is that of Yhwh, whether the spirit of promiscuity expresses the animus of Yhwh, remains to be seen.

The two similes of v. 14—'For I am like a lion to Ephraim, and like a young lion to the house of Judah'—match those of v. 12. Their relationship may be incremental or even consecutive, as Jeremias suggests (1983: 83): moth damage and creaking joints may be healed, but not the depredations of a ravening lion. The two verses may also be read as complementary: God is both like a moth and a lion, representative of two extremes of destructiveness among the creatures, of subversion from within and aggression from without; between them, Israel is trapped. The lion symbolizes God at his most dangerous, and thus the fragility of existence. That God experiences himself most fully in his violence is suggested by the threefold repetition of the word 'I': 'I am like a lion...I, I will tear...', of which the first is the emphatic form *'ānōkî*. But there is also an interesting inversion. The second half of our verse is echoed in Deut. 32.39: 'For I, I am he, and there is no God beside me; I bring death and I give life, I crush and I heal, and there is none who delivers from my hand'. The two verses are close enough to suggest a conscious allusion, and some such text must underlie the people's expectation of deliverance in 6.1-3. The context of Deut. 32.39 is God's turning his wrath against Israel's enemies. The presence of a text like this behind or alongside ours suggests that something is missing, that our text is askew, for it lacks the essential element of transformation, the capacity to change violence into vivification. The threefold I's endorse the violence, but with each assertion, each commitment of egoistic energy into the triumph, there is a depletion of conviction. Why does God insist so much? This is evidenced by the vague 'I will go' which follows 'I will tear'; in an analogous position, Deut. 32.39 has 'I will heal'. The anticlimax produces a momentary deflation, as well as a question: where will he go? The duality of the metaphors, of moth and lion, like all metaphors for God, expose grounds of dissimilarity; the analogies between moths, lions and God break down. The paradox of commensurability and incommensurability of moths and lions repeats itself, infinitely magnified, between them and God. Any simile is ambiguous, establishing relationships of likeness and difference; between God and the creatures this ambiguity is absolute. We then wonder about the nature of God's 'I', so strongly asserted, behind its conflicting personae and the metaphors it seeks out so as to be able to communicate.

The next verse presents a failure of nerve. God returns to his place for his supposed prey to seek him out. No matter how fully he enters into the role of the lion, this does not seem to be what he wants. There is a contradiction between this verse and v. 5, in which God makes himself scarce when Israel seeks for him. It may, of course, be resolved, with the help of the following passage, by the inadequacy of the people's rapprochement; they come with flocks and herds, rather than a confession of guilt. But it also suggests a duality in God's response, that whatever his rejection of their overtures, he still waits. Similarly, God's retirement to his place imparts a dialectic of absence and presence, absence for the sake of presence.

Hosea 6

(1) Come, let us return to Yhwh, for he tore and he will heal us; he struck and he will bind us up.
(2) He will revive us in two days; on the third day he will raise us up and we will live in his presence.
(3) And we will know and we will pursue knowing Yhwh; like the dawn his rising is sure; and he will come like rain to us, like the latter rain that pours upon the earth.
(4) What shall I do with you, Ephraim? What shall I do with you, Judah? Your love (*hesed*) is like the cloud of morning, like the dew that quickly passes away.
(5) Therefore I hewed with prophets; I slew them with the words of my mouth; and your judgments are light that goes forth.
(6) For I desire *hesed* more than sacrifice, and the knowledge of God more than burnt offerings.

God's return to his place in 5.15 is matched by the people's return in 6.1; they seem to fulfil his wish and seek his face. Commentators suggest as reasons for the inadequacy of their overture the lack of a confession of guilt and that they treat Yhwh as a nature god, whose return is as inevitable as the rain or the dawn. Nevertheless, the problem won't simply go away, since the desire to return, no matter that it is induced by extremity, is real; it is a desire for normality, for the familiar rhythms of seasonal and cultic life. God's 'place', on this view, is inside the people and the land of Israel. It may be identified, for instance, with a shrine, such as Bethel, which literally means 'House of God'. To posit God as being outside the people, and to align this with the difference between God's conception of loving-kindness and knowledge and that of the people, makes the return to God a journey to something outside the human domain and tangible human values. The people seek to correct the misappropriation of Deut. 32.39, to restore the familiar text and its consolations. Their universe is one of complementarity, authorized by tradition and experience, between God and humanity, life and death, light and dark. Parallelism, alliteration, rhyme and repetition inform a poetic text whose message is reassurance, that everything fits. The violence of 'he tore' (*ṭāRāP*) slides effortlessly into the certainty that 'he will heal us' (*yiRPā'ēnû*), the abrupt monosyllable 'he struck' (*yak*) echoes, attenuated, in the first syllables of 'he will bind us' (*yaḥbᵉšēnû*) and 'he will revive us' (*yᵉḥayyēnû*). In v. 2 the ease of restoration to life 'in two days' is formulaically completed by a third day, in which 'we will live' is augmented by 'he will raise us up' and the specification that life will be 'in his presence'. The cumulative effect is repeated in v. 3, where 'we will know' is expanded into 'we will pursue knowing'. 'Knowing Yhwh' complements 'we will live in his presence'. The intimacy of knowledge corresponds, reciprocally, to the conception of life as led before his benign gaze, and both anticipate the simile comparing the inevitability of God's theophany to the dawn. Illumination, the familiar metaphor aligning vision and consciousness, is coterminous with the conjunction of daylight and the divine presence. Knowing God is as pervasive, and as unconscious, as awareness of daylight; it becomes our natural element.

But the correlation may also be reversed: the knowledge the people 'pursue' is the confirmation of old certainties, and the reduction of the divine presence to humdrum reality. They 'pursue' knowledge, but the pursuit becomes an end in itself; the retrogression from 'we will know' to 'we will pursue knowing' transfers the emotional charge to the excitement of the chase. Excitation is proportional to the relief when the rain/divinity comes. But in fact the knowledge is coming of its own accord. The pursuit is consequently pointless, an arousal or gratification for its own sake. The erotic metaphor is less important than its transferability. Pursuit suggests the male activities of hunting and war, as well as amorous rapaciousness. However, intertextually, it is a female propensity. In the Song of Songs the woman is the active partner, who seeks her lover in 3.1-4 and 5.5-6; in 1.4 the collectivity of women pursue the man. In Hosea it is the woman/Israel who pursues her lovers (2.9). Our text then confirms the feminine identification of Israel and evokes the romantic interplay of God and Israel in 2.16-25. As there, knowledge of God is reflected in the fruitful interaction of heaven and earth. The rain, as fertilizing celestial fluid, has its obvious phallic correlate. Critics, such as Fisch (1988: 149-50), who stress the confusion between Yhwh and Baal in this passage, emphasize this association. However, the rhythm of arousal and release—the relief at the advent of the rains—applies as much to Israel as to God. The rain is both inseminatory and, like the day, all encompassing. The image of God as matrix, object of Israel's pursuit and knowledge, reverses that of impregnation. The reversibility of gender positions that affects both Israel and God makes the difference between them uncertain. Israel's focus on the pursuit rather than the attainment inserts God, as the object of desire and knowledge, into its own wishful fantasy, as the instrument of comfort. This is confirmed by a pun: the word for 'pours' in 'as the latter rain *pours* upon the earth' also means '*teaches*'. Israel's desire for knowledge is matched by God's instruction, which is as effortless and enveloping as the rain. Again there is an echo of Moses' song in Deuteronomy 32, which is compared to the rain and the dew (Deut. 32.2-3). There the fertilizing effect of the song, as part of the dialogue of heaven and earth, contrasts with its content; the music is not altogether pleasant to its hearers, since it predicts the destitution as well as restoration of Israel. It is the point of reference for the subsequent history and the prophetic books. By correcting and completing God's partial misquotation in 5.15, and interpreting positively the comparison with rain, the people exclude its darker ramifications. In v. 5 the words of the prophets are the words of death. But there is another cross-reference. In Hos. 10.12 the metaphor is repeated in an unavailing call to proper repentance, in which God pours/teaches righteousness in response to the people's efforts to cultivate virtue. The two texts match each other; 10.12 exposes the inadequacy of their words in our passage, precisely because they are not substantiated by effort and fundamental change.

What the people find is not certainty but divine equivocation: 'What shall I do with you, O Ephraim? What shall I do with you, O Judah?' (v. 4). Repetition raises the question of the possible difference between Ephraim and Judah, although they are mirroring terms throughout the passage. Ephraim and Judah are equally culpable, equally court Assyria, and are equally subject to divine judgment. Yet, as the reader knows, Judah is the survivor; God does different things with Judah and Ephraim. The difference between Judah and Ephraim, those fratricidal mirror-images, is that of God's hesitation, his alternative futures. Repetition takes time, prolongs the moment of divine bafflement,

Hosea 6 89

as he turns from one to the other. God, as the voice that underlies and infuses the voices of the poem, has his crisis of doubt, a question of the possibility of speech and action on which the poem is based. The presupposition of the prophetic discourse, that there is a divine action to be heralded, founders. But it is also ambiguous whether God's claim to helplessness responds to the people's solicitation in vv. 1-3 or to the review of prophetic history in v. 5. On the one hand, God cannot simply come at the people's call as automatically as the literature of trite religious confidence would lead us to expect (a sentiment manifested in various ways in the Psalms; for example, 'the king who answers us on the day we call' [Ps. 20.10]); on the other hand, capital punishment for perfidy no longer satisfies. Hosea represents a hiatus, a sudden qualm, in the line of death-dealing prophets.

Accordingly, the phrase following God's access of doubt—'and your love (*ḥesed*) is like a morning cloud, like the dew that goes early away'—can be interpreted in two ways. It may be because human affections and ties are so transitory that God cannot trust himself to them; the evaporation of *ḥesed* then corresponds to God's loss of words. Alternatively, human weakness both provoked the monotonous sequence of lethal prophets, and generates a realization of its pointlessness. God's indulgence, or exhaustion, results from a belated recognition of human incapacity. (Similarly, in the story of the Flood, the human propensity for evil both motivates the Flood and justifies its not being repeated [Gen. 6.5; 8.21].)

The morning mist is deceptive, because its shade and dampness are transient, and associated with illusory shapes and concealments. The *ḥesed* of the people is characterized thereby as false, if comforting, in contrast to the true *ḥesed* of v. 6. The image of dew complements that of rain in v. 3; they are seasonally contrasted, and also oppose the rain that comes from the heavens to the moisture that appears on the earth. If the rain and the rainy season are figures for the approach of God, the dew is analogous to the *ḥesed* with which the people disguise themselves. The dew is a symbol of transformation in Hosea: from being an epitome of impermanence it becomes an image for God himself (14.6). In the immediate context, however, the similes in our verse correspond to those at the end of v. 3. Images of the dawn pass backwards and forwards between God and Israel. In 5.15 God anticipates that in extremity the people will seek his presence betimes; one of the verbs used is derived from the word for 'dawn', the time when eager clients solicit their patron. These human embodiments of the dawn, however, transfer the metaphor to God in v. 3. Their importunity, they hope, will converge with the certainty of his manifestation. In v. 4 the image reverses itself: the dew burns off because of the heat of the sun, whose rising is compared to the appearance of God. Thus the ostensible simile (*ḥesed* as fleeting as the dew) overlays a more pervasive and commonplace one: the dew as a figure for human impermanence. One may collapse the overt and implied similes; there is a rhetorical shift from the passing affections of the people to their own transience. *Ḥesed* becomes a synecdoche for the body itself. In v. 5 the shift is confirmed, as the image of dawn is transferred back to God, identified with his attribute of justice (most critics read 'my judgment goes forth as the light' instead of the Masoretic 'your judgments are light that goes forth', but the difference between the two readings is in fact insubstantial). Dawn then becomes a figure for death, juxtaposed with the fatal words of the prophets, instead of the new life the petitioners expect in vv. 1-2.

There are other wordplays. In v. 3 the pursuit of knowledge culminates in God's 'coming forth' (*môṣā'ô*); in 5.6 the quest for God is unsuccessful. The failure to 'find' (*yimṣā'û*) God in 5.6 is corrected by God's envisaged epiphany. What they find instead, however, is the emanation of a hostile justice. In v. 4 there is another allusion to the same verse. The word for 'morning' (*bōqer*) in 'morning cloud' is another permutation of the consonants *q, r, b*, that we found in *qereb* ('midst') and *rāqāb* ('rottenness') in 5.4 and 12. Just as the word *rāqāb* represents an immanent dissolution in the midst (*qereb*) of the body politic, so does the morning cloud shred in the light of the sun. Since *ḥesed* refers primarily to a relationship with God, that which should provide organic coherence is delusive. In 5.6 the people seek God with their flocks and 'with their herds' (*bibqārām*). The word for 'cattle' (*bāqār*) replicates the consonants of *bōqer* ('morning'). Similarly, the word for 'their sheep' (*ṣō'nām*) in that verse is a metathesis of *môṣā'ô* ('its coming forth') and *yimṣā'û* ('they found'). The journey to find God, 'with their flocks and their herds', underpins the speech of vv. 1-3; both converge on the rejection of sacrifices in favour of true knowledge and *ḥesed* in v. 6. The people play at the Exodus, just as they do at the pursuit of knowledge. What God wants, however, is not re-enactment or performance. True knowledge and *ḥesed* remain undefined,

Hosea 6 91

beyond the horizon of familiar regressions and formulae. Equally, God's desire (*ḥāpaṣtî*) transforms and upstages his habitual 'hewing' (*ḥāṣabtî*) of the malefactors. The prophets clear the terrain for the practice of *ḥesed* and the cultivation of knowledge; the relationship between *ḥāṣabtî* and *ḥāpaṣtî* is both one of opposition and succession. At the same time, God's repeated question in v. 4 (repetition as an index of anxiety?), and the variation in the allusion to 1 Samuel that I discussed earlier, suggest that the old answers are no longer appropriate.

Wordplay generates metaphors and cross-references, and is one of the instruments wherewith the text is constructed. But it also creates uncertainty, as one term is transposed into its opposite, and a sense of the music of language, which sidesteps any stable, determinate meaning. This is especially true of Ephraim (*'eprayim*), which is associated with the lion-like (*kᵉpîr*) predatory (*ṭārāp*) God and with the search for healing (*rp'*). The use of terms like *ḥesed* and the knowledge of God with different meanings for the different participants in the discourse ruptures the flow of language, since all words, at least as used by human beings, become suspect. The images, such as that of the dawn, that are interchanged between the speakers both constitute the dialogue and destroy it, as they change signification; an image of life becomes an image for death. The rhythm of the passage is comprised of feints, tactical withdrawals, abortive initiatives, and inconclusive advances. What God desires instead of sacrifices is *ḥesed* and knowledge of himself; the verb, as well as the comparison, suggest a theocentric universe, a God who is nourished on these attributes. Both, however, are relational terms; that which supports God's well-being is the discourse with human beings. The gratification of God as the centre of attention is counterbalanced by the affirmation of human subjectivity.

(7) And they, like Adam, have breached the covenant; there they dealt treacherously against me.
(8) Gilead is a city of workers of evil, tracked in blood.
(9) Like bandits lying in wait are the company of priests, on the way to Shechem they murder, for they have committed depravity.
(10) In the house of Israel I have seen horror; there is the harlotry of Ephraim, Israel is defiled.
(11) Also, O Judah, a harvest is set for you, in my restoring the fortunes of my people.

6.7-11 is transitional, in that it introduces the theme of assassination and political anarchy that dominates the next chapter, while it is linked to 5.1-7 through refrain (Ben Zvi 2005: 126). The verses, however, are short, abrupt, and lack logical coherence, reflecting the dislocation of their represented world. While the sequence is fractured, its components form multiple connections, both within the text of Hosea and outside it. They direct us from the surface to underlying patterns.

Verse 7 immediately presents us with a problem. Our Hebrew text reads, 'And they *like* Adam have breached the covenant'. Most critics emend this, however, to 'And they *at* Adam have breached the covenant'. The emendation is justified by the ease with which the Hebrew characters k ('like') and b ('at') are confused, and by the arguments that no covenant was made with Adam, that references to the story of the Garden of Eden are anomalous in early biblical literature—the assumption is that Hosea did not know the creation traditions (see, however, Murray)—and that, if one reads it as 'like Adam', 'there' in the second half of the verse is anchored nowhere. Adam (modern Damiya) is a ford of the Jordan where, according to Josh. 3.16, the waters were held back when Israel crossed into the Promised Land. Hosea, then, in their view, would be alluding to some long-forgotten contemporary breach of covenant.

This is a much less interesting reading of the text than 'like Adam'. It does not seem probable that Hosea would not have been acquainted with some version of the Adam story (they go back, after all, to Sumer). Furthermore, the word 'Adam' is ambiguous, referring both to the first human and to the human race in general. On the second of these interpretations, this verse would support God's equivocation in v. 4: since it is integral to human nature to break covenants, correction is wasted (Ben Zvi 2005: 145-46. Ben Zvi provides a detailed defence of the double meaning of Adam and the reference to the garden of Eden story). The prospect the book predicts and/or seeks to avoid is universal bereavement (9.16). A trajectory passes from the innate or primal fault to the ultimate extinction.

But there may be a more direct link with the Garden of Eden story. God desires 'knowledge of God', according to v. 6, contrasting with his insistence on blind obedience in 1 Samuel 15. Adam's contravention consists in the acquisition of divine knowledge against God's will. Our text offers a reversal of the Eden story. Knowledge of God will return us to a paradisal condition

(2.22-25; ch. 14). Breach of the covenant, by inference from v. 6, comprises substituting sacrifices for knowledge of God and *ḥesed*. This is supported by the parallel between 'there they dealt treacherously against me' in our verse, and 'they dealt treacherously against Yhwh' in 5.7, since the context for the latter is the search for the Lord with flocks and herds in 5.6.

To know, according to the Genesis story, is constitutive of humanity, whatever its cost in mortality and dissimulation. The knowledge that God desires is in some respects the reverse of the knowledge of the garden of Eden, the product of relationship not rivalry, which finds expression, so the parallelism suggests, in acts of *ḥesed*. Yet if the knowledge of good and evil is all-inclusive, knowledge of God must come under its purview, perhaps as an ultimate horizon. This might lead us to the ambiguity of God's motives in Genesis, but also to the priest's rejection of knowledge and forgetfulness of Torah in 4.6. These latter-day Adams have abandoned what it is to be human.

The word 'Adam' rhymes with the word for 'blood' ($dām$) at the end of v. 8, which itself recalls the welter of blood in 4.2. Forgetfulness of the covenant results in the reduction of human beings to blood and the structured cosmos to violent dissolution, associated in 4.3 with the Flood. The problem is why, amid all the intertextual references to the origins of Israel's perfidy, there should be a sudden throwback to those of the human race. The book is full of references, especially at the beginning of sections, to the uniqueness of God's relationship with Israel and his discovery of it in the wilderness (9.10; 10.1; 11.1; 13.4). The fleeting ghost of Adam suggests another genealogy for Israel, its interconnectedness with the rest of the human race. It raises the question of the identity of Israel, of its dual origination, posed, for instance, by the priest's mother in 4.5. If being human, for the priest as well as the people, consists in forgetting the quest for knowledge that defines humanity and the bonds of *ḥesed* wherewith society is constituted, then God teaches them the Torah which restores to them their humanity. Paradoxically, divine origination is a means of reconstituting human origins.

There is one other possible citation of the story of the Garden of Eden. There is a prediction in 10.8 that 'thorns and thistles' will grow on the Israelite altars. The phrase only occurs elsewhere in the Hebrew Bible in Gen. 3.18, as part of the curse which God imposes on the earth for Adam's sake. A comparable image, though using different words, occurs in 9.6. A passing homology between Israel and the Garden of Eden is possible, though thorns growing on ruins is a standard topos for desolation in prophetic literature.

The Adam figure informs the references to Gilead and Shechem in the next two verses. Even if one reads 'like Adam' as 'at Adam', there may still be an adversion to the crossing of the Jordan; breach of the covenant would be coterminous with entrance into the Promised Land, and thus into history. At any rate, both verses are recondite: we do not know who the 'evildoers' of Gilead are or what they have done (it should be noted that the word *'āwen* has a very wide semantic range, including mendacity, idolatry, and illusion), while the incident(s) at Shechem is likewise inaccessible. Both have multiple intertextual associations. In the case of Gilead, we have discussed some of these in the context of 5.1. The connection with Jacob's treaty is tightened by the phrase 'tracked with blood', since the word for 'tracked' (*ᶜaqubbâ*) is a pun on Jacob's name (*yaᶜaqōb*), and foreshadows the extensive meditation on Jacob's name and nature in ch. 12. Those who follow in Jacob's footsteps leave a trail of blood. But Gilead, immediately focalized as a *city* of evildoers, is reminiscent also of Jehu's revolution, which broke out in the city of Ramoth Gilead (2 Kgs 9), and hence of the blood which Yhwh threatens to 'visit' in 1.4. Gilead recurs in Hosea in 12.12 (Eng. 12.11), again in conjunction with a word for 'evil' or 'folly' that is used here. There the word for 'evil' (*'āwen*) is a transformation of that for the vigour (*'ôn*) with which Jacob confronts God. Again, the trajectory from Jacob to his descendants is a reversal.

Shechem is associated with crimes of sexual and homicidal violence; the story of Dinah (Genesis 34) is closely reflected in that of Abimelech (Judges 9). The verse obviously intensifies the accusations against the priests in 4.7-8; their predations no longer have a mask of sanctity. Murder is generalized into an indictment for 'depravity' (*zimmâ*). *Zimmâ* is a term for sexual transgression, in particular if it crosses the boundaries between generations. A man who prostitutes his daughter desecrates her and fills the land with *zimmâ* (Lev. 19.29); intercourse with mother and daughter (or granddaughter) is likewise characterized as *zimmâ* (Lev. 18.17; 20.14). The heinousness of the latter offense is evidenced by the penalty of burning that is prescribed for it; the same penalty adheres to a promiscuous priest's daughter (Lev. 22.9). Our verse may be correlated with 4.13-14, where cultic occasions invite indirect *zimmâ*, prostituting daughters and brides through setting them a bad example. *Zimmâ*, however, could be a vague term of abuse, a prelude to v. 10, inclusive of or contrasted with murder. At any rate, the combination makes the priests the antithesis of guardians of sacred order: they breach the boundaries of life, sex and time. They are thus harbingers of chaos, social as well as political. Their ancestor, Levi, massacred the inhabitants of Shechem (Gen. 34.25), thereby breaching a covenant and earning Jacob's curse (Gen. 49.5-7). But they are also, so the sexual insinuation suggests, guilty of the same sexual shamelessness ($n^eb\bar{a}l\hat{a}$, Gen. 34.7) that Levi avenged. ($N^eb\bar{a}l\hat{a}$ and *zimmâ* are used as coordinated terms for sexual abuse by another vicious Levite, the husband of the woman murdered at Gibeah, in Judg. 20.6.)

The delinquencies of the priests contaminate Israel or at least ensure that they cannot fulfil their purgative function. The next verse takes a God's eye perspective, unifying the Trans- and Cisjordanian halves of the country, represented metonymically by Gilead and Shechem, under a single condemnation, prefatory to the narrowing of the focus on the capital city, Samaria, for the first time in the book. Verse 10 is a reprise of 5.3; whereas 5.3 concerns God's unmasking Israel's impurity, v. 10 turns to his emotive reaction, and replaces the semantics of time with those of place. 'There' in v. 10 echoes '*there* they dealt treacherously with me' in v. 7 to enclose the intervening verses as an evocation of a single location. The contexts of 5.3 and 6.10 correlate two strikingly juxtaposed instances of the verb 'return' ($\check{s}\hat{u}b$), which, as we have seen, is germinal to the interaction of God and Israel in 5.15 and 6.1. The impurity of Israel in 5.3 results in their being unable to return to God as well as their refusal to do so, despite their search for him with their flocks and their herds; 6.10, however, is followed by 'in my restoring the fortunes ($b^e\check{s}\hat{u}b\hat{i}$ $\check{s}^eb\hat{u}t$ [the latter word may also mean 'captivity']) of my people'. Human impotence is replaced by divine initiative.

Once again, too, Israel and Judah are coupled together; the word 'also' at the beginning of v. 11 seems to append Judah as an afterthought ('Also for Judah, a harvest is set for you!'). The metaphor of the harvest would seem to be entirely conventional, except that we do not know what it means. It is an example of a metaphor whose apparent triteness is subverted by its lack of reference. On the one hand, the conjunction 'also' aligns it with Ephraim and Israel as an entity worthy of judgment; the harvest then would be the consequence of misdeeds. On the other hand, it is conditional also on the following phrases, concerning God's restoration and healing of Israel. Judah then would share in Israel's ultimate harvest of God's bounty. As in 6.4, two competing programmes, one resulting in annihilation as a logical conclusion from the rhetoric of the preceding verses, and the other envisaging a miraculous and inexplicable transformation through God's inability to carry out his destructive intentions, converge. The second possibility, as in v. 4, is derived from reversing the direction of the argument: reading from the future, and from a return, too, to an acknowledgement of relationship, that they, Israel and Judah, are 'my people'. If in 4.6 'my people' are destroyed for want of knowledge, here their restoration is contingent on God's reclaiming his knowledge of affiliation.

Hosea 7

(1) When I would heal Israel, the iniquity of Ephraim is revealed, and the evils of Samaria, for they have acted falsely, and a thief would come, and robber bands outside.
(2) And let them not say in their hearts, 'I have remembered all their evil'. Now their deeds will surround them, they are constantly before my face.
(3) In their evil they make the king rejoice, the princes in their deceit.
(4) All of them are adulterers, like a baker's oven, burning; he desists from stoking it, from kneading the dough until it is leavened.
(5) The day of our king: the princes have sickened from the heat of wine; he puts forth his hand with the scoffers.
(6) For their heart has drawn close like an oven in their conspiracy; all night their baker sleeps; in the morning it blazes like a flaming fire.
(7) All of them are heated like an oven; they consume their judges; all their kings fall. None calls among them to me.
(8) Ephraim is mingled among the peoples; Ephraim is like an unturned cake.
(9) Strangers have consumed his strength, but he does not know; indeed, hoary hair is cast upon him, and he does not know.
(10) And the pride of Israel will answer in his face; and they will not turn back to Yhwh their God and they will not seek him, despite all this.
(11) And Ephraim was like a silly thoughtless dove; they called to Egypt, they went to Assyria.
(12) Wherever they go, I will spread upon them my net; like the birds of the heaven I will bring them down; I will chastise them at the very rumour of their assignations.
(13) Woe to them, for they have fled from me; disaster to them, for they have rebelled against me, when I would redeem them, and they spoke lies against me.

(14) And they did not cry to me in their hearts, but they wail on their beds, over the corn and the new wine; they estrange themselves, turn against me.
(15) And I trained, I strengthened their arms, and they plotted evil against me!
(16) They turn again, but not above; they are like a deceitful bow; their princes fall by the sword, by the wrath of their tongues; that is their scorn in the land of Egypt.

Whatever be the case at the end of ch. 6, the intimation of return, the desire to 'heal' Israel at the beginning of 7.1, is transitory and founders on God's reality sense, his awareness of the irremediable evil and deceitfulness of Israel. The movement is precisely the same as that which connects ch. 11 and ch. 12; the vision of return at the end of ch. 11 is immediately countermanded by a recognition of the mendacity of Israel (12.1). Both passages are further linked by the verb 'surround'. If in 12.1, Ephraim 'surrounds' God with deceit, in 7.2 the Ephraimites' deeds 'surround' them. A closer parallel is 5.15–6.1; when, in 5.15, God retreats from his destructive purpose in order to elicit Israel's response, their overture in 6.1 releases a paroxysm of doubt. The correlation with the end of ch. 11 points to the sharper interpretation of $š^eb\hat{u}t$ in 6.11 as 'captivity', corresponding to the pattern of destruction, banishment and restoration that pervades chs. 1–3. The cumulative references to a reversal on the other side of disaster anticipate the contrast between ch. 13 and ch. 14, and represent an irrepressible hope despite all demurral. On the other hand, that every flicker of promise is immediately retracted makes the last chapter less certain a conclusion. We do not know if the exhortation to return to the Lord (14.2) will be regarded, or whether God's vision of reconciliation will not be undercut by further second thoughts. The turn between 6.11 and 7.1, like that between 11.11 and 12.1, 5.15 and 6.1, suggests an alternative structuring of the book, in which sections are demarcated by moments of hope. This would be confirmed by the common attribution of a major structural break between chs. 4–11 and 12–14. If the transition between chs. 11 and 12 is comparable to that between chs. 6 and 7, then it should mark a similar rupture. The 'alternative structure', substituting a happy for an unhappy ending, opens out an indefinite future, and thus undermines historical and poetic closure. In the gap between God's intended retreat ($'āšûbâ$) and the people's breathless attempt to fill it by returning to him (nāšûbâ) in 5.15–6.1, there is a surreptitious pun on the word for dawn ($y^e\check{s}ah^arun^en\hat{\imath}$), which may be a metaphor for this opening beyond the end of a history defined by beginnings and ends, births and deaths. The dawn, which may or may not prove false, is the fugitive figure beneath the desire for importunity ($y^e\check{s}ah^arun^en\hat{\imath}$), the poetic entreaty and tortuous logic of the book, as it searches through the dynamics of its political and religious world for knowledge—the knowledge of God—and an end to its restless turnings and returnings, traced by the protean word šûb, 'return'.

The dominant images in ch. 7, at least until v. 12, are those of the oven (7.4-9) and the dove (7.11-12). Both induce a focus on the heart of Israel/Samaria, from complementary angles: whereas the oven represents the heart in its deviousness, compactness, and intensity, the dove 'has no heart' (7.11)—the heart in the Hebrew Bible being the organ of sense as well as sensibility (I translate with 'thoughtless'). Its flight indeed is away from its very centre. The oven and the dove are opposed images of concentration and diffusion. Since they are juxtaposed images for Israel, they must also reflect each other, contributing different but interacting insights into Israel's personality. The heart is in some way no heart. The self-absorption and destructiveness of Israel's internal politics is transposed to the diplomatic arena, as becomes clear, for instance, in 7.16. The word for heart is the subject of numerous wordplays, and continues to be of concern also in the last part of the chapter (7.11).

The process of internalization, the insistence in this central chapter on the heart of Israel, becomes evident in the first two verses. Verse 1, as many commentators note, recapitulates the words and images of 6.7-11: 'the robber band' (6.9; 7.1), the parallel between 'doers of evil' (6.8) and 'doers of falsehood' (7.1), as well as some less tangible thematic connections. However, in doing so, it reverses them. Attention narrows from the whole country to Ephraim—which may be a synecdoche for the whole or only the central region—to the capital city, Samaria. From murderous priests acting like 'robber bands' we turn to the inhabitants who are fearful of 'robber bands outside' and who are presumably confined to their houses. The replacement of 'doers of evil' by 'doers of falsehood' directs us to the disparity between deed and thought, to the intentions of the perpetrators; attempts to disguise these are unavailing, since 'the iniquity of Ephraim is revealed' (niglâ). Ultimately, it is trying to hide from God.

The word for 'revealed' is associated with sexual exposure, for instance in the incest code in Leviticus, and hence with the nexus linking prostitution and shame (e.g. 2.12); it also resonates with the first two consonants of Gilead (*gil'ād*). This introduces us to an intricate associative network. Gilead is phonically as well as geographically correlative with Gad, one of the Transjordanian tribes; Gad, according to the Bible, is etymologically derived both from *bāgad*, 'act treacherously' (Gen. 30.11 [reading the *kethib* for the meaningless *qere*, *bā' gād*, 'a troop has come']; cf. Hos. 6.7) and *gᵉdûd*, 'band' (Gen. 49.19; cf. Hos. 6.9; 7.1). The transfer of the qualities of Gilead onto Ephraim explicates why it cannot be healed; the normative therapeutic relationship of God and Israel, supported by the similarity of the words for 'healing' (*rop'î*) and 'Ephraim' (*'eprayim*), is ruptured.

From the fear and deception of the inhabitants of Samaria in v. 1, we turn directly to their heart in v. 2, to a wish-fulfilling inner dialogue: 'All their evil I have remembered'. It is framed, however, by the divine negation: 'Let them not say in their heart...'. Their subjectivity is pre-empted by God; the obvious messages, that the troubles are not over, that the soothing thought will be taken amiss, that the motions of 'return' without profound change are unavailing, arise in a context of utter exposure. The word for negation, *bal*, 'Let not', reverses and implicitly cancels that for heart, *lēb*. If God interposes himself in and prospectively revokes the dialogue of the heart, there is no space for human autonomy; the heart is denied the privacy and strategies of defence that are the condition of its existence. The heart protectively surrounds itself with deeds, which are congruent with the raiders around the city, with their own acts of marauding, and with the evanescent *hesed* that invests them in 6.4. A phonological metaphor links the heart to the deeds which surround it. 'To their heart' (*lilᵉbābām*) conjoins two 'l's, two 'b's, and a concluding 'm'. The two 'l's recur in the word for 'deeds' (*ma'alᵉlêhem*), the two 'b's and the 'm' in that for 'surround them' (*sᵉbābûm*). The constituents of the heart are distributed in its actions; all are under the sign of negation. The pervasive duplication suggests repetition: the heart meditating to itself, its habitual deeds, its encirclement. The same combination and duplication occurs, however, in v. 8, towards the end of the extended metaphor of the oven: 'Ephraim is mingled (*yitbôlāl*) among the nations'. The figure of the heart is finally reversed in one of dissolution.

While God ominously remembers their evil, the same evil continues to unfold, and to delight their king and princes. Verse 3 is ambiguous; the evildoers and deceivers may be lulling their rulers with ill-intentioned adulation, or the latter might actually take pleasure in crime and subterfuge. At any rate, their felicity is oblivious to or sustained by the malfeasance it ostensibly controls. The introduction of the rulers, for virtually the first time in the main Hoseanic corpus, is thus a succinct portrait of misrule. In the next verse, the subject, 'all of them', presumably includes in the indictment the kings and princes with the other inhabitants of Samaria; the difference between subject and object is closed. They are 'adulterers'—the charge may be literal, in keeping with the list of offences in 4.2 and the focus on promiscuity in that chapter, or it may be metaphorical, in the sacred or political domains. Thus there are two subjects, the anonymous 'they' of vv. 1ff. as including and differentiated from the kings and princes, and two levels of interpretation (Ben Zvi 2005: 150). These indeterminacies affect our understanding of the simile of the oven which follows. It changes frame of reference, so that not only do we make provisional identifications for the figures in the tableau, only to see them displaced but not entirely divested, but the image itself is subject to several revisions and is finally transformed into an antithesis. The difficulty, however, is not an index of confusion, but of the confusion of the human situation, of the capacity of any state of affairs to change to another or to its opposite, and of apparent protagonists to disclose their vicariousness. The simile apparently describes adultery; the oven would accordingly either represent the human body as the repository of seditious desire or the body politic as constituted by adulterous liaisons. If adultery is a figure for social disintegration, since marriage is the basic social institution, this society is atomized and self-destructive. The baker on this model would either be the king, nominally responsible for its administration, or God. This, however, is paradoxical: if the baker is charged with producing good bread, then God/the king would be obliged to destroy it. Alternatively, the baker could be the conspirators, who patiently wait for their plot to hatch (Mays 1975: 105-106). It should be noted, too, that wordplay links the words for 'baker' (*'ōpeh*) and 'adulterers' (*nā'ªpîm*) with 'Ephraim' (*'eprayim*). If the conspirators or the king are representative of Ephraim, then the body politic merges with the figure of the baker.

A further level of complexity arises because the simile illustrates the primary metaphor of the book, that of sexual betrayal. As a second order figure, the simile promises to be regressive, to introduce images at a further remove, distracting us from the world of the book to a different imaginative domain that supposedly mirrors it. The simile corresponds, as I have noted, to the heart (v. 6) and is consequently structurally central. If the simile breaks down, if it fails in its mirroring function, then it suggests a fundamental incoherence, precisely because of the effort of its construction and its structural significance. Metaphor, which is normally an instrument of integration, of putting together the *disiecta* of the world, is then in the service of disintegration and dissimilarity.

The simile is carefully structured: v. 3 corresponds to v. 5, dealing with the king and princes, while v. 4 matches v. 6, pairing images of the oven with complementary descriptions of the baker's inactivity. Verse 7 caps the simile through the convergence of its two threads, before its surprising turn in vv. 8-9. There are, however, a number of subtle transfers that undermine its fluency. One is between male and female personae. It is a man's world, in which kings and princes drink, celebrate, and are overthrown; adultery, moreover, seems to be a male affair, perpetrated, so the global 'all of them' indicates, by the kings, princes, and malefactors of vv. 1-3. The word for 'oven' (*tannûr*) is grammatically masculine; the word for 'burning' (*bō'ērâ*) which qualifies it is inexplicably feminine (though commentators attempt to explicate matters by emending and redividing the text in various ways, especially since the preposition *m* before the word for baker ['*ōpeh*] is difficult). Comparably, in v. 6 the masculine word for 'fire' ('*ēš*) is combined with the feminine one for 'flame' (*lehābâ*). The instability of gender is reminiscent of that of Ephraim in 4.16-19. The slippage may be misogynistic, in keeping with the habitual image of prostitution in the book, or simply realistic. At any rate, the circularity of male discourse is broken.

A second transfer is from the image of the oven to that of the dough in the second part of v. 4. The leavening of the dough corresponds to the firing of the oven, as an internal volatile process; it too may serve as an image for adultery, literal or metaphorical. As we read on, the literal meaning is progressively displaced by the metaphorical, without vanishing entirely, as the subject—conspiracy and assassination—becomes clear. We draw, of course, on our background knowledge of the last years of Israel for the context, the assassination of four kings in twelve years. Images of oven and bread intertwine, converge and diverge throughout the passage. But the most important shift is in the referents of the images. If in v. 4 the bread may be identified with the conspiracy, in v. 7 it designates its victims, and in vv. 8-9 Ephraim as a whole. In v. 4 the depiction of the baker is apparently positive; in v. 6 it is negative. One looks unavailingly for some stability and consistency in the images. A hypothesis that seems to be excluded by one verse (for example, that the baker is God) may be revived a moment later.

The difficulty is intensified by the elliptical and sometimes multivalent language; a glance at the variety of English translations, mostly highly reconstructed, will illustrate this. An example will suffice. In v. 4, according to most interpreters, the baker 'desists from stoking' (NJPS) the fire while the bread rises. This is either because the bread will be baked on the embers or because fresh fuel will be added when ready. The word for 'stoking', however, may also mean 'waking'. Andersen and Freedman (1980: 457) hold that he falls asleep during the leavening process, and that this verse is accordingly correlative to v. 6. But the word may also mean 'from a city'. Though clearly inapposite to the baker, this peripheral meaning hints at the political dimension of the image, suggestive perhaps of a king who relaxes his vigilance over his capital city.

Verse 5 returns to the subject of the king and his court, and thus lends support to the identification of the baker with the king. The verse amplifies the satire on the royal fools' paradise which began in v. 3. The bliss of king and princes concentrates on one paradigmatic day, 'the day of our king', presumably a day of celebration of the monarchy, of the royal accession or birthday. For a moment it takes the perspective of the conspiratorial celebrants, whom we already know delight the court with their deceptions, so that their acclamation of 'our king' has an ironic twist. The joy of the princes in v. 3, fed by mendacity, merges with their drunkenness in v. 5; drunkenness is a standard trope for dissolute rulers, and combines a focus on their behaviour at the king's feast with their general state of intoxication. It juxtaposes two puns: $heh^e l\hat{u}$ could mean 'they began' or 'they became sick'; the word for 'the *heat* of wine' may also denote 'poison'. Ecstasy and morbidity thus coincide; the princes are addicted to their undoing. That the king throws in his hand with the scoffers indicates the dominant mode of thought and conversation at the celebration. Scoffers habitually deride all social institutions and values; a court constituted by scoffers will be utterly cynical. There may, however, be a more particular object of scorn. If the king came to the throne through the assassination of his predecessor, his accession would be symptomatic of the absence of a belief in human values. Laughter would be directed at the demise of the previous monarch; hence the association of joy with evil, deception, and the malignancy of scoffers. In that case, the last laugh may be on the king.

There is little to add on vv. 6 and 7. The oven returns as an image for the heart in its insidiousness, which bursts out in flame and consumes kings and judges. If the king in vv. 4 and 5 may be identified as the baker, a reading confirmed by his sleep in v. 6, then the baker becomes the bread, or perhaps fuel. Things change into their opposites; the waning of the fire while the bread rises suggests these as alternating images of destruction and nourishment; if the oven signifies adulterousness, the cessation of stoking would correspond to a quietening of turbulence. In fact, the withdrawing of the embers concentrates the fire in the heart and makes it more dangerous. The heart is characterized by its closeness, which is both secretiveness and retraction from relationship. It seeks opportunities to aggrandize itself, transforming itself from 'heart' (*lēb*) to 'flame' (*lehābâ*), and to consummate its enmity. The scornful laughter of v. 5 conceals watchfulness. The metaphor of ambush reflects that of the priestly highway robbers in 6.9 and internalizes it; the crimes of the country at large originate in and are compressed in the heart.

The heart, however, opens out. The word, as I have already mentioned, is reversed in that for the 'mingling' (*bālal*) of Ephraim with the nations, as well as in the insistence on its unchangeable nature, that it is 'a cake unturned' (*bᵉlî hᵃpûkâ*). The sudden expansion of horizons universalizes the image; the oven becomes the world, the bread its peoples, and the baker God. On one level, it refers to deportations, both those that may have already taken place (Galilee and Gilead were annexed to the Assyrian Empire and much of their population deported in c. 733 BCE) and those that would follow the fall of Samaria (whose turn came in 722 BCE); on another level, it anticipates the description of Ephraim's frenetic foreign affairs in vv. 11-12, and thus the heart defined by its interactions with the outside world. The verb 'to mingle' is associated with the vocabulary of cereal offerings, always with reference to combining flour with oil, and more important, with the story of the Tower of Babel, the name of which is a play on the word 'confuse' (*bālal*), 'for there Yhwh *confused* the language of all the earth' (Gen. 11.9) (Sweeney 2000: 80). Ephraim in its pride (v. 10) imitates the story of the Tower of Babel; internal dissension leads to dispersion. The metaphor of blending recalls that of kneading in v. 4. If the rising dough there is a figure for the fermenting conspiracy, the plotters here become victims of their own designs, as has already been intimated by the ambiguity of 'all of them' in vv. 4 and 7.

The second half of the verse, 'Ephraim is a cake unturned', parallels the first, since it emphatically repeats the subject, 'Ephraim', in the initial position, as well as the phonological correlation of *bālal* and *b^{e}lî*. Yet they apparently couple opposites; whereas the first is an image of admixture, the second is one of stagnation. The unturned cake likewise opposes a burnt side to a raw one, corresponding to the incinerated rulers and the conspiracy respectively. Both perhaps testify to the baker's sleep in v. 6. In the next verse, the contraries multiply. 'Strangers have consumed its strength', even though one would have thought that it would be inedible. The strangers are equivalent to the peoples in the previous verse, and thus an image of synthesis is replaced by one of predation. They replace the people who devour their rulers in v. 7; behind the internal dissension of Ephraim is the external threat. Parallel to this clause is the 'hoary hair' that is cast on it in the second half of the verse; this may, as Andersen and Freedman suggest (1980: 467, following a proposal of Paul, 1968: 119-20), refer to mould, corresponding to the unpalatability of the bread in the previous verse. Alternatively it could represent cinders, in the aftermath of the conflagration, or even flour, sprinkled on the dough consequent to Ephraim's being blended with the peoples. All three possibilities are subsumed under the image of old age; the metaphor of the life cycle is superimposed on those of bread and the oven. Ephraim's senility is manifested in the repeated phrase, 'And he does not know'. Ignorance of his weakness, exploitation and age is a prelude to the final ignorance of death.

The contraries are capable of resolution: Ephraim's assimilation to the nations is its condition of being unchanged; its inedibility is consequent upon strangers devouring it. There is a continuum between the motif of consumption, together with the possible connotation of mould, and that of necrosis. Yet they also resist compatibility. The transition, for example, from the neglected cake to its unfastidious devourers remains abrupt and perplexing. Like the *pseudosorites*, the apparently logical chain that is actually a figure for disconnection, the metaphor, reinforced by its obtrusive parallelism, constructs a world that disintegrates as one tries to focus on it.

The subject of the metaphor is entropy, political upheaval within, territorial dismemberment without. Its artfulness, its skill in shaping and interweaving its constituents, is in opposition to the world it has to communicate. Hence it has a dual function, to replicate the chaos of the world and to organize it. This gives the images a double-edged quality. If the oven is a simile for adultery in v. 4 and for the transgression of social boundaries comparable to the mingling of Ephraim among the peoples in v. 8, in v. 6 it is a figure for the heart in its 'closeness', its refusal to relate. There the metaphor of ambush suggests an inherent subversiveness, that instead of being the organic centre of society, the heart is that which always threatens to surprise and suborn it. The association of the heart with treachery is supported by wordplay and rhyme: *qēreḇû kattannûr libbām be'orbām* (literally 'they have drawn their heart close in their ambush'). In v. 7 the heat of the oven is duplicitous and destroys the society it nurtures. Juggling identifications for the various figures, such as the conspirator, king, and God in the role of the baker, will tend to telescope them: God, for instance, will become the arch-conspirator, as the oven unfolds to include the world.

At the centre of the tableau, the king dips his hand in with the scoffers. A king who does so is an anti-king, who mocks the social order he guarantees. Alliteration links this image with that of the baker: the kneading and fermentation of the dough (*millûš bāṣēq 'ad ḥumṣātô*) is repeated and compressed in the word for 'scoffers' (*lōṣeṣîm*). In the body politic their agitation is equivalent to that of the leaven; the strongly marked double 'ṣ' might be onomatopoeic, imitative of their laughter. At any rate, at the heart of the carefully constructed metaphor is subversive speech, an anti-poetry, coterminous with the speech in the heart in v. 2. The liquid and continuant texture of the double 'l's and 'b's of v. 2, expressive of the lulling complacency of the heart, is reversed in the sharply etched double 'ṣ' of *lōṣeṣîm*. The same heart that placates itself tears its society apart.

The conflagration occurs in the morning, and concludes the sequence of images of the morning that began in 5.15. Whereas there and in 6.3 the dawn was a sign of hope, and in 6.4 and 6.5 of disappointment and the coming judgment, here the catastrophe is self-induced. A fire that blazes forth at morning reflects its incandescence; the association is strengthened by the assonance of the words $bōqer$ ('morning') and $bō'ēr$ ('burns') which are virtually juxtaposed to each other. If the dawn is a metaphor for the counter-structure, the hope on the other side of history, the fiery dawn here is its antithesis.

The metaphor concludes with Ephraim's descent into unconsciousness, as 'grey hair' is cast upon it and strangers eat it away, both figures for morbidity, matching perhaps those for God as inner and outer destroyer in 5.12 and 14. Not knowing is, of course, the opposite of the knowledge that the book seeks to impart; it is also the parodic opposite of metaphor. If metaphor constructs the world and affirms its unity, not knowing reduces it to nothingness. With the repeated judgment 'And he does not know', a stillness is imposed upon the scene into which the complex significance of the metaphor is drawn and nullified.

But the end is not the end, at least in a poetic continuum such as Hosea. In its ignorance, 'The pride of Israel answers in its face'. The phrase is identical to one in 5.5, where likewise it is juxtaposed to Israel's lack of knowledge. There they do not know the Lord; now they do not even know themselves. In 5.4 their deeds do not allow them to return to the Lord, but they nevertheless seek him, a search whose inadequacy is the subject of the ensuing discussion. Here they neither return nor seek the Lord; instead they court Egypt and Assyria, just as Ephraim and Judah send emissaries to the king of Assyria in 5.13. The parallels between the two passages suggest that they play against each other. In particular, that even in the utmost extremity they *still* do not seek Yhwh implies that they had never sought him. In that case, the search in 5.6 is dismissed as no search at all. The contradiction, however, remains; that they did seek for Yhwh, no matter how inadequately, cannot simply be negated. Instead, each instance is transposed onto a different semantic field: the one to pilgrimage festivals, the other to foreign affairs. The one is superimposed on the other: the true pilgrimages are to the great powers, the dialogue of Israel with itself is but a vehicle for their communication.

The pride that talks only to itself is exposed as foolish and helpless through the simile of the dove in vv. 11-12, which complements that of the oven. In the Hebrew Bible, folly is not a common attribute of doves—or even of birds in general (I can only think of the partridge in Jer. 17.11 and the ostrich in Job 39.13-18). Doves are associated with love and beauty in the Song of Songs and elsewhere (e.g. Ps. 68.14), and with the pathos of their voices, as in Hezekiah's lament (Isa. 38.14). Both associations contribute to the image here. They call with love and longing to Egypt, contrasting with their failure to call on Yhwh in v. 7, while the word for 'foolish' (*pôtâ*) is commonly used for seduction (e.g. in 2.16). The solicitation of Assyria is even more foolish and desperate than its counterpart in 5.13, since the quest of love from the one who will destroy Israel is less rational and legitimate than that for a cure. The narrative form ('And Ephraim was...') is another point of contact with 5.13. By setting the quest in the past, it is a distancing, parabolic device, that makes Ephraim exemplary of folly. By turning Ephraim, if only momentarily, into an historical entity, it already assumes its fall, which, combined with the plaintiveness of the dove, is responsible for the tone of lament that Jeremias (1983: 97) rightly detects here. The lament, however, is immediately foreclosed, as the past merges with the present, and the lamenter claims to be the destroyer. Here too the passages are parallel as well as distinct. In 5.14-15 God adopts the guise of a ravening lion, an external threat, so as to express his failure of nerve, his desire for Israel to seek him, while here he is a fowler, who literally brings Israel down to earth. God is then an internal constraint, intercepting foreign travel; the dove's missing heart is manifested in its flight from its centre. God then takes the place of the heart that excludes him in v. 2; Israel's failure to seek God in v. 10 is a non-recognition of his presence.

The passage correlates with and completes 5.1-2, concluding the set of allusions to 5.1-7. In 5.1 the addressees have been 'a net spread out over Tabor'; now they are victims of the same metaphor. God, in 5.2, promises to be a chastisement to them all; v. 12 presents the fulfilment, whose appropriateness is reinforced by a pun, since the word for 'I will chastise them' is nearly homophonous with that for 'I will bind them' (Andersen and Freedman 1980: 473). The penalty for Israel's turpitude in ch. 5 is its plight in ch. 7. But there is another association, with 11.11. There the dove, in tandem with the 'bird', flies back from Assyria and Egypt, in a vision of restoration that may also be correlated with 3.5. The dove is adduced because of its homing instincts, and is coupled with the image of God as lion that we found also in 5.15. The dove then embodies the possibility of redemptive transformation. (I omit all discussion of the last phrase in v. 12—which reads literally, 'like the very rumour of their assignations'—because of its obscurity.)

The last section is both a very compressed summary of the chapter, reverting especially to the concerns of vv. 1-2, and a preview of developments in subsequent ones. As in 5.15–6.6 and 6.11–7.1, God desires to redeem Israel, but is frustrated by its mendacity and dissembling. 'They deal falsely' in v. 1 corresponds to their 'lies' in v. 13; their speech to their heart in v. 2 is amplified by their failure to cry out in their heart in v. 14; the treachery that pervades the entire unit is finally revealed as rebellion against God. The flight to Assyria and Egypt is a flight from God, the fowler of v. 12. God is the point of convergence of the lies, subterfuges, palace revolutions and diplomatic duplicity of the chapter, the point, then, of estrangement, identified, as we saw in v. 12, with the heart the dove lacks. God, as the heart, is the repository of memory, which Israel regards in v. 2 as a punitive and exhaustive inventory of evil. In v. 15, however, the memory becomes the agent of nostalgia, foreshadowing God's recollection of himself as parent in ch. 11, and hence the conflict between affection and exasperation that belies Israel's understanding of God as an implacable but gullible nemesis.

The imagery of night returns, too. In v. 6 the baker sleeps all night, while the conspiratorial heart hatches its plot; in v. 14 the heart is detached as 'they wail on their beds'. Nocturnal prayer, presumably when sleepless, is part of the stock repertoire of Psalms (e.g. Pss. 4.5; 6.7; 42.9), but insomnia is associated also with the machinations of evildoers (e.g. Micah 2.1). Here the two motifs are combined: the insidious heart, surrounded by its deeds according to v. 2, uses prayer as a pious sound barrage. Prayer is collateral with the deeds. The associations are underpinned by phonemic correlations. The word for 'night' (*laylâ*) is recollected in that for 'they wail' (*yᵉyēlîlû*), and reproduces the double 'l's that we found in v. 2. The onomatopoeic effect, however, is reversed: whereas the double 'l's and 'b's of v. 2 metaphorically mimic the lulling speech of the Samarians, as they insulate themselves with their deeds, *yᵉyēlîlû* metaphorically supports the vocalic oscillation of wailing. In turn, the double 'l' of *yᵉyēlîlû* corresponds to the double 'r' of the following verb, *yitgôrārû*, 'they gather, estrange themselves, strive'. (Many commentators read *yitgôdādû*, 'they gash themselves', following the Septuagint and several manuscript variants; 'd' and 'r' are almost indistinguishable in Hebrew, and thus easily confused, so the choice between the two possibilities is purely contextual, what makes better sense in context; for a discussion, see Andersen and Freedman 1980: 475.) Both 'l' and 'r' are liquids; the inarticulate wailing of prayer is confused with the noise of quarrels. From being a sign of quietness, the double 'l's, combined with other closely related duplicated consonants, become a sign of uproar. The wailing, at present purely *pro forma*, may be predictive; lamentation, so the introductory 'Woe' of v. 13 suggests, is at hand.

The wailing is 'over grain and new wine', either because of the dearth or devastation of those crops, as most critics assume, or simply as accompaniments or aids to ritual clamour. The occasion might correspond to the festival of 4.11-14, or possibly a funeral feast or *marzēaḥ* (Jer. 16.5; Amos 6.7; for a good and representative discussion of the *marzēaḥ* feast, see Paul 1991: 210-12). In 9.1 'threshing floors of grain' are associated with prostitution, suggesting another dimension to the wailing on the beds in our verse (see Sweeney 2000: 82-83). 'New wine' is deceptive, according to 9.2, and 'takes away the heart' in 4.11; together with prostitution, it is the medium of self-delusion as well as lies against God, just as it deceives the princes in v. 5. The collocation can be traced back to ch. 2, where 'grain and new wine' are among the products the people falsely attribute to Baal. Reading *yitgôdādû*, 'they gash themselves', for *yitgôrārû*, 'they gather together', 'estrange themselves', or 'strive', intensifies the Baalistic connotations (see Jeremias 1983: 100-101, and Andersen and Freedman 1980: 475; self-laceration as a practice of the prophets of Baal is evident in 1 Kgs 18.28, and prohibited by Deut. 14.1).

In v. 15 we turn back to God, introduced somewhat obtrusively by the first person pronoun *ʾanî* 'I', and to his memory. Already in v. 13, the contention that 'I would ransom them', endorsed by the emphatic first person form *ʾānōkî*, 'I' (see above on 5.14), contrasts the people's centrifugal flight and rebellion with God's commitment and history of redemption, exemplified archetypally in the Exodus. In 13.14 'I will ransom them' recurs in the context of deliverance from Sheol, the always ambiguous possibility of reclamation beyond death. To the impulse towards restoration and healing in 5.15 and 6.11–7.1, the passage adds the temporal span, from birth to death, and initiates the meditation on God's formative experience with Israel that will increasingly preoccupy the book. It focuses, however, on the training and strengthening of Israel, evoking traditions of holy war. As a paternal office, military training inducts the son into the male fellowship of arms, or perhaps the noble sport of hunting. 'I trained' (*yissartî*), moreover, is formed from the same verb as 'I will chastise them' (*'ay^{e}sirēm*) in v. 12; that which is now chastisement was once paternal care. The chastisement in v. 12 is equivalent to the binding of the dove, whose only wish is to be free. Israel's bond with God would then be contrary to its natural inclination, in v. 13, to fly from him. This is confirmed by another play on the same consonantal cluster; in v. 14 their solicitations illustrate their turning away (*yāsûrû*) from God. The transformation of 'I will chastise' into 'I trained' is indicative of God's ambivalence: chastisement evokes affection, whose memory induces resentment at their ingratitude (for the pun, see Ben Zvi 2005: 152).

The recollection is the occasion for the elaborate simile of the last verse. Unlike the complexly structured and referentially ambiguous simile of the oven, and that of the dove which depends for its effectiveness on an intertextual network, the simile of the deceitful bow works through substitution, one scene giving place to another, in a regress which, if not infinite, at least takes us back to Egypt. The strengthened arms and training of Ephraim prepare it to be a faithful soldier of Yhwh; the helpless and heedless dove of v. 12, grammatically feminine, becomes a skilful and self-reliant warrior, a figure for Israel's independence. The thought process and reading time of the text is reversed in historical time: the warrior has become a dove. This is coterminous with its thinking evil thoughts against Yhwh. The apparently innocuous dove is guileful and seditious, and indeed metonymous with all the treachery and subterfuge of the chapter. In the immediate context, for instance, it 'calls on', cultivates, Egypt, while 'going to', pretending to be a loyal vassal to, Assyria. It thus conforms to a feminine stereotype, according to which deviousness disguises itself as silliness. As with the daughters and brides in 4.14, the dove evokes sympathy because it has 'no mind' and is irresponsible. But this sympathy itself is the vehicle for the punitive desire of the fowler and for sexual transformation, since Yhwh wishes, so the thought process suggests, to turn chastisement into training, feminine into masculine.

The evil thoughts of the people—as perceived through the divine lens—corroborate their perception in v. 2 that God tallies their evil. The motif of exposure, as in v. 1, combines with the hope of return. 'They return', but 'not above'; interpretations and emendations of this expression vary greatly, as a glance at translations will show. The main lines are that 'above' refers to God, or that *'al* ('above') should be corrected to *bā'al* ('Baal') or to *yā'al* ('that which does [not] profit'). The deceitful bow reverts to the theme of the chapter; it may be deceptive because it breaks, because it aims badly, or because it boomerangs. (The verbatim recurrence of the simile in Ps. 78.57 might confirm this interpretation, since there the participle that qualifies the deceitful bow could be construed as 'turned inside out'; for a comparison of Hosea with Psalm 78, see Day 1986.) At any rate, if Israel is the divine archer's bow, the image suggests a failure to fulfil God's commission; that they do not return above may refer to the arrows' falling limply to earth. The comparison transposes the attributes of the warrior in v. 15: the arms that Yhwh strengthened are equivalent to the wooden frame of the bow, the hostile thoughts to its deceptiveness. It is, however, immediately undercut by the following phrase: 'they fall by the sword of their princes'. The bow may be broken by the sword; if the sword of the princes recalls the succession of assassinations in v. 7, and resonates with the phrase, 'all their kings have fallen', then they are the agents of self-destruction. The sword replaces the bow as the main object of attention. It is, however, immediately dematerialized; the sword emanates from 'the wrath of their tongues'. But this is somebody else's speech: 'their scorn in the land of Egypt'. We now know the destination of their return at the beginning of the verse, introducing a motif that will become increasingly prominent. The chapter ends in mordant laughter, echoing that of the conspirators in v. 5. They are now its victims.

Hosea 8

(1) To your palate a shofar like an eagle over the house of Yhwh, because they have broken my covenant, and they have rebelled against my Torah.
(2) To me they cry, 'My God, we have known you, Israel'.
(3) Israel has rejected the good; the enemy pursues him.
(4) They enthrone kings, but not from me, make princes, and I do not know it; their gold and their silver they have made into idols for themselves, in order that it should be cut off.
(5) Your calf has rejected, O Samaria, my anger is kindled against them; until when will they be incapable of innocence?
(6) For he is from Israel, and he—a craftsman made him and no god is he—for the calf of Samaria will be splinters.
(7) For they sow the wind and reap the whirlwind; its standing corn—it has no flower and produces no flour, and if it does—strangers will swallow it.
(8) Israel is swallowed up; now they have become among the nations like a vessel in which there is no delight.
(9) For they have gone up to Assyria, a wild ass wandering alone; Ephraim tenders its love.
(10) Even if they tender among the nations, now I will gather them in; and they will writhe a little under the burden of the king of princes.
(11) For Ephraim multiplied itself altars for sinning; they had altars for sinning.
(12) I wrote for it myriads of my Torah; they were considered as if they were alien.
(13) The sacrifices of my gifts, they sacrifice flesh and eat, but Yhwh does not desire them; now he will remember their iniquity and he will visit their sin; they will return to Egypt.
(14) But Israel forgot its maker, and it built palaces, and Judah multiplied fortified cities, and I will cast fire on its cities and it will consume its palaces.

Once again, as in 5.8, we hear the shofar, cutting through the reverberations of the princes' vicious tongues. The recourse to the shofar is addressed directly to the prophet, rather than to watchmen, presumably of border towns; the shofar is a summary of his warning, a representation of his speech as well as an extension of his mouth. (Some critics—e.g. Wolff 1974: 137—hold that the addressee is a military officer. Since the passage is a first person speech by God, the second person singular form of the command would make the prophet the most probable, or at least most immediate, recipient of the message; cf. Utzschneider 1980: 107-108; Macintosh 2000: 192; Ben Zvi 2005: 168 leaves the addressee open.) The urgency is expressed through the abruptness and ellipsis of the command: 'To your palate a shofar...'. From Ramah, Gibeah, and other towns associated with prophecy and sacrilege in 5.8 we focus on the house of Yhwh itself. The shofar is invasive as well as expressive, which accounts for the otherwise baffling detail of the palate; the palate is associated with taste, with intimate kisses in the Song of Songs, and thus the prophet's interiority. The eagle may resemble the lookout in sharpness of vision and protectiveness; it may, on the other hand, signify the enemy, depending on whether one reads 'on' or 'against the house of Yhwh'. (For a similar ambiguity in Isaiah 31.14-15, see Exum 1981: 336-37. For an intertextual comparison of Isa. 31.4-5 and Hos. 11.11, see Eidevall 1993.) In that case, warner and enemy are conflated; Yhwh and the prophet are bivalent, destroying Yhwh's house as well as guarding it. Yhwh's word, his hostility to Israel, is inserted into the prophet's mouth, and imparted by it. Foreshadowed is the tension between Yhwh and the prophet in 9.10-17 and the reflection on the divisiveness of the prophet in society in 9.7-9, in which the metaphor of 'watchman' is repeated. If our phrase opens a potential gap between prophet and God, as well as prophet and people, through the ambiguous metaphor of the watchman, it also reflects God's vacillation on the role of the prophet that we discerned in 6.4-6, the dissonance between Hosea, as a latter-day Samuel, and the succession of prophetic axemen to which he is heir. The ambiguity of the image of the eagle, poised between defence and attack, expresses this. In the next two chapters, the house of God is a recurrent figure, ultimately emptied of its worshippers (9.15). It is represented in our chapter by the focus on the calf, in vv. 5-6. Destruction of the calf (v. 6), exile and exclusion (9.4, 15), the animosity embodied by the prophet (9.8), would support the aggressive interpretation of the symbol of the eagle, perhaps associated with the winged disk as the emblem of Assyria. But the alternative, that the eagle protects God's house, remains possible, to contribute to the culminating consideration of prophecy in 12.11-14.

In v. 2 the people cry, 'My God, we have known you, Israel'; their claim to knowledge corresponds to their profession of desire to pursue knowledge in 6.3, and is equally facile (Eidevall 1996: 129). Like 6.1-3, their exclamation, evoking the totality of Israel and proceeding from the personal appeal to the collective consciousness, is a parody of liturgy, whose hollowness is revealed by Yhwh's disclaimer of knowledge in v. 4. In ch. 5 what God knows is that Israel does not know him (5.3-4); he makes known Ephraim's doom (5.9). Here, in an apparent reversal, Israel asserts knowledge of God, while God avers ignorance. The two texts comment on each other; Israel's credence is a symptom of its actual unawareness; God's perspicuity is manifested in his studied refusal to grant any notice to Israel's transient appointees as kings and princes.

Stylistically, the opening verses are characterized by compression, as in the prefatory simile, brevity, and syntactic disjunction, expressive of urgency, expostulation, and the swiftness of retribution. In contrast, the last part of v. 1 is a carefully composed parallelism, whose smoothness is undergirded by the alliteration of $b^e r\hat{\imath}t\hat{\imath}$ ('my covenant') and $t\hat{o}r\bar{a}ti$ ('my Torah'). The house ($b\hat{e}t$) of Yhwh should incorporate covenant and Torah; it is imperilled by the rupture of those systems of communication between God and humanity, especially if, as the ensuing discussion suggests, it is preeminently implicated in the rebellion. The parallelism, introduced by a conjunction 'because' ($ya'an$) almost always used in contexts of covenant breach or fulfilment, adduces the language of covenantal oratory, such as Deuteronomy, and indeed several critics regard it as a Deuteronomistic intrusion (e.g. Jeremias 1983: 104; cf., however, Holt 1995: 54-56 and Keefe 2001: 108). It suggests world-order, the time needed for rhetorical expansiveness. The breach of this order in turn reflects back on other passages, such as the conjunction of knowledge with Torah in 4.1 and 4.6, breach of covenant with the failure of knowledge in 6.6-7, and the juxtaposition of rebellion with the mendacious cry to God in 7.13-14. Of this, the quotation from the people in v. 3 is presumably illustrative. Thus a chain of parallel terms is established that both represent structure and its dissolution. Strategically, these frame the intervening passages, with their detailed exposition of Israel's dereliction. Through evoking the ideal, they compound its absence.

In the next verses, both registers—the abrupt speech of crisis, and the poignant allusion to the rhythms of the covenant—interplay with each other. Once again, we turn to the kings and princes; no sooner is the subject introduced, than we switch to that of idols, and focus on the calf and the capital city, Samaria. The successive subjects function as metaphors for each other: the kings and princes are made and unmade by the people, just as they manufacture idols, of which the calf is exemplary. Within the political round there is the proliferation of icons, and within this the symbol of political and sacred power in the kingdom. The kings and princes would then be phenomenal manifestations of the numen of the calf. This is supported by homophony, noted by several commentators, between 'they make princes' (*hēśîrû*) and 'they turn away' (*hēśîrû*), either in the sense that their appointing princes—'officers', as suggested by the NJPS, is a more accurate translation—is a form of turning aside from God, or that no sooner do they make kings or princes than they depose them. To be a prince, the pun would suggest, is already to be passé, to transfer allegiances, whether from the king or God.

In 2.10 Yhwh's gifts of silver and gold are employed to make Baal; much the same formulation describes the making of images here. The images, and pre-eminently the calf, are thus equivalent to Baal. There is, however, an appended phrase, which reads literally, 'in order that it should be cut off.' 'In order that' (*l^ema'an*) rhymes with 'because' (*ya'an*) in v. 1, both familiar from the field of covenantal promise and infraction. 'It should be cut off' (*yikkārēt*) suggests primarily the penalty of 'excision' (*kārēt*), which, as Jacob Milgrom (1991b: 405–408) points out, refers solely to the sacred domain, and is exacted by God rather than human beings. But the same verb is also used for the making, literally 'cutting', of covenants. Covenants are made and unmade with the same breath. That Israel should act 'so that it should be cut off' is improbable; the double meaning suggests confusion, that their piety is in fact faithlessness, as well as the insinuation, commonplace in the rhetoric of covenantal reprobation, that they are responsible for their own demise. The brief reversion to covenantal language alludes to the rhythm of the formula of v. 1, the long time of God's memory and promise, in the context of the rapidity of events and the fabrication of images. In its succinctness it imparts summary judgment.

The 'calf of Samaria' is anomalous, since the biblical evidence situates golden calves in Bethel and Dan (1 Kgs 12.28-30). Except for this passage, there is no trace of the cult of a calf at Samaria, and analogy with 10.5-6, in which the calf is situated in Bethel, would suggest that that is the case here. Critics are divided between those who think that there was actually a calf in Samaria, that Bethel and Samaria are metaphorically equated, and that the reference is to the inhabitants rather than to the city itself. Another problem is that the polemic against the golden calves as the paradigmatic apostasy of the Northern Kingdom reflects, most critics assume, a southern perspective. No trace of it can be found in Amos or in narratives about Elijah and Elisha. The golden calves would, they argue, have been equivalent to the cherubim in Jerusalem, and constituted the pedestal of Yhwh; no divinity was ascribed to them (for a detailed discussion, see Utzschneider 1980: 88-110; cf. Ben Zvi 2005: 181). They could not be identified with Baal.

It makes little difference whether the location of the calf was in Samaria, or merely subsumed under its political or poetic aegis. In either case, the sacred and royal centres are closely linked; the shrine can become an instrument of government or legitimation—as we see, for example, in the insistence of Amaziah, priest of Bethel, that his is a royal sanctuary, in pointed contrast to its being a divine one (Amos 7.13). Samaria has already been characterized in the previous chapter as a city of false dealing and conspiracy; now these qualities are transferred to the calf. The images are made by the conspirators; their silver and gold signify either their misbegotten gains or their status, and at any rate an attempt to invest in the sacred, to procure it. The calf, at the centre of the entourage of images, is lifeless, if beautiful, made by a craftsman (v. 6), the product of human ingenuity and aesthetic sense. As a symbol for Samaria it represents cultural achievement, brutishness, and petrifaction.

If the calf was conceived as Yhwh's pedestal, Hosea's charge that it is deified seems unfounded. More generally, the polemic against idols and their association with Baal would apply to all cult images, including those that came to be canonically authorized. The opposition of Yhwh to calf, setting life against death, intangibility against materiality, resists domestication of the divine. Making a calf into Yhwh's pedestal at the centre of one's kingdom ensures that his feet are on the ground, founded in the rhythms of farm life. Cutting the link means that immanence is no longer representable. Yhwh then becomes wholly unpredictable, if not 'other', then unfamiliar, inaccessible to conventional wisdom and theurgy, exemplified by v. 2 (for discussions of the calf image, see Zevit 2001: 451-53 and Keel and Uehlinger 1998: 191-94).

The immobile calf is in apposition to the wilful cow of 4.16, but also to another, this time female, calf, which represents the ideal Ephraim in 10.11. In contrast to the calf of Samaria, it is a vital image, which recollects the unity of Israel in the service of God. Moreover, it shares a word with the description of the golden calf, but transforms its meaning. *Ḥārāš*, which means 'craftsman' here, reappears as 'ploughs' in 10.11. From being a means of self-glorification, it becomes the instrument of fertility.

Verses 5-6 have a circular structure: the outer ring describes and predicts the fate of the calf; the middle one contrasts God to the calf as anti-god; while the inner one focuses on Israel. The rings interconnect and flow into each other, as when the heat of the divine wrath (*ḥārâ*) echoes in the word for craftsman (*ḥārāš*), suggesting that the rage, with its underlying metaphor of fire, is directed against and threatens to undo the golden work. An inner ring within this structure is to be found in v. 6, which reads literally, 'And he—a craftsman made him, and no God is he'. The calf, isolated through the strong pronoun 'he', is delimited on both sides; it is an invention of Israel, but denied divine status by God.

The enclosure makes the passage an inset tableau, emblematic of the overall concerns of the chapter, spatially as well as structurally. From the calf, presumably at the most sacred point in Yhwh's house, emanate the multiplication of altars, the restless journeys to Assyria, the desperate cries of the surrounding verses. If the calf is an emblem for the integrity of the people and its connection with God, its shattering is manifested in the whirlwind of v. 7 and in the fissiparous activities that the wind introduces. The linkage between calf and people is evidenced by the repetition of the word 'rejected' in vv. 3 and 5. The people rejects goodness, according to v. 3; the calf 'rejects', in v. 5. (There are a large number of proposed translations and emendations of this phrase. I think that it is simplest to retain the Masoretic, 'Your calf has rejected, O Samaria', with an unspecified object, thus preserving the parallel with v. 3.) The lack of specification of the object suggests that this is its fundamental attitude, corresponding to the stereotypical wilfulness of the cow in 4.16. The centre of the people's devotion is a rejection of God. In contrast, in 10.11 the calf is characterized by goodness, since God rides 'on the goodness of her neck'; the irony is intensified by the proverbial stiffness of biblical necks.

The calf, at the centre of the people and the chapter, corresponds to the heart and its metaphor, the oven, in ch. 7. The heart and the oven are likewise enclosures, concealing conspiratorial designs and fire; similarly, the description of the oven is circular—delimited by the repetition of 'all of them are adulterers/ burn like an oven' in vv. 4 and 7—and yet intricately connected with the rest of the chapter. The oven is the alimentary base of the community, the calf its sacral one; the oven harbours fire that destroys it, the calf is made by fire and attracts divine wrath.

The following sections also have their equivalents in ch. 7. The harvest that is swallowed up by strangers and that represents Israel's admixture among the nations in vv. 7-8 reproduces the paradoxical imagery of mingling and consumption of the inedible cake or flour in 7.8-9, while the simile of the lovesick wild ass in vv. 9-10 corresponds to that of the dove in 7.11-12 as a figure for Ephraim's diplomatic adventures. Both are caught in Yhwh's constraints.

The structural parallels between chs. 7 and 8 may be summarized as follows:

    7.2/8.2: Israel's quoted speech.
    7.3, 5/8.4: kings and princes.
    7.4-7/8.5-6: calf and oven.
    7.8-9/8.7-8: admixture and swallowing by the nations.
    7.11-12/8.9-10: courtship of the nations.

In vv. 7-8 two main rhetorical strategies serve to disorient the reader, to produce a combination of furious energy and paralysis, familiarity and dissonance, typical of the chapter. The first, as O'Connor points out, is pseudosorites, the false logical chain; the agricultural cycle is disrupted at every point, and only imaginative will links one stage to the next. The first phrase, 'They sow the wind and reap the whirlwind', has become proverbial, and indeed is typical of the simple reciprocities of Wisdom Literature; the world is governed by a basic order, for which agriculture provides a reassuring metaphor. The rhyme, in Hebrew, of 'flower' ($\d{s}ema\d{h}$) and 'flour' ($qema\d{h}$), is similarly reminiscent of aphorism; the world order conforms to the order of language. The continuities represented by Wisdom literature and agriculture are the background for discontinuity, whose message is the end of normal time.

The second strategy is the ambiguation of the metaphor, or a vacillation between literal and metaphorical meanings. The consequence is not only that meaning bifurcates, and thus is rendered uncertain, but that there is an effect of displacement, as one construction gives way to another that encompasses it. The ambiguities develop from the initial proverb, in which it is indeterminate whether the wind and whirlwind are objects or adverbs. It may be, as Andersen and Freedman argue (1980: 481), that the wind and whirlwind represent weather conditions; the seed is blown away, the harvest devastated. They translate, 'They will sow when it is windy; they will reap in a whirlwind'. In that case, one loses the boomerang effect, dear to Wisdom literature, produced by regarding them as objects. Andersen and Freedman hold that this familiar interpretation would only make sense if wind and whirlwind are themselves metaphors; one would then have a metaphor within a metaphor, a regress that they claim is atypical of Wisdom literature. But not, surely, of Hosea's subversion of it! 'Wind' or 'spirit' has been previously associated with the 'wind' or 'spirit' of promiscuity that infuses, binds, and impels the people in 4.12, 19, and 5.4. To sow the wind, then, would be to impregnate licentiousness, a sexual metaphor already suggested by O'Connor (1989: 245-46), one which would involve a further regress, since to fornicate fornication makes the woman merely a vehicle for the sexual drive, which in turn instigates more insemination. The 'wind' or 'spirit' of promiscuity, as Jeremias points out (1983: 108), is a figure both for idolatry and foreign entanglements, and thus links the concerns of the previous and following sections. But it would be mistaken to limit its application to those domains. The conjunction of sexuality and agriculture corresponds to the activities of the priests in 4.10; as there, cultivation breeds sterility. Furthermore, one must not eliminate the adverbial sense of the metaphor. To sow in the wind, like casting bread on the waters in Eccl. 11.1, suggests speculation in the uncertain flow of events, as in 12.2. The two possibilities are not mutually exclusive. If the wind is the seed, it is also that in which it is sown. Implanting wind in wind is an ethereal exercise, connoting emptiness as well as the dissolution of their efforts.

In the rest of the verse, the wind/seed primarily retains its literal, agricultural significance, culminating in consumption by strangers at the verse's end. Israel is the subject of sowing and reaping. But in v. 8 Israel itself is the seed which is swallowed up. There is thus displacement from literal to figural, from the national to the international context. The sequel, 'Now they have become among the nations like a vessel in which there is no delight', seems to contradict the image of assimilation. The vessel is a container, which has nothing in it. Its contents may be that which the strangers have devoured; it becomes an empty shell. One may note that the word for 'delight' (*ḥēpeṣ*) has the same root as that for God's 'delight' in *ḥesed* in 6.6. That which has vanished from Israel is its *ḥesed*. The image of the seed is transformed into the husk.

In vv. 9-10 the metaphor of the wild ass corresponds to the dove in the matching section of ch. 7. Solitude and indomitability typify the wild ass in the Hebrew Bible; its freedom here, in the liminal space of the wilderness, is surrendered to its pursuit of Assyria's favours. Jer. 2.24 suggests that this amorous susceptibility is proverbial. The wild ass is a masculine figure, complementing the femininity of the dove, and repeating the oscillation of male and female personae that characterizes Ephraim in 4.16-19. The depiction of the dove then has a male counterpart, the lover whose desire subjugates him to the feminine, construed as omnipotent, mercenary—since it receives his gifts—and consequently untrustworthy. The two figures risk humiliation, breach natural or social bounds; the woman is not demure, the wild ass invites capture. But these are also cultural conventions, illustrated, for instance, by the Song of Songs, whereby the world of love inverts patriarchal order. The alternating images of Ephraim as male and female, corresponding to alternating images of Assyria as the male and female object of love, fascination and military power, confirm a misogynistic program, since both reinforce negative feminine stereotypes: the wild ass/male lover is emasculated, the dove/woman is duplicitous beneath her apparent simplicity. Yet both hint at a possible subversion of that program, if one converts the language of prophetic condemnation into that of love poetry.

The word for 'wild ass' (*pere'*), as most commentators note, is another wordplay on that for Ephraim (*'eprayim*). The wild ass contrasts, in gender as well as habitat, with the cow (*pārâ*) which symbolized Israel/Ephraim in 4.16, and which introduced the bovine imagery that focused on the calf. They constitute two sides of Israel's identity, as indigenous and alien, domesticated and untamed, both of which have been traduced.

Dove and wild ass between them invert the process of God's reconciliation with Israel in 2.16-17. Israel had been under the misapprehension that its prosperity was the gift of its lovers (2.7, 15); now it returns that gift. The dove is open to suggestion (*pôtâ*); in 2.16 God uses that propensity to persuade her (*m^{e}patteyhâ*) to return to him, and takes her into the wilderness, the home of the wild ass. There he speaks to her heart, supplying the organ missing in 7.11.

Verse 10 presents a number of difficulties, especially in its second half, as a glance at different translations will show. It can best be approached through a comparison with the corresponding verse in 7.12; God's bringing down the dove(s) is recalled in his gathering the lovers and/or their gifts. This, however, is an anticipation of a further stage in the process, since his gathering is not merely, or only temporarily, to the land and himself, as in 7.12, but a prelude to the gathering into Egypt and death in 9.6. In v. 8 Ephraim among the nations is like an unregarded vessel; their gifts among the nations will come under this general disapprobation. Instead, 'they writhe a little under the burden of the king of princes'. (I adopt here, with most commentators, a slight emendation of the verb *wayyaḥēllû*, 'they will begin' to *wayyaḥîlû*, 'they will writhe'.) 'The king of princes' may be a variant of the Assyrian royal title and thus correspond to the parody of the imperial epithet 'The Great King' in 5.13 (Paul 1986); the princes are not merely subordinate monarchs, as in the Assyrian formulary, but the unruly nobles of the previous chapter, whose intrigues lead to their subjugation. The succession of kings and princes in v. 4 is foreclosed by the imposition of the authority of the 'king of princes' here. Implicitly in 5.13 and explicitly in 11.5 Assyria is acknowledged as their true king. There is a further disabusal. Israel is accused of sending love gifts to the nations; the burden of the king of princes is presumably tribute. The gifts are then compulsory, the love in fact pain. (This is to say nothing of the problematic 'a little', which suggests that the pain is but a foretaste; in that case, 'they will writhe' may be combined with *wayyaḥēllû*, 'they will begin'.)

The last section of the chapter combines these themes, and returns to the concerns of its beginning: the threat against Yhwh's house, the betrayal of the Torah. Concentration on the sacred and political centre is replaced by centrifugal images of multiplication, of altars, cities and laws.

Ephraim multiplies altars (v. 11); paradoxically, the altars are for sinning. We go back to the world of the priests in 4.6-10, with their inversion of sacred values. The proliferation of altars is proportional to the goodness of the land in 10.1; here it is a manifestation of its rejection of the good in v. 3. The phrase, 'altars for sinning', is repeated. Verbatim repetition otherwise occurs in Hosea only in questions expressive of doubt and impossibility (6.4; 9.14; 11.8). Here it is anomalous, inexplicable in terms of unique emotive import or informational gain. A repeated message always differs from the message itself, if only by its secondariness. The disjunction between two instances of the same moment opens a gap, allowing slippage to a different rhythm. Time slows down, permitting one to dwell on the enormity of the paradox and the centrifugal progress of Israel's history. The repeated thought in which the altars multiply and history develops contrasts divine and human time, reverberating with God's irony and grief. At the beginning of the chapter, perfect parallelism recalls the time of the covenant and sets the rhythm of divine and social order against the abrupt sentences and dislocations of the present. Here the lag between the two parts of the verse induces a sense of entropy, since nothing happens, despite the febrile political and agricultural activities, the acceleration of time through compression and its interruption through aporia that characterize the previous verses. Proliferation, as in 4.7, is not a sign of piety and prosperity, but of disintegration. In v. 13 the parallelism, 'he will remember their iniquity and visit their sin', restores the time of the covenant, in which God's memory goes back and redresses the broken order; its formulaic nature is confirmed by its repetition in 9.9 and its echo of 4.10. In between the two allusions to the breach and vindication of the covenant, there is a moment of suspension, intensified by temporal retardation, between two halves of a parallelism. In the next verse (v. 12), God endeavours to fill the gap through writing 'weighty matters/myriads of my Torah'; obviously the myriads match the numerous altars, as well as the Torah against which the people rebel in v. 1. (For Torah here as a written, authoritative document, see Ben Zvi 2005: 178.) The central house of Yhwh, as the focus of danger and invective, is diffused over the many altars, the single violated Torah in many directives (Ben Zvi 2005: 173, from a postmonarchic perspective).

Writing fixes speech, impressing it visibly, just as an altar establishes a topos for the divine presence; it becomes a point of reference for subsequent interpretation and repetition. The myriad and weighty inscriptions, presumably instilling *ḥesed* and the knowledge God wishes to impart, fail to communicate; they are regarded as strange. They testify to the urgency, and perhaps detail, of the message, and the defamiliarization of God. A God who manifests himself in writing supposes a literate audience, an ability to puzzle out significance, and the poetic reconstruction of the world, in contrast to the God, as in vv. 5-6, whose primary symbol is the calf, and who confirms natural order. God's failure to communicate through writing corresponds to the people's inability to communicate through sacrifice in v. 13. Like the priests' offerings in 4.7-8, the sacrifices serve only to feed themselves, while God remains unmoved. If the word for 'favour them' (*rāṣām*) is normally used in priestly writings for the acceptance of sacrifice, his disinclination here suggests a divestment of priestly order.

In 7.15 God trains Israel, who think evil against him; here the myriads/weighty matters of Torah presumably correspond to his instruction, while the thought that his script is alien emanates from their enmity. Thus in both chapters speech about God at the beginning is reversed in their thought at the end. In 7.2 the people claim that God 'has remembered all their evil'; in 7.15 they think or plot 'evil' against him. In 8.2 they affirm 'My God, we know you', while finding him mystifying in v. 12. The framing reversal completes the structural parallels I noted earlier; if in ch. 7 the history of Israel is construed as rebellion, conspiracy, and turning God's weapons against himself (or themselves), here it is one of non-cognition, through misapprehension of conventional icons or rituals. The two conceptions are not exclusive; they take us from or ascribe the immediacy of political rancour to the circumambient lack of consciousness.

In v. 14 the image of proliferation is transferred from altars and texts to cities and fortresses; Israel and Judah are again coupled, recalling, as in v. 1, the military context of 5.8-15. The cities and palaces are burnt, victims of their own sacrificial economy; those who eat the flesh are themselves consumed. The transposition from altars to cities, feasters to food, duplicates that in vv. 7-8, in which Israel is both seed and sower. Commentators frequently point out the parallel with the refrain in Amos 1.3–2.5, 'And I will cast fire on X, and burn the palaces of Y', suggesting either direct borrowing or later insertion. It is adapted, however, to the rhetoric and imagery of the chapter. In v. 6 the calf is made by a craftsman, and is not God; here Israel forgets its maker. I have already noted the correlation between the calf and the heifer in 10.11, who ploughs God's field; that passage in turn closely reflects the reversion to the multiplication of altars in 10.1-2, intertwined with the motif of the calf in 10.5-6. The intertextual net associates the calf, altars, and the agricultural cycle. Amnesia, combined with the motif of the calf as no-god, attracts the divine wrath in v. 5, where the calf is cognate to the oven as the product of fire. The fire spreads from the oven to the entire political order it represents, from the calf to the cities whose emblem it is.

There is another fate: 'they return to Egypt' (v. 13), preceded by the evil tongues of their princes in 7.16, and reversing the ascent to Assyria in 8.9. Covenant time goes back to its beginning.

Hosea 9

(1) Do not rejoice, O Israel, to exultation like the peoples, for you have whored away from your God; you have loved a harlot's hire on all the threshing floors of grain.

(2) Threshing floor and wine vat will not shepherd them, and the new wine will deceive them.

(3) They will not dwell in the land of Yhwh, and Ephraim will return to Egypt, and in Assyria they will eat defiled food.

(4) They will not pour out libations of wine before Yhwh, and they will not make pleasing their sacrifices to him; it is like mourners' bread to them; all its consumers will be defiled, for their bread is for their life; it will not come into the house of Yhwh.

(5) What will you do on the day of assembly, on the day of the festival of Yhwh?

(6) For behold, they go from pillage; Egypt will gather them, Memphis will bury them; their precious silver objects, thorns will inherit them, thistles in their tents.

(7) The days of visitation have come, the days of reckoning have come; Israel will know; foolish is the prophet, mad is the man of spirit, over the greatness of your iniquity and much enmity.

(8) Ephraim is a watchman with my God; the prophet is a fowler's snare across all his paths, enmity in the house of his God.

(9) They have dug deep, they have made a pit, as in the days of Gibeah; he will remember their iniquity, he will visit their sin.

Chapter 9 may be divided into two halves or tableaux, vv. 1-9 and 10-17, marked in the Masoretic Hebrew text by a paragraph division. The two halves match each other as follows:

Verses 1-9	*Verses 10-17*
v. 1a: Israel's false joy	v. 10a: God's false joy
v. 1b: Cultic prostitution	v. 10b: Cultic prostitution

vv. 3-4: Consequence: loss of sacrifice	vv. 11-13: Consequence: loss of children
v. 5: Central question	v. 14: Central question.
vv. 6-9: The prophet in God's house	vv. 15-17: Being driven from God's house.
Their 'precious silver objects' (*maḥmad*)	The 'precious' fruits of their womb (*maḥmad*)
Being a watchman with 'my God'	Being rejected by 'my God'

We will look at the two halves separately.

The chapter begins with a series of negatives: 'Do not rejoice' (v. 1), 'will not shepherd them' (v. 2), 'they will not dwell' (v. 3), 'they will not pour out libations of wine...they will not make pleasing their sacrifices to him', 'it will not come into the house of Yhwh' (v. 4). These lead up to the central question: 'What will you do on the day of assembly, the day of the festival of Yhwh?' (v. 5). The festival of Yhwh is the time of rejoicing (Deut. 16.11, 14, 15) over the products of the earth; the concatenation of threshing floor and vat would identify it as Tabernacles (Deut. 16.13; cf. Macintosh 1997: 337, Sweeney 2000: 95). But this is an anti-festival, when joy is turned to mourning, libations are not poured out, sacrifices are not sweet, and the harvest is not brought into the house of Yhwh. Tabernacles is a pilgrimage festival, when celebrants journey to 'the place which Yhwh chooses' (Deut. 16.15); the distinctive feature of the festival, the dwelling in *sukkot* or 'booths' in memory of the sojourn in the wilderness (Lev. 23.43), is recalled in the 'tents' in which thorns grow in v. 6 (cf. 12.10). This is an anti-pilgrimage; instead of dwelling in Yhwh's land, Israel returns to Egypt and goes to Assyria, where it eats 'defiled' bread. Sacred history is reversed: if Egypt is the antonym of Yhwh's land, the return, marked by a wordplay between 'dwell' (*yēšᵉbû*) and 'return' (*šāb*), results in a parody.

Israel is not to rejoice 'like the peoples'; one imagines all peoples celebrating their harvest, except Israel. Becoming 'like the peoples' is a pervasive fear in the Hebrew Bible, associated with the monarchy (Deut. 17.14; 1 Sam. 8.5) as well as worship. The addition of 'to exultation' to 'Do not rejoice' suggests a manic glee; a number of critics (e.g. Jeremias 1983: 115; Rudolph 1966: 171) hold that the word for exultation (*gîl*) denotes Canaanite ritual ecstasy, a possibility supported by its use in 10.5, where idolatrous priests are the subject. (See, however, Ben Zvi's

128 *Hosea 9*

cautionary note [2005: 197].) Ritual, sexual and alcoholic intoxication converge; as ever, new wine (*tîrôš*) is falsely euphoric, and takes away the heart (4.11). Celebration of the new vintage would be especially characteristic of the autumn harvest festival, the more so if, as 1 Kgs 12.32 suggests, it took place a month later in the northern kingdom than in the south, i.e. in October-November. New wine, being petillant, might have been extra intoxicating.

However, in 7.8-9 and 8.7-8 Israel is the harvest that the peoples consume; Israel is 'mingled' among the nations (7.8). The metaphor of prostitution draws on the amorous traffic of 7.11-12 and 8.9-10. Just as Israel gave love gifts to the nations in 8.9-10, so it loves the harlot's hire in v. 1; the wooing of Assyria and Egypt in 7.11 culminates in their burial in Egypt and eating mourners' bread in Assyria. Prostitution 'from your God' recalls especially chs. 1–3 and 4. In particular, Israel regards her vine and fig tree as her 'harlot's hire' in 2.14, and in 2.10-11 does not know that corn and new wine come from Yhwh and will be reclaimed by him. Prostitution with the indigenous gods is then equivalent to becoming 'like the peoples'. There is an even closer correlation with 4.11-12; in both Israel plays the harlot 'from under' or 'from' God, and in both this is associated with the deceptiveness of drink. The licentious feasts at the high places in 4.13-14 are thus aligned with the celebrations at the threshing floors; one may note that threshing floors were often on heights, to catch the wind, and might also be public places (cf. 1 Kgs 22.10). One may postulate, from Ruth 3.1-5, at least a literary connection with sexuality.

The word for 'prostitution' has not occurred since 6.10, and vanishes for the rest of the book. Its isolated resurfacing intensifies the reversion to the concerns of a previous part of the book, and makes them emblematic of the political, personal and prophetic crisis that dominates the latter part. The high places compose a pastoral prelude, with only intimations of approaching disaster. Its recollection here, in the shadow of the burning palaces, both serves to superimpose the two segments or visions, and to ironize cultic normality; people still think they live in the pastoral, and do not notice that it is collapsing around them.

The joy over corn and wine echoes the cries over the same comestibles in 7.14, whose various interpretations I have already discussed. This suggests that chs. 8 and 9 are parallel, variant continuations of ch. 7. If ch. 8 begins with the ambiguous image of the shofar, which both protects and heralds danger for the house of Yhwh as a figure for the prophetic message, ch. 9 adumbrates that message. The house of Yhwh over which the prophet stands guard is empty of sacred food (v. 4) and the scene of enmity (v. 8). This suggests a correlation with 8.13, where Yhwh does not accept the people's sacrifices. The parallel between ch. 8 and 9.1-9 is confirmed by the conclusion, 'he will remember their iniquity, he will visit their sin', which summarizes the two passages; the reward, 'they will return to Egypt', in 8.13 is repeated and expanded in ch. 9.

In 4.16 Yhwh 'shepherds' or 'would shepherd' Israel 'like a lamb in a broad pasture'. As we saw there, he suffers from a zoological error, since Israel actually behaves like a wilful cow. In v. 2, in a startling but identical metaphor, threshing floor and vat 'do not shepherd them'. The word for 'shepherd' could also mean 'befriend' (Wolff 1974: 149) without any serious change in meaning. In either case, 'granary' and 'vat' are personified as shepherds or friends; a pastoral image, in the former instance, is overlaid on a sedentary one. The two conceptions need not necessarily conflict; Yhwh presumably was perceived as caring for Israel through the produce of the land. That threshing floor and vat do not graze them, and wine deceives them, like Yhwh's category mistake, suggests, however, a shared misapprehension.

In the next two verses, the pattern of reversal continues. They eat unclean food in Assyria, either because Assyria itself is an impure land, the obverse of the land of Yhwh, or because purification requires contact with Yhwh's house, the ritual communication that is insistently broken off. Egypt and Assyria are in tandem; playing off the great powers against each other results in deportation to both. Eating defiled food not only evokes the subsistence diet of deportees, but their exile from God. The food does not partake in the transformation of impurity into purity, the profane into the sacred, represented by sacrifice, or in the rhythms of the festive year. Absorbing impurity means becoming irredeemably impure, which amounts to political and religious anomie.

This need not happen only in exile; the interruption or non-reception of libations, the failure of sacrifice to please, may also be experienced in the land. Verse 4 would then correspond to 8.13, in which the ingestion of sacrificial meat meets with no divine approval. In that case, God's rejection of sacrifice would be an internal exile, of which depopulation would be a consequence or correlate.

The food of exile or sacrifice is like mourners' bread, which defiles those who eat it. In the purity code, death is the antonym of God and the most intense source of impurity. Those who share a meal with mourners participate in their grief, and sympathetically contract the contagion of death. The mourning would presumably be for the loss of independence and the divine absence. Assyria, where the impure food is eaten, thus becomes a figure for death, an association that becomes more explicit in the case of Egypt in v. 6. Eros, the wooing of Assyria and Egypt, turns to Thanatos. The irony is confirmed by two puns. The word for 'mourning' (*'ônîm*) represents virility in 12.4; phallic desire is fatal. Another form of same word means 'folly' (*'āwen*), whose fruit the exiles endure. It is probable that this vocalization, introduced by the Masoretes, was not original, and that, at least in the northern Israelite dialect, the word was an exact homonym of *'ôň'ônîm*. The second pun is on the word *napšām*, 'their soul, life, appetite' in the phrase 'for their bread is for their soul/life/ appetite'. This could mean that it is solely to appease their hunger, as most recent translations interpret it; or that, as in 8.13, the sacrifices are for their own enjoyment; or that they eat it at the risk of their lives.

In 11.5 the text asserts that Israel will not return to Egypt. The contradiction is evident, and is explicated in various ways by commentators: for instance, by a change of mind by Hosea, or by the use of Egypt as a metaphor for Assyria. The contradiction is duplicated in 11.8-9 by the contradiction within God between his destructive impulses and his desire to mitigate them. If Egypt represents the subjugation from which God liberated Israel and is consequently the archetype of the other peoples, return to Egypt would close the circuit of Israel's history. The contradiction opens the closed circuit, and is equivalent to the vacillation elsewhere in the book between destruction and continuance.

After the central question, 'What will you do on the day of assembly, the day of the feast of Yhwh?', v. 6 returns to the desolation of the land and the return to Egypt. The feast is an anti-feast, the gathering into death. Egypt is apparently a place of refuge from pillage; it is in fact a cemetery. The association of Egypt with death is supported, as most commentators note, by the prominence of tombs in its landscape, especially around the old royal capital of Memphis, and by its funeral cult. The negations of vv. 1-4 are replaced by emptiness; instead we have rhyme and alliteration that match *tᵉqabbᵉṣēm*, 'will gather them', with *tᵉqabbᵉrēm*, 'will bury them', just as in v. 3 Ephraim rhymes with *miṣrayim*, 'Egypt'. Ephraim merges with Egypt; Egypt's apparent security is a guise for its morbidity. But there is also a displacement; in 8.10, Yhwh 'gathers them', using the same verb, just as in 7.12 he is the fowler who intercepts the dove on its flight between Egypt and Assyria. As I have noted, his retrieval of Israel is a prelude to their deliverance to Egypt; it also makes God and Egypt metaphorically equivalent to each other.

Egypt offers flight from the threat of Assyria; historically, we know that it was the weaker power, and incapable of supporting its allies (Ben Zvi 2005: 159-60). It is thus a false opposite to Assyria, whose spectre is raised only to demonstrate the impossibility of resistance. In 8.10 God's imposition is paired with Ephraim's submission to the Assyrian burden. Egypt, as the place of origins, holds out hope for a new beginning, that, once the Assyrian danger has passed, Israel can be restored. In fact, it is an old death. Assyria, however, suggests an alternative to the figure of return, that on the other side of destruction and horror, although they eat impure food, there is a future.

Egypt is paralleled by Memphis, the great city is composed of graves; in the next half verse, the two imperial entities are matched by two words for 'thorn'. Thorns inherit the treasures of silver instead of children; the land is so forsaken that not even Assyrians or brigands plunder it. In 10.8 two other words for 'thorn' occur; they grow upon the altars whose proliferation is condemned in 8.11 and 10.1. The collocation of thorns and thistles, as we have seen, is found also in Gen. 3.18, and thus evokes a post-Edenic desolation.

The last section of the first part of the chapter (vv. 7-9) turns to the figure of the prophet; most critics dramatize it as a dialogue between the prophet and his audience, but without any real justification. According to them, it is the audience who call the prophet insane and foolish; the last part of v. 7 and v. 8 are his angry response. The section reverts to 8.1-3 and thus encloses 8.1–9.9 in a frame. In 8.2, the people claim to know 'my God'; now they come to that disenchanting knowledge. Once again we focus on the house of God and its sentinel; the visitation against which the shofar warns is finally at hand.

The days of visitation and recompense have arrived, and expose the true nature of the day of assembly and of the feast of Yhwh. The announcement concludes the prediction of the people's fate in foreign lands, and anticipates—through the word 'visitation'—the formula 'He will remember their iniquity, he will visit their sin' in v. 9. Between the two there is prophetic self-reflection.

It is the prophet himself who claims to be mad and senseless, driven so by the greatness of their sin and the disaster he foresees. The motif is familiar in prophecy, especially in Jeremiah, and is expanded in the next section (Morris 1995: 146-47). Madness and prophecy are related etymologically as well as phenomenologically (the verb *hitnabbē'* means to 'rave' as well as 'prophesy', for instance in 1 Sam. 18.10). The prophet sees clairvoyantly and attempts to make sense of a world that disintegrates. His madness mirrors and expresses that of his contemporaries; it may correspond to the delusive joy of v. 1. The epithet, 'the man of spirit', implies possession; such a person is subject to the spirit's impulses.

The problem is complicated by the next verse. The prophet 'is a fowler's snare across all his (Ephraim's) paths'. The prophet then corresponds to God in 7.12, and the judiciary in 5.1. It recalls also the prophet's function as the vindicator of divine wrath in 6.5, whose performative word is lethal. Since he is part of the people, he sets a trap for himself. He does so because he is emblematic of the people. Ephraim is the watchman with my God, charged with maintaining divine order in the world. If it acts as a trap for the lookout point in 5.1, the prophet, in turn, traps it. (For the rhetorical raising and dashing of traditional hopes here, see Ben Zvi 2005: 193.)

Verse 9 begins, 'They have dug deep, they have made a pit/ corrupted themselves, as on the days of Gibeah'. Again there may be a reference back to 5.2, in which the same verb, 'they have dug deep', occurs in the context of a near homophone of *šiḥētû*, 'they have made a pit/corrupted themselves', and a noun, *šēṭîm*, that could be read as the nefarious place name, Shittim (for these interconnections, see Morris 1995: 71). Gibeah occurs previously in 5.8, linked through the expression 'Blow the shofar at Gibeah' to 8.1, and thus to the image of the watchman in 9.8. Gibeah, we saw, recalls both the near-annihilation of Benjamin after the paradigmatic sin of Judges 19 and the fraught beginnings of the monarchy. Here it is followed by the refrain 'He will remember their iniquity, he will visit their sin', which prefaces the return to Egypt in 8.13. Gibeah and Egypt are metaphori-

Hosea 9 133

cally consequent; inhumation in Egypt is the external effect of an inner corruption. Gibeah adumbrates the failure of the premonarchic polity and the kingdom that succeeds it. It becomes a symbol for Israel's entire alienation from God, as well as the archetypal conflict between prophet and king. The displacement from God's gathering them to asylum in Egypt is reversed; Israel suffers from 'enmity in the house of its God', equivalent to the sin of Gibeah. Similarly, in v. 6 the retribution is equally exile in Egypt and desolation in the land.

The enmity comes from God, and conforms to the similes of moth and rottenness in 5.12. That there is a trap 'across all its paths' not only requites the trap laid at Mizpah in 5.1 but the endemic hostility of bandits and conspirators, for instance the fellowship of murderous priests in 6.9 and the regicides of ch. 7. Verse 9 suggests, in proverbial fashion, that they dig their own pit. The watchman, Ephraim, is careless of where he puts his feet. If the metaphor makes Ephraim prophetic, the prophet himself is the arch-Ephraimite, who preserves its prophetic identity and guards it on its journey (12.14). That the prophet is a trap is a recurrent theme in the prophets, found in Amos 3, Isaiah 6, 8.15, and 28.13. His mission is contradictory; the paradox is symmetrical to the one that renders his clairvoyance madness, his knowledge folly. If true knowledge is delusive, and its communication entraps those it is designed to enlighten—if enlightenment is a trap—the prophet's situation must indeed lead to madness, whether the madness be an inability to make sense, a fracture of personality pulled by contradictory demands, or a destruction of ego boundaries.

The prophet is an agent of God, a trap laid by God. Consequently it is God who propagates the metaphorical equivalence of folly and prophecy, madness and spirit. It is God for whom reality verges on insanity.

(10) Like grapes in the wilderness, I found Israel, like a first fruit on a fig tree; in its beginning I saw your fathers; they came to Baal Peor; they consecrated themselves to shame, and their abominations were like their love.
(11) Ephraim—like a bird their glory flies away, from birth, from pregnancy, from conception.
(12) For even if they raise their children, I will bereave them from humanity. Indeed, woe to them in my turning away from them.

134   *Hosea 9*

(13) Ephraim—when I saw it, like Tyre planted in a meadow—
and Ephraim, to bring out its sons to the slaughterer.
(14) Give them, Yhwh, what will you give? Give them a
bereaving womb and dry breasts.
(15) All their evil is in Gilgal, for there I hated them; over their
evil deeds I would drive them from my house; I will no
longer love them; all their princes turn astray.
(16) Ephraim is smitten; their root is dry; they cannot produce
fruit. Even if they give birth, I will kill the precious fruit
of their womb.
(17) My God has rejected them, for they did not listen to him,
and they shall be wandering among the nations.

In the second part of the chapter we return once more to beginnings, to God's discovery of Israel in the wilderness. Most critics see here the beginning of a new phase in the book, characterized by a reflection on Israel's early traditions. 'Like grapes in the wilderness' in v. 10 is matched by 'Israel was a luxuriant vine' in 10.1, and by God's recollection of his adoption of Israel in 11.1. At the same time, the beginning of the second half of ch. 10— 'From the days of Gibeah you have sinned, O Israel'—corresponds to the end of the first half of ch. 9. This should make us suspicious of any such neat divisions, and indicate also an intertextual connection between Gibeah and Egypt, inner dissolution and foreign subjugation.

The death of children is the distinctive feature of the tableau, anticipated only by the sterility of the priests in 4.4-10, and perhaps by the failure of the harvest in 8.7-8. It is the reverse of the imagery of sexual abandon elsewhere in the book. Clearly, too, the fate of Ephraim's children recollects their names in ch. 1. The motif resurfaces in the final verse before the concluding vision of return, in which infants are shattered and pregnant mothers ripped open (14.1). Nevertheless, in the intensity of its focus the passage is unparalleled; it is the only point, apart from the introductory narratives, in which the prophet's voice unambiguously separates itself from that of God: he speaks his own prayer. This may be set in the context of the prophet's experience in vv. 7-9, combined with Ephraim's prophetic mission. One might thus be justified in seeing the passage as more personal than any other.

Its structure is circular: v. 10 matches v. 17, since God's discovery of Israel in the wilderness is reversed by his rejection of them and their wandering among the nations (Krause 1992: 198) while the centre is dominated, as O'Connor has shown (1987a: 166-68; 1987b: 250-52) by an elaborate pseudosorites, or false logical chain, in which the process of reproduction is interrupted at every step, and yet continues. Verse 11 presents the pseudosorites from the woman's point of view, and in reverse (birth > pregnancy > conception), v. 16 from that of the man (impotence > sterility), while in v. 14 it is reflected in the prophet's words (bereaving womb > dry breasts).

From madness and horror, typified by Gibeah, we go back to God's first experience of wonder. The simile, 'Like grapes in the wilderness I found Israel', represents God as thirsty, as infused with a sudden rush of sensual pleasure; the grapes are a source of life. Its lifelessness makes the wilderness into a recess into uncreation; if the wilderness is a symbol for God's experience, the world, before God's chancing upon Israel, was a wasteland. In 2.17, in the wilderness God gave Israel 'her vineyards', as a prelude to her reentry into the land. The transfer of imagery is typical of the metaphorical interchange: through giving itself to God, being incorporated in God, Israel is constituted as itself. This may be confirmed by the elaboration of the accompanying simile, of the fig tree. Both 'first fruit' (*bikkûrâ*) and 'at its beginning' (*bᵉrē'šîtāh*) are associated with the offering of first fruits, and with the motif of Israel as God's firstborn (Exod. 4.22). 'In its beginning' may either refer to the 'first fruit' or to 'Israel'; if the latter, there is another transfer of gender between male and female personifications of Israel, since the suffix of 'in its beginning' (*bᵉrē'šîtāh*) is feminine. What God sees, desirously, is a matrix, and a birth. Vision is linked to the beginning, also through word play, since *bᵉrē'šîtāh* ('In its beginning') and *rā'îtî* ('I saw') alliterate. The vision, across a maximal distance, contrasts with its obscuration by Israel's later history and the consumption of the fruit. However, the vision is liable to be deceptive; grapes in the wilderness are too good to be true, like mirages and Dead Sea fruit. Figs are too readily interpreted as gifts of the 'lovers' (2.14), whose fee Israel loves, according to v. 1.

'In its/her beginning' God saw 'your fathers', a patrilineal succession that imparts itself genetically to the present and suggests a human origin in remote antiquity. Israel, on this model, is only illusorily the divine partner, founded as well as found in the wilderness; it consists of patriarchs about their own business. As soon as the ancestors reached the edge of cultivated land, they fell for its sexual and numinous temptations. The word for 'they consecrated themselves' (*yinnāz^{e}rû*) would normally connote people who take Nazirite vows, involving abstention from grapes and wine, and hence from Dionysiac celebrations; becoming Nazirites for Baal comprises a complete reversal of normal values. They become 'disgusting as that which they love', suggestive of the crossing the boundaries of repression and anticipating the impure food eaten in Assyria.

'Ephraim, like a bird their glory flies away'—literally, 'like a bird it birds itself'. The repetition establishes one of the distinctive features of the passage: excess combined with fragmentation. Already the single word 'Ephraim' is starkly isolated by the simile. In the next half line, each of the three terms, 'from birth, from pregnancy, from conception' is disjoined from the others; the lack of connection is reinforced by the reversal of time. The bird repeatedly materializes as bird, only to disappear over the horizon; similarly, Ephraim is momentarily envisaged in its glory, before it vanishes. 'Their glory' might refer to Yhwh, or to demographic, political and economic splendour (for its many connotations, see Ben Zvi 2005: 194); that it is used for the process of generation is a surprise. The simile represents glory as a winged creature and thus corresponds to symbols of divine transcendence; at the same time, the word for 'glory' (*kābôd*) is related to that for 'heavy' (*kābēd*). The loss of glory renders Ephraim insubstantial, as well as robbing it of its significance, as under, or part of, God's protective aura.

Glory is stripped away from Ephraim, reducing it to its reproductive functions. The list is extremely elliptical; it may either mean that there will be no birth, pregnancy or conception, or that these events will be without glory. All that will be left is a joyless continuance, and even that may be cancelled. Disruption continues in the next verse, with its jump from conception to growth suddenly cut off, and its twinning of the concessive 'For even if…' with the emotional interjection: 'For indeed woe to them!' Conception and maturity juxtapose extreme ends of the reproductive process; regression to the very beginning of life is pointless, because it cannot save from the omnipresence of death. 'I will bereave them from Adam/humanity' emphasizes the double movement; the verge of extinction is also a recollection of the first human's mortality, and makes Adam into a figure of grief, suggesting that to be human is to be bereft. (Indeed, Andersen and Freedman 1980: 543 suggest an allusion to Cain's fratricide of Abel.) Both parents and children are lamented, parents because they are deprived of offspring, children because, cut off from the human race, they have lost the hope of a future. Correspondingly, woe is ascribed to them because God has turned away from them. In between the absent God and bereaved humanity/Adam, their state is isolated, insubstantial; the emptiness is perhaps communicated through the immateriality of the words: 'for indeed woe to them!' The relationship between parents and children extends back to the carefree fathers with their determinative sin in v. 10, as well as to Adam.

Verse 13 presents unusual problems, since the Hebrew text, which literally reads, 'Ephraim, just as I saw like Tyre planted (fem.) in a meadow', is very strange; other possibilities are 'rock' and 'palm tree'. Tyre was an island city and thus unlikely to be planted in a meadow; the comparison may be with its impregnability and wealth (Kuan [1991] thinks there may be a reference to an Assyrian siege of Tyre). Thus the readings 'Tyre' and 'rock' converge; the rock is a metaphor for durability, and is a frequent attribute of God. The word for 'planted' is almost always used for trees planted in a fertile, well-watered place, and may thus be correlated with Tyre in its ocean fastness, as well as the arborial imagery associated with Ephraim in v. 10 and the possible meaning of 'palm tree'. The feminine form $š^e tûlâ$, 'planted', likewise echoes the feminine persona of Israel in v. 10, especially since it seems grammatically anomalous here. As in v. 11, the subject, Ephraim, is isolated as a single initial word; in the second half of the verse, the form is repeated. The two halves are conjoined as two visions of Ephraim, that are collapsed into each other. They measure the trajectory of the flight of Ephraim's glory in v. 11; if the first half enables us to perceive how it was envisaged by God, the second encapsulates utter destitution. The phrase 'just as I saw' evokes God's vision in v. 10. His perception 'in its/her beginning' is elaborated in a fully articulated design for Ephraim's future in the land, combining the political and economic security and splendour suggested by Tyre with the theological implications of the metaphor of the rock and the agricultural prosperity of the date palm in the well-watered meadow, in contrast to the maritime Tyrian emporium. 'Planted in a meadow' may also have sacred connotations, as in Ps. 92.14, in which the righteous are 'planted in the house of Yhwh'. Trees frequently grew in temple courtyards; the word for 'meadow' or 'pasture' is applied to God's sanctuary (e.g. Exod. 15.13; 2

Sam. 15.25), to the land as God's pasture, or even to God himself (Jer. 50.7). The concatenation of motifs, together with the metaphorical concentration of terms from very different domains, testifies to the intensity of God's hopes.

The sentence that begins 'just as' is left uncompleted; we expect a matching conclusion: 'so...' That it is omitted makes the second half of the verse equivalent to the first; the grief over the children is implicitly equal to God's expectation. The horror of surrendering one's children to slaughter focuses on the refinements of the conquerors' cruelty, and thus is inescapably literal, but it is also the nation's fate and God's fate. His vision of the matrix turns to desolation and disillusion; the 'woe' that is attributed to the parents in v. 12 is then his too.

One would have thought this a propitious moment for prophetic intercession; instead it merely retraces God's prediction, to the extent of mirroring the pseudosorites, as O'Connor shows. Dialogue between the prophet and God generally dramatizes conflict between them. It may be elicited for the sake of the retort, as in Amos 7–8, Isaiah 6 and Jeremiah 1. It may express the prophet's reluctance and self-doubt, especially in Jeremiah and Second Isaiah. Here there is no response and no evidence of conflict. The prayer complies with God's instruction to Jeremiah: 'And as for you, do not pray on behalf of this people...' (Jer. 11.14). Nevertheless, it focuses attention on conflict within the prophet, and the difference between his voice and that of God who speaks through him. The difference turns into that between the voice of desire, whose imperative is 'Give', and the second thought, 'What will/can you give?', which may either express an inability to know what it wants, or a disbelief that God can give anything. The conflict between desire and its negation is repeated in the second half of the verse. Desire is for womb and breasts, figures that combine sexual desire with the desire for propagation and infantile dependence. Womb and breasts comprise the entire libidinous realm. That the womb is 'bereaving' conflates the source of life with death. If in v. 12 it is God who bereaves them, here it is the mother herself. The action of leading one's children out to slaughter begins in the womb, is transmitted genetically. Bereaver and bereaved are identical. Similarly, the desiccated breasts transpose nourishment into starvation. If God is the provider of gifts, addressed as such by the prophet, and the breast is the bestower of food for infants, God and the breast are equivalent. Conversely, in v. 10 Israel was for God a matrix, a source of life in a dry land. The word for 'shrivelled' ($ṣōm^eqîm$) is a form of that for 'raisins' ($ṣimmûqîm$). God's discovery in the wilderness has reached its conclusion; the grapes, if not sour, have become inedible.

The prayer may be, as several critics suggest (e.g. Davies 1992: 229), the least of evils, conforming to the biblical cliché that miscarriage or infant death are sometimes preferable to the miseries of life. A second meaning of the word for 'womb' ($reḥem$)—'compassion'—may be invoked in support of this interpretation; for these children abortion is euthanasia. However, this is to ignore the mirroring function of the petition. The citation of part of the pseudosorites suggests the whole. It also belittles the intensity—communicated through the threefold repetition of the word 'give'—and gravity of the request. If all desire—sexual as well as poetic—is pointless, if the emissary has nothing to ask, then the only valid desire is for impotence. The problem is that love always bereaves itself, that to be human is to breed death. At one moment the prophet acts his part, craves life, reprieve, to be satisfied with the divine infusion; at the next, he suffers from a sudden incapacity, a loss of confidence, when words fail. This is the poetic problem of the book: how to create a world of significance when there is none, when the unravelling of significance is the meaning, and the sexual problem, when desire, in all its forms, e.g. the conspirators of ch. 7, turns into an agent of death.

The central question, 'What will you give?', corresponds to God's self-interrogations in 6.4 and 11.8. As the epigone of the prophets, as we have seen in discussing 6.5, Hosea may experience an access of uncertainty, a hesitance about being as remorselessly fatal as his predecessors. Here the vacillation is the opposite, an inability to intercede. It meets, however, God's crisis of indecision. In between both is a state of irresolution, an indeterminacy—an oscillation between giving and not-giving, fulness of communication and its exhaustion—which allows a precarious balance between rapport and distance.

The last three verses are more public, returning to the themes of temple, politics and exile, and less dense. In v. 15 'All their evil' is repeated in 'because of the evil of their deeds'; 'for there I hated them' is simply reversed in 'I will no longer love them'; 'their princes turn astray' seems unmotivated by the rest of the verse. Verse 17, apparently spoken by the prophet, is an anticlimactic sequel to v. 14, to which it bears little relation. Neither 'My God rejects them' nor 'for they have not listened to him' seems adequate to the antecedent verses. 'They shall be wandering among the nations' correlates with 'they have wandered away from me' in 7.13, perhaps suggesting the closure of a larger unit (Ben Zvi 2005: 191).

Gilgal is antithetic to Baal Peor, geographically—since they face each other on opposite sides of the Jordan—and connotatively. If Baal Peor represents the paradigmatic sin on the eve of the conquest, Gilgal is the site of the Israelites' first encampment after crossing the Jordan, marked by a cairn of twelve stones representing the unity of Israel, and a hill of foreskins as a sign of the covenant (Josh. 4.20; 5.3). That God condemns Gilgal is tantamount to rejecting their entire experience in the land. Gilgal is also associated with the founding of the monarchy (1 Sam. 11.14), accompanied by Samuel's awful warning (1 Sam. 12), and with Saul's loss of the kingdom (1 Sam. 13.15). Gilgal is then a counterpart to Gibeah in v. 9, since Gibeah was Saul's royal residence and the scene of the crime that symbolically destroyed the unity of the twelve tribes memorialized at Gilgal; the two sites delimit the age of divine rule in Joshua and Judges. In 4.15 pilgrimage to Gilgal is discouraged; in 12.12 it is destined to become rubble; its appearance here perhaps anticipates plays on the sounds *gil* and *gal* in 10.5.

Gilgal, in particular, recalls the word *gîl*, 'exultation' in v. 1, thus contributing to a circular structure; the chapter begins with Israel exulting like the nations, and ends with their dispersal among them (for the envelope structure, see Ben Zvi 2005: 192). Festive joy would normally be celebrated at Gilgal. Now, however, no offerings are brought there (v. 4) and its worshippers are driven out. Israel's love of a harlot's hire in v. 1 and at Baal Peor in v. 10 is repaid by God's ceasing to love them.

The vagueness of the indictment, 'All their evil is at Gilgal', makes it impossible to determine for which crime it is condemned, and thereby narrow the associative field (as in 5.1 and 6.7-9, some critics, such as Rudolph 1966: 198, hypothesize a long-forgotten contemporary scandal). 'All their princes turn aside' evokes the homophony between the word for prince (*śar*) and that for 'turn aside' (*sārar*) which I noted in 7.14 and 16, and establishes a further link between the two passages; the deviations of the princes presumably motivates God's turning away (*śûrî*) in v. 12. In ch. 7, too, the Samarians' accusation that God has remembered 'all their evil' is followed by a focus on the misdeeds of the princes.

Verse 16 repeats the pseudosorites, as O'Connor argues, since the dry root and failure of the crop may signify male impotence. It intertwines this motif, however, with that of the deceptive harvest of vv. 1-2 and the promising fruit of v. 10. The threat to kill 'the treasures of their womb' echoes the abandonment of the silver treasures in v. 6. As many critics note, the word for 'fruit' ($p^e r\hat{\imath}$) is a pun on that for Ephraim; that for 'their root' ($\check{s}or\check{s}\bar{a}m$) also alliterates with 'their princes' ($\acute{s}\bar{a}r\hat{e}hem$).

In v. 17, as at the end of the first section, in v. 8, the prophet acknowledges Yhwh as 'my God'. If in v. 8 'Ephraim is a watchman with my God', here God has rejected them, because they have neglected their charge. Ephraim suffers from a failure of vision, but this is also true, as we have seen, of God's first sight of Israel.

The two tableaux of the chapter intermesh: the question 'What will you give?' corresponds to and inverts 'What will you do on the day of the festival?' The first tableau turns the festival into a day of mourning for a land inherited by thorns. In the house of Yhwh the prophet is a trap into which the people fall and whose clarity of vision is madness. The second tableau goes from death to birth, transfers the imagery of the aftermath, eating the melancholy bread of exile, to the horrors of conquest. At its centre is the prophet, whose voice is heard in its individuality, only to be at a loss for words. The trap the prophet sets is his own perdition, his bereaving womb or compassion, the poetic and sexual desire that destroys itself as soon as it is spoken.

Hosea 10

(1) Ephraim is a luxuriant/damaged vine; it sought to make fruit. According to the abundance of its fruit it multiplied altars, according to the goodness of its land it beautified pillars.
(2) Their heart is smooth; now they will be found guilty; he will break the neck of their altars, he will shatter their pillars.
(3) For now they say, 'We have no king, for we do not fear Yhwh, and the king—what will he do for us?'
(4) They have spoken words, vain oaths, forged covenants; their judgment will flower like poisonous weeds on the furrows of the field.
(5) For the calves of Beth-awen the resident of Samaria shows dread; for his people mourn over him, and his idolatrous priests rejoice/wail over him and over his glory, for it has been exiled from him.
(6) Also he has been taken to Assyria, as a present for King Contentious; disgrace Ephraim gains; Israel is abashed because of its policy.
(7) Perished is Samaria, its king, like a chip upon the waters.
(8) And the high places of Awen shall be laid waste, the sin of Israel. Thorn and thistle will rise up over their altars, and they will say to the mountains, 'Cover us', and to the hills, 'Fall upon us'.

10.1-8 closely reworks Ch. 8, as many critics have noted. At its centre, as in 8.4-6, are the twin figures of king and calf, connected to the capital, Samaria; in both, tribute is paid to the Assyrian monarch, whose royal titles expose the factitiousness of Israelite royalty, and in both the proliferation of altars is evidence of sin and provokes destruction. Both have concentric structures, spatially as well as verbally, and thus enact, centrifugally, the dispersal of political and sacred authority. 10.1-8, in particular, is a perfect ring composition, as Jeremias (1983: 127) and others have pointed out:

vv. 1-2: altars
vv. 3-4: king
vv. 5-6: calf
v. 7: king
v. 8: altars

'Ephraim is/was a luxuriant vine': the chapter begins, like the previous section, with a reflection on Israel's promising and disappointing history. If, in 9.10, God initially found Israel like grapes in the wilderness, the vine is coextensive with the land and Israel's settlement on it. In Ps. 80. 9-14, which may well be a northern Israelite composition, Joseph is a vine transplanted from Egypt, whose gigantic growth is imperilled by wild beasts. One may suppose an intertextual relationship between the two.

The word translated as 'luxuriant' is obscure, the meaning derived from the context and the Greek translation. But it may also mean 'empty', and thus points to an underlying theme of the passage: the hollowness of Israel's prosperity, rituals, politics and language. In v. 4 it speaks meaningless words, vain oaths, frames alliances, and justice grows like weeds, while in reality it has no king and does not fear God (v. 3). Like 9.1-4, the opening verses are under the sign of negation.

The noun 'vine' is treated as masculine, in contrast to normal usage. Once again we have an unexplained slippage of gender. In 9.10 Israel was feminine, its fruit a source of nourishment for God; here its masculinity is grammatically regular—and 'vine', as some commentators suggest, adapted to conform to it—but it does suggest an alternation, a contrast between present and past, and an inability to reduce Israel to a single persona.

The verb that completes the phrase ('fruit it would make equal/produce for itself') is likewise disputed; its most common meaning, 'to be equal, like', introduces a play of equivalences, and suggests calculation and expectation, that the fruit would be commensurate with the size of the vine. (Many commentators suggest a homophonic pun with $šaw'$, 'falsehood, vanity'.) In the following half verse, the pairing of the quantity of fruit with the number of altars, the quality of the land with the workmanship of pillars, is sustained by rhyme between the words for 'quantity' ($rōb$) and 'goodness' ($ṭôb$) and syntactic and semantic parallelism (cf. Morris 1995: 59).

Parallelism is an indicator of poetic order, which corresponds to the symbolic order maintained in the land, whose prosperity is reciprocated with altars, and whose benevolence is transferred to sacred pillars. Rudolph (1966: 192) remarks on the shift of the word 'good' (*ṭôb*) from the material to the aesthetic domain, and the high quality of masonry in 8th-century Israel. But the image of natural piety responding to divine favour should arouse our suspicion in view of our experience of the book; in particular, the phrase 'it multiplied altars' has already occurred in 8.11, and thus connects the two chapters together. In 8.11 the proliferation of altars is 'for sin', and is co-ordinated with alienation from the multitude/principles of teachings and the fortification of cities. The two contexts may be juxtaposed, to disturb the complacency of the apparent idyll.

The metaphor of the vine and its fruit passes from Israel and the land to the altars and pillars. The geography of local shrines replaces the vine; the altars could be seen as the fruit of the land. Intertextually, Psalm 80's charge that God has destroyed his vine is counteracted by exposure of the vine's 'emptiness'. The metaphor of vine and fruit, having served its purpose—for instance linkage—fades out, and is transposed into the far more elaborate one of agriculture.

Verse 2 begins with an ambiguity: the people's heart may be either 'smooth' or 'divided'. Some commentators suggest an allusion to Jacob's 'smoothness' in Gen. 27.11 (e.g. Sweeney 2000: 103). We return to the motif of the perfidious heart in ch. 7; the piety conceals flattery or duplicity. In exchange, God breaks their altars and shatters their pillars. The word for 'breaks' is derived from a word for 'neck' (*'ōrep*) and normally means 'to break the neck of an animal', especially a bovine (e.g. Deut. 21.4). The implied metaphor assimilates the altars to the calf or calves of vv. 5-6 and the heifer of v. 11, on whose neck Yhwh rides. It may perhaps be supported by the term 'horns' applied to the projections at the corners of altars, and the associative field of horns and cattle as symbols of power and pride throughout the Hebrew Bible. (For the reference to horns, see Wolff 1974: 174.) The word *'ārap*, however, has a second meaning: 'to drop dew', used also of prophetic speech (Deut. 32.2). Although scarcely primary in our context, since 'altars' cannot be its direct object, this possibility opposes to divine violence and the diffusion of altars the distillation of dew, as a symbol of transience and divine blessing in the book (6.4; 13.3; 14.6), and the prophetic word. It may also be that, in view of the parallel with v. 11, *'ārap* here means less 'to break' than 'to vault over' a neck, in an assertion of power.

Verses 2 and 3 are interconnected by the word 'now'; the guilt that is acknowledged or established in v. 2, consequent on their false or divided heart, is illustrated through their speech. From the land as a whole we pass to the consciousness of its inhabitants. Commentators differ on whether *ye'šāmû* refers to punishment or acknowledgement, and suggest a pun with *šmm*, 'destroy'. The passage clearly relates to God's hope for their confession of guilt in 5.15, and their inadequate response in 6.1-3. In 6.1-3 God's return is regarded as being as inevitable as the rain. Here all they can express is the absence of fear of God and the impotence of the king. There is no apparent hope for reconciliation: normal means for inducing divine favour are abandoned, and the admission that 'we do not fear Yhwh' is not matched by any impulse towards contrition. Elsewhere the people proclaim their belief that they know God (8.2) and their sense of his implacable scrutiny (7.2). The emphasis on prayer and ritual shows that they attribute responsibility for catastrophe to God. To all appearances, in their extremity, they are profoundly God-fearing. Davies (1992: 236) points out that the concept of the 'fear of Yhwh' occurs only here in Hosea. If their knowing is an unknowing, their acknowledgement here is that they have not attained the prerequisite of knowledge, the awe or reverence out of which knowledge arises.

'Fear of Yhwh' evidently refers to his kingship, given the context, since that they have no king is substantiated by insubordination to the divine king and contempt for his human counterpart. In 8.3 the kings are controlled by the people; their 'making princes' is equivalent to, perceived at the same moment as, their removal of them, and the transience, or insignificance, of the kings is such that they are unknown by God. Here the recognition that the royal appointees are worthless is coupled with the awareness of the immense distance between the people and God. The hierarchy, in which the political order is subsumed under the divine aegis, dissolves, resulting in anomie. They may not fear God, but in the absence of divine and human protectors, they are without horizons and are defenceless. That they have no king is a lie; according to 11.5, their king is Assyria.

A succession of words, oaths, covenants, the political vacuum is filled with language, whose proliferation, like that of the altars, is a sign of its emptiness. The oaths are 'vain', testifying only to the lack of fear of God. The list recalls that of 4.2, which likewise begins 'making oaths and deceiving'; structures of meaning then subvert meaning and trust. A closer relation is with 8.1-4. There the kings and princes are paired with idols, 'in order that it should be cut off'; the word for 'be cut off' (*yikkārēt*) has the same verbal root as that used here for the framing of covenants, especially the one with Yhwh, the breach of which is noted in 8.1. The covenants in our verse are usually interpreted as foreign alliances, corresponding to the diplomatic entanglements of the previous chapters; their unreliability and perfidiousness contrasts with the covenant of Yhwh. The compression, which Jeremias (1983: 129) calls 'staccato-style', imparts the intense pressure of speech and its lack of referential object; the only qualifier in the entire sequence is the adjective 'vain'.

It is consequently a surprise when the verse opens out: 'and justice will flower like poisonous weeds on the furrows of the field'. Justice presumably is equivalent to the justice which is a trap in 5.1, used for exploitation and hence injustice; the systematic inversion of values continues. We are back to the image of the land and its fruit in v. 1. If the fruit God desires is justice, and is associated with the altars in vv. 1-2, the harvest is venomous.

Verses 5 and 6, like the corresponding ones in ch. 8, concern the Golden Calf, at the centre of the house of God and subject to his wrath. In contrast to ch. 8, the fate of the calf here is exile, and a portent for that of its followers. The passage is thus parallel to 9.4-6, in which, instead of the feast of Yhwh, the people eat the bread of mourning in Assyria. As many commentators note, v. 5 especially is characterized by an insistent inversion of terms. Bethel, which literally means 'the House of God', has become Beth-Awen, the house of wickedness or folly (cf. 4.15; 5.8); its devotees, instead of dreading it, dread for it; its priests have become idol priests; the normal word for 'exult' (*yāgîlû*) has turned to grief.

The inset passage begins with an anomalous feminine plural, 'For the calves of Beth-Awen'. There was only one calf at Bethel, which is always described as masculine, as it is in 8.5; as the verse continues, moreover, its gender and number are normalized. Some critics are constrained to see here an abstraction, as it were, 'calfishness' (Jeremias 1983: 127; Rudolph 1996: 196). Andersen and Freedman (1980: 555) see it as a plural of majesty.

In contrast, Ben Zvi (2005: 212) suggests that the feminization is polemical.

As in 8.5-6, the nexus between the calf and Samaria is emphasized by the latter's particular devotion: 'For the calves of Beth-Awen, the resident(s) of Samaria show dread'. Their sacred awe obviously contrasts with their fearlessness of Yhwh in v. 3; the calf and Yhwh are antonyms, contradicting their continuity in official ideology. The word for 'resident(s)' is in the singular, but governs a plural verb; it may be taken as a collective term for the inhabitants of Samaria, or as a title for its king, in parallel with the mention of the king of Samaria in v. 7. Similarly, v. 4 could refer interchangeably to the people or the succession of kings, without substantial difference of meaning. But the word from which 'resident' ($š^ekan$) derives also has divine connotations, and is used repeatedly for Yhwh's indwelling. Yhwh's presence is transferred to the calf; indeed, some critics hold that 'the one who indwells in Samaria' is an appellation of Yhwh, in tandem with the calf, and thus the object of the verb 'dread' (Utzschneider 1980: 116; Andersen and Freedman 1980: 556).

In v. 8 'the high places of Awen' are laid waste; like the 'calves' in v. 5, the word for high places is feminine plural, and like them, it is anomalous, since high places are associated with local cults, while Bethel was the state sanctuary. Local cults are also represented by the 'altars' and 'pillars' of vv. 1-2; altars reappear in parallel to 'high places' in v. 8. Thorns and thistles grow over them; comparably, Yhwh breaks the altars which correspond to the fruit of the land in v. 2, and poisonous weeds grow in the furrows. In the ring composition of vv. 1-8, v. 8 repeats the identification of periphery and centre, the transformation of the house of God into that of Wickedness or Folly, and the agricultural metaphor of vv. 1-4.

The thorns and thistles that grow on the altars recollect the prickles and briars that take possession of the inhabitants' tents in 9.6. (Hebrew is blessed with a large number of synonyms for 'thorn', of which Hosea takes full advantage. At least five words for 'thorn' appear in this short text. Their exact identification is unknown.) These diverse thorns complete the set of parallels between ch. 9 and vv. 1-8. The central image of mourning over the abandoned or desecrated cult common to the first part of both chapters is intensified by the ironic and complex play on the word $yāgîlû$ ('exult'), which is likewise shared by both of them. The 'idolatrous priests' of the calf 'exult' ($yāgîlû$) over its glory, presumably as they are accustomed to do, fulfilling their role, in their own eyes, as orthodox ministers of Yhwh. (Many critics propose a secondary meaning of 'show distress' for *yāgîlû*; as Ben Zvi 2005 remarks, the anomalous use of the verb communicates conceptual incoherence.) Their rejoicing, however, has a bitter taste, since its glory 'has been exiled from it'. It is immediately replaced, however, by the word *gālâ*, 'exiled'; the word play suggests rejoicing suddenly cut off, or a grieving for that which is banished. *Gālâ*, however, is also a pun, since it may mean 'to uncover'. In that case, the motif of exposure, associated in the Hebrew Bible with sexual shame, combines with that of captivity.

In 9.1 Israel is admonished not to rejoice to exultation (*gîl*) 'like the peoples'; here the rejoicing by the 'idolatrous priests' exemplifies cultic assimilation. Some propose an echo of ritual lamentation for the dying-and-rising god (Jeremias 1983: 130; Sweeney 2000: 105). The joy over the deceptive harvest in 9.1-2 corresponds to that over Israel's luxuriant vine in v. 1. In 9.15 the word *gîl* recurs in the name of the covenant site, Gilgal, which has become the scene of God's hate. Furthermore, the exiled glory of the calf correlates with the glory of Ephraim that flies away in 9.10.

The relationship of the two chapters may be schematized as follows:

Chapter 9	Chapter 10
v. 1 *gîl* over the harvest	vv. 1-2 Israel as luxuriant vine
vv. 4-6 Exile, mourning	vv. 5-6 Exile, mourning, *gîl*
v. 6 Thorns growing over tents	v. 8 Thorns growing over altars
v. 10 Their glory flies away	v. 5 Glory exiled

The visions are nevertheless very different. In ch. 9 the focus is on the people, the children, and the prophet; in ch. 10 it is on the priests and the calf. Chapter 10 is a reversal of ch. 9: the calf is exiled, not the people. The motif of the return to Egypt disappears; Assyria is the sole hostile power. The prediction that the people will subsist in the land without political or sacred institutions is reminiscent of ch. 3, with which there are several lexical and conceptual correlations (Jeremias 1983: 128).

In v. 6 the calf is brought to Assyria; the title 'King Contentious' has already been encountered in 5.13. This, it appears, is the culmination of the search for healing that began there, and was maintained through the love gifts of 7.11 and 8.9. The word for 'present' (*minḥâ*) suggests appeasement, and is a technical term for meal-offerings to Yhwh. The idol itself, the image of God, becomes an offering to the Great King, confirming his suzerainty; the fractious epithet offers little hope for the success of the gift. The confession or establishment of guilt in v. 2, for which Yhwh hopes in 5.15, is only accomplished by the deliverance of the object of guilt; the offence—the courting of Assyria—is also the cure.

Israel experiences shame, as the corollary of the acknowledgement of guilt; the phrase is repeated, without much variation in meaning. The amplification has a conclusive effect; this is the consequence of the preceding developments. 'Israel is abashed because of its policy', the latter term encompassing the words, oaths and negotiations of v. 4, that have proved futile.

After this summary, the last two verses of the tableau are an appendix, detailing the results of the desolation and shame. Verse 7 returns to the fate of Samaria and its king. In Hebrew the two entities are abruptly juxtaposed, suggesting the violence of the image. This is intensified by two puns. The first, with which the verse begins, combines the meanings of 'perished' and 'compared'. 'Perished is Samaria, its king' may also be 'Compared is Samaria, its king, to a chip upon the water'. The simultaneity of comparison and dissolution enacts the transitoriness and insubstantiality of the king and capital. No sooner are they imagined than they disappear. This is confirmed by the simile, 'like a chip (or, foam) upon the waters'. However, the word for 'chip' or 'foam'—since, in this sense, it only occurs here, its exact sense is uncertain—normally means 'wrath'. Water effaces all disturbance; one may suspect a proverbial background for this expression. Wrath and power amount to a chip—or froth—that is carried away by the water.

The chip, in turn, may be linked with the thorns and thistles that grow upon the altars, the aftermath of abandonment. But these, as I have already suggested, echo Adam's fate in Gen. 3.18. It is a post-Edenic landscape; instead of the offerings that are normally made upon the altars, thorns rise up upon them. The verb 'to rise up' also means 'to offer' (cf. Jeremias 1983: 131). Altars were situated on hills and mountains, whither the spirit of promiscuity drove Israel to engage in hedonistic sacrifice in 4.11-14; conversely, they desire these hills and mountains to fall upon them. The motif of burial is transferred from Egypt, in 9.6, to Israel itself.

150 *Hosea 10*

So far, we have found that the calf is metaphorically linked with the altars, through the use of the verb *'ārap*, 'break the neck'. The altars express gratitude for the fertility of the land; cult and political order are symbolized by cultivation. The furrows of the fields produce poisonous weeds instead of corn, injustice instead of justice. Reciprocally, weeds grow on the altars.

(9) From the days of Gibeah, you have sinned, O Israel; there they stood; would not war overtake them at Gibeah, against the sons of iniquity?

(10) In my desire when I would chastise them, and nations would be gathered against them, in their being bound up, because of their two transgressions.

(11) Yet Ephraim was a trained heifer, who loved to thresh; and I passed over the goodness of her neck. I would ride Ephraim, Judah would plough, Jacob would prepare the field.

(12) Sow for yourselves in righteousness; reap in *hesed*; till for yourself tillage. It is time to seek Yhwh until he should come and rain down righteousness for you.

(13) You have ploughed wickedness; you have reaped miscreance; you have eaten the fruit of deceit, for you have trusted in your ways, in your many troops.

(14) Tumult shall rise up against your people; all your fortresses shall be ransacked, as Shalman sacked Beth-Arbel on the day of war, mother dashed to pieces over her children.

(15) Thus will he do to you, Bethel, because of your great evil. At dawn the king of Israel shall indeed be destroyed.

'From the days of Gibeah' introduces the second part or tableau of the chapter with another retrospective. Like 9.10, it locates the origins of Israel's sin. In contrast to 9.10, however, the primal sin is incurred in the land instead of on its threshold. Furthermore, 'from the days of Gibeah' matches 9.9, in which Israel is corrupted 'as in the days of Gibeah', in the context of conflict in the house of Yhwh. Centre and periphery, archetypal alienation outside the land and disintegration within it, are metaphorical counterparts, and transpose one into the other. As we have seen, Gibeah and Egypt are also correlates; return to Egypt is consequent upon depravity like that of Gibeah. Our verse matches the previous one, at least lexically; Gibeah corresponds to 'hills'

($g^eb\bar{a}$'$\hat{o}t$), while 'You have sinned, O Israel' parallels 'the sin of Israel'. 'The sin of Israel' explicates 'the high places of Awen'; the latter may refer, as we have seen, both to the cult of the high places, and hence the local shrines on hills and mountains, and to the central sanctuary in Bethel. Bethel, the house of God, is not necessarily the house of Yhwh in ch. 9. Nevertheless, the two polemics counterpoint each other. The calf may well be the cause of God's being an object of enmity. The culmination of the passage, whose horror is magnified through being unspoken, only imagined through the speech of the victims as the obverse of their preferred fate that the land should collapse on its inhabitants, infuses eschatology with origins, the 'hills' with Gibeah.

The sin of Gibeah, like that of Baal Peor, combines sexual crime with a vengeful war of extermination. Gibeah, however, differs from the story of Baal Peor as a civil war resulting from rape. Moreover, none of the parties involved acts honourably. Gibeah has already figured in 5.8, where the affirmation of Benjamin, the exterminated tribe in Judges 19–21, contrasts with the desolation of Ephraim in 5.9. The transfer of the semantics of Gibeah to Israel as a whole, with its convergence of sexuality with violence, is already anticipated.

Verses 9-10 are among the most recondite in the book. Most translations and interpretations are the result of emendation and guesswork, which I will not attempt to emulate. The Gibeah story seems to be imagined at a point before hostilities have begun, when the Benjaminites are still confident that war will not reach them. (Sweeney 2000: 107 thinks it refers to their actual survival.) It thus attracts the irony of hindsight. God declares that he will chastise and bind them; his will is coordinated with the gathering of the peoples, who are accordingly equivalent to the tribes in Judges 20. Alliteration links the words for 'I will chastise them' ('$ess^or\bar{e}m$) with 'their binding' ('$osr\bar{a}m$) and 'they will be gathered' ($uss^ep\hat{u}$); there is some correlation between the end of v. 10 and the equally obscure conclusion of 7.12, in which God, in the guise of a fowler, 'binds' or 'chastises' Ephraim 'like a rumour to their assembly'.

In v. 11 a new image is introduced: Ephraim as a docile and willing calf. Like 9.10, it is a nostalgic retrospective, that contrasts God's hopes for Israel with their disappointment. God chanced upon the calf, and used it for his service. The calf clearly is the contrary of the Golden Calf in vv. 5-6, as well as previous animal images for Israel. As a symbol for Ephraim, it contrasts with the Golden Calf as the symbol for Samaria and its rebellion against God. The calf is 'trained'; its training corresponds to the teaching and knowledge of God whose rejection and neglect is otherwise lamented. It loves to thresh: such love is the antithesis of love elsewhere in the book, in particular the love on threshing floors in 9.1. Some critics (e.g. Jeremias 1983: 134) hold that the calf likes its work because it can feed on the grain (cf. Deut. 25.4), but this limits the scope of the love to self-interest, as well as ignoring the idealization of pristine Ephraim that is the point of the scene. The love complements the training and suggests affection for its master, hope for a reward, pleasure in its exercise. A plough horse might similarly be imagined to enjoy ploughing. It may be that threshing is easy work (Rudolph 1966: 202), preceding the calf's initiation into hard field labour; nevertheless, one would suppose that it would follow the harvest and that the calf's training would encompass all its activities. That threshing is specified as an activity the calf loves perhaps encapsulates a particular moment of bovine felicity. There may also be an association with friskiness, since the calf could tread freely on the threshing floor.

God 'passed over' the goodness of her neck; the word 'goodness' recalls the 'goodness' of the land in v. 1. (I translate 'goodness' literally; most commentators interpret as 'fine' or 'well-formed'. Similarly, 'passing over' may mean that God chanced upon the calf, as in 9.10 [Macintosh 1997: 408] or placed a halter on it.) If the goodness of the neck is a synecdoche for Ephraim's goodness at its inception, Ephraim and its land are complementary; the good calf works the land, whose fruitfulness is thus assured. In vv. 1-2 the goodness and fruitfulness are transformed into altars and standing stones. God breaks the neck of the altars, which are metaphorically correlated with the Calf of vv. 5-6. In 8.3 Israel rejects 'goodness'; in 8.5, the Calf adumbrates that rejection (see above, pp. 118-19). Correspondingly, in 12.12 the altars become like heaps 'on the furrows of the field'; the same phrase, 'on the furrows of the field' occurs, as we have seen, in v. 4. The ruined altars have multiplied on the fields in which justice is turned into injustice. In contrast, the calf in vv. 11-12 is set to prepare land whose harvest is a metaphor for moral order ($ṣ^e dāqâ$) and goodness ($ḥesed$), though with equally disastrous results (v. 13).

The goodness or beauty of the calf's neck is difficult to explicate aesthetically or morally. It is, however, a focusing device, which concentrates our attention on God's passage; we experience the strength, sleekness and suppleness of the neck through God's eyes and perhaps God's hands. This mandates understanding the verb as 'pass over' rather than 'pass by', 'spare', etc., and the following verb, *'arkîb*, in its normal sense of 'I will ride', in contradistinction to most critics and translations (e.g. Macintosh 1997: 418, 'harness'). The image of God riding the calf recalls the disavowed function of the Golden Calf as God's pedestal, as well as God riding clouds (Ps. 68.5; Isa. 19.1) or cherubim (Ps. 18.11). The task of representing God's presence in the world is transferred from the calf to the people.

The triad Ephraim–Judah–Jacob recollects the pairing of Ephraim and Judah in chs. 5–6. Ephraim and Judah may be equivalent, yoked together in the plough team. Ephraim, however, could be God's vehicle, while Judah ploughs alongside it, or Judah may direct the plough. The ambiguity corresponds to that which informs the relationship of Ephraim and Judah throughout the book: they are mirror images. Judah is the junior partner, but also the possible survivor. The third member of the team, Jacob, as the common parent of the two kingdoms, lends probity to their equivalence; Israel is the instrument of God's cultivation. On the other hand, there may be a progression, from Ephraim to Judah to Jacob. This would depend on whether the verb usually translated 'harrow' is simply parallel to 'plough' or implies a separate agricultural activity. (It occurs only three times in the Hebrew Bible, and in Isa. 28.25 it is also parallel to 'plough'.) Two wordplays also link this passage to previous ones concerning the calf. The first, the pun between *ḥāraš*, 'craftsman' in 8.6, and *ḥāraš*, 'plough', has already been discussed (p. 118). The second is the alliteration between *yᵉsaddēd*, 'to prepare a field', and *yᵉšōdēd*, 'to destroy' in v. 2. Once again the two halves of the chapter reflect each other. The field that Jacob should have tilled is covered with the debris of altars and pillars. In 12.12, this image is juxtaposed with Jacob's flight to 'the field of Aram', a prototype of exile.

In v. 12 the bucolic retrospective merges with the present, as the divine narrative is replaced by prophetic imperatives and the immediacy suggested by 'it is time to seek Yhwh'. Sowing and reaping, righteousness and kindness (*ḥesed*), follow each other; natural rhythms are coordinated with those of proper human relations. It is rare indeed for Hosea to have any positive proposals, even if the vision is countermanded in the next verse.

There is a possibility of change that may avert catastrophe. Comparable to this verse is 12.6, in which similar ethical imperatives are juxtaposed with God's speech to Jacob in the now corrupted theophanous site of Bethel. Here the field that Jacob prepares is elaborated allegorically, without losing its literal reference; both the first two phrases are accordingly ambiguous. Righteousness and kindness may be the seed and the harvest, or the principles by which the land is farmed. The superimposition of a benevolent social order on agricultural well-being is reminiscent of the false pastoral of vv. 1-2, and the vacuity of language and politics in v. 4. Instead of duplicitous oaths and covenants, there are relations of kindness and righteousness; the injustice that is like poison on the fields is transformed into the justice based on $ṣ^ed\bar{a}q\hat{a}$ or 'righteousness', with which it is paired in 2.21.

In ch. 8 the scene with the Golden Calf is followed by a passage concerning sowing and reaping, characterized by the interruption of time, and dispersal on the wind; rhyme emphasizes discontinuity. Here the antithetic metaphor of the calf as Ephraim is succeeded by one of sowing and reaping in which time is an ally; correspondence between sowing and reaping is matched by one between the righteousness which is sown and that which God 'pours down' or 'teaches', between the human search and the divine response. Rhyme, between 'sow' ($zir'\hat{u}$), 'reap' ($qiṣr\hat{u}$) and 'till' ($nîr\hat{u}$), sustains divine and human harmony, and contrasts with the loquaciousness of v. 4, introduced by the same rhyme, $dibb^er\hat{u}$, 'they speak'.

The exhortation recalls that of 6.1-3, and the ensuing reflection on $ḥesed$, God's desire, and the role of the prophet. In 6.1-3, the people determine to return to Yhwh, whose response, they believe, is as inevitable as the rain and the dawn. Here the same image recurs, with the same pun between 'pour' and 'teach' ($yōreh$), except that the word 'righteousness' ($ṣedeq$) is added. The penitents in 6.1-3 simply want to return to their familiar world; they are happy to pursue knowledge of God—or to claim that they will do it—without intrinsic change (see above, p. 87). The prophet, as part of the succession of prophets, and in particular as an avatar of Samuel, exposes the inadequacy of their overture. As we have seen, he also changes the prophetic message. Ṣedeq may also mean 'vindication'; that God will 'rain/teach' righteousness not only supposes a transformation of human action, but a correspondence between this and external affairs. If, in 6.4, God despairs over the transitoriness of Ephraim's and

Judah's affections and loyalties, in the context of their rivalry, here his hope is predicated on their partnership.

Fairness, the Golden Rule, and natural justice are approximate equivalents or illustrations of ṣᵉdāqâ or ṣedeq (there is no clear semantic differentiation between these forms, though the first is feminine and the second is masculine). On this basis, ḥesed may be established, implying both loyalty and gratuitous goodwill. The sequence culminates in 'Till for yourselves tillage' (my translation attempts to preserve the duplication of the Hebrew words nîrû 'till' and nîr, 'tillage'). Most commentators understand this to refer to breaking up fallow ground, but the object is much more likely to be the field that Jacob cultivates in v. 11, since it is the same land, infused with the same qualities. Ṣᵉdāqâ or ḥesed are not a new message; the repetition of the word 'till' suggests a recurrent process.

In 2.21, ṣedeq and ḥesed introduce complementary pairs of attributes with which Yhwh betroths Israel. The betrothal is accompanied by God's answering the heavens, by the gifts of rain, fertility, and compassion. Verse 12 expands on and diffuses this vision; God's gift of righteousness and fertility is preceded by its cultivation, by historical and prophetic toil. It may adumbrate the prophet's message, whose apparent vagueness is only diminished when delineated against everything that is not righteous and benevolent: the calf, the kingdom, and their attendant evils.

Verse 13 either expresses the disappointment of God's hopes, if v. 12 is taken to be a repetition of the original charge to Israel, or the background against which change is still possible. The fruit of deceit recalls the fruit whose yield was expected in v. 1, as well as the deceptive new wine in 9.2. Those who eat of the fruit of deceit are themselves liable to be deceived.

The last verses revert to the theme of war. The fruit of deceit is explicated by Israel's trust in its way and in the multitude of its warriors. Military strength corresponds to the altars as well as the fruit of v. 1, but also to the proliferation of fortresses in 8.14. In v. 14 the fortresses return, and are likewise faced with destruction, as are the pillars of v. 2. In 8.14 the fortresses are paired with the altars and are evidence for Israel's amnesia, just as trust in one's own way and resources disavows the divine direction of v. 11 and the reciprocity of v. 12.

The identity of Shalman is unknown, as is the location of Beth-Arbel, and its exemplary sack. Shalman may be an abbreviation of Shalmaneser V (727–722 BCE), corresponding to the Assyrian monarch to whom the calf is delivered in v. 6. In favour of this possibility is his actual destruction of Samaria; he would make a fit subject for v. 15. Alternatively, he may be identical with a contemporary Moabite king of that name. (For a sceptical discussion of various proposals, see Ben Zvi 2005: 219.) The contemporary allusion matches the paradigmatic sin and annihilation of Gibeah; the day of war has already arrived, and mothers are shattered with their children. The latter image, isolated in its horror, recalls 9.13 and 14. With its compression of the image of maternal love with the terror of infants, the mother's desire to protect her children, and murderous glee, the detail is transferred directly to the conquest of Samaria in 14.1. It corresponds to, and fulfils, God's rejection of wife and children in ch. 2; the sadistic fantasy of that chapter is realized in human violence.

After this, the prediction of the fate of king and cult in v. 15 is anticlimactic. Their juxtaposition corresponds to that of the king of Samaria with the high places of Awen in vv. 7-8. The verb applied to the king, 'to be destroyed/compared', also links the two passages, with the same double meaning. No sooner is he thought of than he vanishes. The true name of Bethel is evoked for the first time; the house of Iniquity or Folly is revealed as the house of God at the moment of its destruction. Complementarily, as Rudolph (1966: 207) points out, the feeble king is poignantly entitled 'king of Israel'. The conclusiveness of the doom, and the verse, is emphasized by two parallel doubled words: Bethel is laid waste literally because of 'the evil of its evil'; the verb 'to be destroyed/compared' is repeated, a familiar mode of intensification. Only one word stands out: 'at dawn'. In 6.3, Israel expected God's advent to be as assured as the dawn; the dawn, as we have seen, is a figure for possible salvation. Here it portends Israel's utter destruction.

Hosea 11

(1) When Israel was a lad, I loved him, and from Egypt I called my son.
(2) They called to them, and so they walked before them; they sacrificed to the Baals, they burned incense to idols.
(3) And I—I cared for Ephraim, taking him in my arms; and they did not know that I healed them.
(4) With bonds of humanity I would lead them, with cords of love, and I was for them as those who lift up the yoke from their jaws, and I inclined to him, I gave him to eat.
(5) He will not return to the land of Egypt, and Assyria, he is his king; for they have refused to return.
(6) And the sword will whirl in his cities and destroy his boasts, and consume, because of his policies.
(7) And my people are dependent on my turning away, and they call above; altogether he will not raise up.
(8) How can I give you over, Ephraim? How can I hand you over/defend you, O Israel? How can I give you over like Admah, make you like Zeboiim? My heart is overthrown within me, altogether my regrets are inflamed.
(9) I will not consummate the fury of my rage, I will not turn back to destroy Ephraim, for I am God and not a man, in your midst holy, and I will not come blazing.
(10) After Yhwh they will go, like a lion he will roar, indeed he will roar, and the children will come trembling from the sea.
(11) They will tremble like a bird from Egypt, like a dove from the land of Assyria, and I will make them dwell in their houses, say Yhwh.

Chapter 11 is a counterpart, and largely a reversal, of ch. 9. The correlations may be schematically presented as follows:

Chapter 9	*Chapter 11*
9.10a Discovery in the wilderness	11.1 Summons from Egypt
9.10b Primal apostasy	11.2 Primal apostasy

9.11-14 Death of children	11.1-4 Israel's infancy
9.3-6 Return to Egypt	11.5 No return to Egypt
9.14 Prophet's question (What can you give?)	11.9 God's question (How can I give?)
9.15-17 Being driven from God's house, exile	11.10-11 Return to their houses

God loves his child, Israel. The metaphor of the child communicates greater affection and kinship than that of the calf, and is less metaphorical, since we remain within the human domain, and since it accords with the assumptions of patriarchal ideology. The God of the fathers legitimates and is the ultimate paternal authority. That Israel is God's child is pervasive in the biblical tradition, especially the Exodus tradition (cf. Exod. 4.22), and as a cliché loses its metaphorical capacity to shock the imagination into a new perception. Instead, it is a root metaphor, so familiar in its assurance that it becomes an article of faith, part of the structural underpinning of the world. In the context of the salvific paradigm of the Exodus, it imparts trust in God's commitment to us.

Hosea revitalizes the metaphor in two ways: first, through great elaboration, and second, through the problem of how it is to be understood, and how it relates to other metaphors for Israel in the book. Is Israel literally God's child, in which case it is not a metaphor at all, or God's child by adoption, as might be implied by 'from Egypt I called my son'? (Jeremias 1983: 141 points out the double meaning of the word 'called' here. See also Ben Zvi 2005: 233.) Is paternity a matter of recognition or procreation? If Israel is God's son, is the reference to creation, or to miraculous birth? In either case, whether filiation is by adoption or by descent, the boundaries between literal and metaphorical are blurred. This reflects the paradoxical dialectic of likeness and difference, immanence and transcendence, whose culmination is v. 9. If Israel is the divine seed, it originates in God, and shares his identity; if it is not, it is fundamentally alien to him.

The problem is complicated by the juxtaposition with 9.10, in which God discovers Israel like grapes in the wilderness. Bach (1952) saw in this evidence for a 'wilderness' tradition independent of the Exodus one. Despite its problems, this thesis indicates two contrary constructions of Israel's initiation. According to the one, God found Israel by serendipity on his progress in a barren world; according to the other they have always been integrally related. One formative experience is the gift of the Torah, the other is history. As we saw, in his gaze on the matrix, God perceives ancestors, who represent the passage of time as well as the propensity to depravity.

In v. 2 God's voice is immediately supplanted by another: 'they called to them'. The subject may be Israel, or the Baalim, or, in tandem with 9.10, the local inhabitants, especially women, who invited the Israelites to join in their worship. (Other possibilities include the prophets; cf. Ben Zvi 2005: 235.) Sacrifice to the Baalim and offering incense recalls the cult of the high places in 4.13-14 and the days of the Baalim in 2.15, where the same verbs are used. The association of sexual promiscuity with cultic deviance contrasts with Yhwh's summons to exclusive filial fidelity. If God is husband in ch. 2, here he is father; there is no trace of specifically maternal imagery (contrary to Schüngel-Straumann 1986: 119-34; cf. the comments of Kreutzer 1989. However, Ben Zvi 2005: 232 notes a reflex of the ancient Near Eastern image of the goddess nursing the king in v. 4). In ch. 2 the children are invited to reject their mother, paradoxically, since both are figures for the same entity. Here God's paternity lacks a maternal counterpart. If the reference is to creation, then it is one in which God has no partner, or the partner is Israel itself, for instance in annunciation scenes to the matriarchs. In 9.10, as we saw, there is a regress to uncreation. God discovers Israel as a matrix in a world that has reverted to chaos. Now creation is the adoption or begetting of a son that excludes the world and the feminine. The matrix from which Israel is extracted is Egypt and connotes oppression.

According to Jay (1992), patrilineality sustains itself through sacrifice. A transcendent birth, in the symbolic order, is held to be more consequential than natural birth. (For example, 'in Rome as in Greece, birth did not give family membership. Should the *paterfamilias* withhold his ritual recognition, legally the child did not exist' [Jay 1992: 45].) Through sacrificing to other gods, the sons are claiming an alternative genealogy for themselves. They thereby release themselves from the paternal domain, a breach emphasized by sexual transgression. If the subjects of 'they called' are women, as in the case of Baal Peor, their gravitation to them, so the comparative particle suggests, is quasi-automatic, inevitable.

In the next two verses God expands on his care for the child Israel, and hence its ingratitude. Reminiscence, however, is as liable to revive past emotions as to stir up anger. God teaches

Ephraim how to walk and guides it through the wilderness (the very rare form *tirgaltî* is usually taken to mean either 'I taught to walk' [NRSV] or 'I led, conducted, drove'; cf. Daniels 1990: 63 and the discussion in Macintosh 1997: 442-43). He either takes it by the arm or in his arms, depending on whether one adopts the Septuagint or the Masoretic text. In the former case, there is a complementary relationship between legs and arms; in the latter, guiding and enabling it to take their first steps in the world is eidetically compressed with the still greater dependence of being carried. One can imagine God patiently accompanying Ephraim and picking it up when it tired. The former reading permits a comparison with 7.15, in which God strengthened Ephraim's arms in the context of military training; directing Ephraim's wanderings and making it self-sufficient are coordinated processes. The latter, conversely, infantilizes Israel, recalling imagery of passivity and ease, such as the eagles' wings on which God alleges he bore Israel (Exod. 19.4; Deut. 32.11). The last phrase, 'they did not know that I healed them', disrupts the nostalgia with an outburst of grievance; it corresponds to v. 2 and the end of v. 5, Israel's rejection of God and seduction by Baal. Temporally, it would refer to Israel's entire history, with its succession of reverses and recoveries, rather than to the wilderness period (Neef 1987: 91, however, refers to God's promise to heal Israel in Exod. 15.26, as well as to the healing of Miriam in Num. 12.13). It does, however, raise the possibility of exculpation, as in 2.10; that they are ignorant mitigates their guilt. In 5.13, in their ignorance that God is their healer, they send to the king of Assyria, paradoxically for a cure from the malignity that God has become (5.12). Now Assyria has assumed sovereignty over them (v. 5), and is the land of morbidity (9.3-4). But the paired voracious similes for God in 5.12 and 5.14, and his dismissal of their plea for healing in 6.1, are countered by the image of his tenderness in v. 4 that recollects his vacillation in 5.15. The reversal of ch. 5 in ch. 11 is completed by the transformation in the significance of the lion in v. 10.

He draws them 'with bonds of humanity, with cords of love'. The love is either that of God—as in v. 1—which attempts to draw Israel to him, or, conversely, their love which attracts them to him. The first would correspond to God's desire, of which Israel is willy-nilly the object; the second would suggest that the bonds are love, that will and constraint are identical. 'Humanity' and 'love' are parallel terms; for the third time the word 'humanity' (*'ādām*) appears, but this time not in the context of guilt or loss, but of love; it is love of which human bonds are composed. If it is God who is the subject of love, his love has a human quality, and anticipates antithetically his assertion in v. 9 that he is not human, precisely in his compassion. God's expectations, his wish that the bonds be indissoluble, conflict with our knowledge from the rest of the book that Israel's love is liable to be abominable (9.10), and the parallel between God's desire to be magnetically attractive, suggested by the verb 'draw' (cf. Song 1.4), and the call of the Baalim in v. 2.

The word for 'bond' (*ḥebel*) is virtually identical with that for 'pain' (*ḥēbel*), as in the birthpangs in 13.13 (Sweeney 2000: 114). Jeremias (1983: 141) suggests that chastisements will be human; in other words, God will not exercise his full wrath. A similar idiom occurs in 2 Sam. 7.14, in which God promises not to renege on the Davidic covenant, whatever the provocation. If the healing of v. 3 encompasses Israel's history, v. 4 interprets its crises as chastisements, whose moderation is a sign of love and of God's corrective will. The bond between God and Israel conceals a history of pain. As in 6.5, the old remedies—the succession of retributive prophets, the alternation of tribulation and reparation—have exhausted themselves. Between the image of the past in v. 4 and the future envisaged in v. 5 there is, it seems, a complete rupture.

The 'bonds' and 'cords', as in Isa. 5.18, reintroduce the idea of a cart, and hence of Israel as a farm animal. The next phrase is interpreted in two ways, depending on whether one reads the crucial word as 'yoke' (*'ōl*), with the Masoretic text, or 'infant' (*'ûl*), with various recent commentators. The two possibilities— infant and calf, lifting up affectionately and removing the yoke—can play suggestively against each other, without necessitating a decision. The last phrase in the verse, 'And I inclined to him, I gave to eat', is amplified by another pun, since the word for 'I inclined' may also mean 'slow' or 'gentle', implying patience and tenderness.

Verse 5 is a surprise, at least in Hebrew, which literally reads 'he shall not return to the land of Egypt', directly contradicting 9.3 and 6, as well as vv. 10-11. (For defences of the Masoretic text here, see Macintosh 1997: 450-52; Ben Zvi 2005: 230-31.) Contradiction is pervasive in Hosea, in which alternative futures are juxtaposed, in particular exile and destruction. The contradiction here duplicates that between the different fates of the calf in 8.6 and 10.5. Rhetorically, the opposition between our verse and 9.3 suggests that the two passages should be read in conjunction, preparing us for God's change of mind in vv. 8-9. In 9.3, Egypt and Assyria are in apposition, though Assyria's dominance is indicated by the greater attention granted to it. In 9.6, Egypt provides no ultimate refuge from death. Our verse is then climactic, since not only is Egypt an inadequate asylum, but it will no longer be available. The polarity of Egypt and Assyria disappears, and the attempt to play them off against each other consequently proves worthless or treasonous. If in 8.13, as in 9.3, return to Egypt is a punishment for sin, undoing the entire history of God and Israel, here it represents mitigation of calamity.

The inability to return to Egypt is justified by their refusal to return to Yhwh, enclosing the central recognition, that 'Assyria is its king'. The three part structure corresponds to that of 10.3, in which the assertion that they have no king, and that the king is impotent, encloses the recognition that they do not fear God. In lieu of the fear of God, they are subjected to Assyrian rule. The inability either to go back to origins or to the one who called them thence results in paralysis.

From the stillness a sword whirls, consuming cities and speech alike; the counsels of which Israel is ashamed in 10.6 now lead to its destruction. (I take the central term $badd\bar{a}yw$ to mean 'his boasts' with Wolff 1974: 192 [cf. Job 11.3; 41.4]. Other proposals are 'villages', 'bolts', and 'oracle priests'.) The verbs flow into each other: 'whirl' ($h\bar{a}l\hat{a}$), 'destroy' ($kill^et\hat{a}$) and 'consume' ($'\bar{a}k\bar{a}l\hat{a}$) alliterate impressively. The word for 'whirl', like that for 'bonds', may also signify birthpangs; the sword—a feminine subject in Hebrew—travails with death. Nourishment is in fact destruction.

Verse 7 is again full of difficulties. The first phrase, 'and my people are dependent on my turning away ($m^e\check{s}\hat{u}b\bar{a}t\hat{i}$)', plays on the recurrent word 'return' ($\check{s}\hat{u}b$), which adumbrates the theme of the possibility of change. The word $m^e\check{s}\hat{u}ba$ usually means turning back or backsliding. Here it could either refer to Israel—so critics usually understand it—or to God. The context, however, would lead us to expect the opposite, that Israel would be dependent on God turning back *to* them, or vice versa (indeed, Rudolph 1966: 211, does propose this as a possible interpretation). Then their prayer amounts to apostasy, a familiar theme in the book, or, if God is the subject, his reconciliation is a self-betrayal. In either case, values are volatile; the same term can alternate between opposite meanings. This contributes to the extreme tension of the verse, in which the bond between God and Israel, communicated through the affective term 'my people', spans an incommensurable gap.

In 7.16, the people 'return, but not above'. There their speech is compared to a deceitful bow, whose arrows fall back on itself. The epithet 'above' recurs in our verse, and, as in 7.16, their words fail to carry across the distance. The voices of the boasts and counsels of v. 6, like those of the princes' scoffing in 7.16, are reduced to an inaudible cry for help, in a land whose devastation corresponds to that of its speech. The last phrase is also ambiguous. It may be Yhwh who does not raise up: some see the word *yaḥad*, 'altogether', as a divine epithet, corresponding to *'al*, 'above' (Andersen and Freedman 1980: 587, repoint it as *Yāḥîd*, 'The Only One'). Alternatively, it may be they who through their combined efforts cannot exalt Yhwh. On either reading, the distance between the transcendent, adduced by the vague substantive, 'above', and human abasement seems insurmountable.

In v. 1 Yhwh calls his son from Egypt, in a primary act of liberation, but they follow after other voices and invoke the Baalim. Now they call to him in their extremity. The parallel between the two parts of the chapter is endorsed by an echo of v. 4. In v. 4 Yhwh says that he was to them 'as those who lift up (or off) a yoke/infant upon (*or* from on) their jaws/cheeks'. The sequence *'ōl* (or *'ûl*) *'al* , 'yoke/infant upon' is almost identical with *'el 'al*, 'to above'. The intimacy supposed by the image of lifting up a child, and Yhwh's benevolence in removing the yoke of oppressors and/or replacing it with his own yoke, his partnership with Ephraim in the plough-team of 10.11-12, contrasts with, and subtends, the abjection that cannot be raised and the height that cannot be attained.

Verse 8 is the turning point. God's self-questioning, nominally addressed to Ephraim, allows us access to a divine disquiet which belies the unity of purpose suggested by the word *yaḥad*, 'in unison', if it applies to God, and his inaccessibility. Our induction to his thoughts, like his knowledge of the voices that cannot be heard by him, collapses the distance imposed by the previous verse. Yhwh's self-reflection corresponds to that of 6.5: 'What shall I do with you, Ephraim? What shall I do with you, Judah?' If, in 6.5, Yhwh's complaint is that Israel's *ḥesed* is transitory, so much the more would destruction negate Yhwh's own *ḥesed*. To the prophet's question in 9.14, 'What can you give?', and his prayer for a bereaving womb, Yhwh responds, 'How can I give?' The gift, which should be a sign of divine generosity, is death; correlatively, the verb in the parallel clause, 'how can I hand you over', would normally mean 'to defend'. God would be countermanding his own nature as benefactor and protector. 'How can I give you?', to translate literally, leaves the receiver undetermined: it could be death, anticipating the protagonist of 13.14, or the Assyrians. Idiomatically, 'to give' in Hebrew may introduce a simile, a fantasy of transformation. This function is foregrounded in the second part of the verse: 'how can I give you over/make you like Admah...?' It raises the possibility of continued existence which is immediately withdrawn: the unstated complement of 'how can I make you?' in the first clause is 'like death' or 'annihilation', of which Admah is an emblem.

Prophet and God are seemingly in dialogue with each other, yet each is talking to himself of his own incapacity. Yhwh cannot respond to the request for a bereaving womb and dry breasts, yet his confusion matches the prophet's, recognizes the impulse of desire for intercession undercut by despair. The conflation of birth and death, desire and destruction, is common to both protagonists, who mirror each other in their speech. It results in a lapse of poetic language, concomitant with the emptiness of the boasts and counsels of the people in v. 6 and the impotence of their prayers in v. 7. The work of the imagination, producing similes, can only express disfiguration, the failure of meaning. Only through poetry, of the utmost tension and ambiguity, can the crisis in poetry be addressed. These antinomies will become most acute in 13.14.

Admah and Zeboiim are the junior partners of Sodom and Gomorrah, only here referred to independently in the Hebrew Bible. As throughout the prophets, the cities of the plain are paradigms for Israel's wickedness and divine retribution. The citation corresponds to the allusion to the Flood in 4.1-3, at the beginning of the central section of the book. Both names are significant. Admah correlates with *'ādām*, 'human being', in v. 4, and is almost identical with the word for 'earth' or 'ground' (*ᵃdāmâ*) from which Adam was taken, while Zeboiim approximates *ṣᵉbā'ôt*, 'hosts', human or celestial armies (uniquely, it is spelt here with an Aleph— *ṣᵉbō'ôim*—making the correspondence closer; it seems to be simply a variant plural). The human bonds with which Yhwh draws Israel, and the equivalence between humanity and love, are reversed in the figure for utter desolation. The former represents Yhwh as bound to humanity and as human in his love, the latter as creating a void. Zeboiim substitutes for a momentary image of multitudes one of vacuity. Like the verb $^{a}maggen^{e}k\hat{a}$ in the first part of the verse, it combines a primary meaning of defence with one of surrender. Interestingly, the two words are in parallel, with a similar double meaning, in Isa. 31.4, a chapter which, as Eidevall (1993) shows, is closely related to ours.

Yhwh's heart is 'overthrown', or literally 'turned upside down'. The same verb is used, as Fisch notes (1988: 142), for the destruction of Sodom and Gomorrah (Gen. 19.25, 29). The fate of Sodom and Gomorrah, and consequently that of Israel, wreaks equal havoc within God. The overturning of the divine heart, coordinated with the word $nih\hat{u}m\bar{a}y$, which means 'regrets' or 'changes of mind' as well as 'compassions' (Janzen 1982: 31), suggests alternation in Yhwh's psyche between wrath and remorse, a temporary exclusion of the fierce anger of v. 9. Its disunity, emphasized by the inchoate plural, is countered by a tendency towards integration: the word $yah\!ad$, 'in unison, together', couples this verse with the previous one. The concentration of Yhwh's warmth responds to the people's collective incapacity. The metaphor of heat imparts an intensification of energy that neutralizes the rage that would otherwise follow, likewise communicated through entirely conventional incendiary imagery.

Verse 9 is one of the strangest in the book. Yhwh will not return to destroy Ephraim, just as the latter will not return to Egypt. Yhwh's estrangement from Ephraim is also one from himself; he will not act on his anger. The distance is equated with that between God and humanity. To be divine is to have self-control, while humans are creatures of impulse, or, alternatively, God admits second thoughts, while humans are inflexible. The insistence on difference correlates with the incommensurable transcendence of v. 7, as opposed to the exposition of God's humanity carefully developed through the analogy with a parent. It is, however, immediately controverted by the following phrase: 'in your midst holy'. God's transcendence—the otherness signified by 'holy'—is his immanence. If God is in our midst, he cannot come back to destroy us, at least not without destroying himself.

The furious energy he holds back with the warmth of compassion is then in us also.

The argument that God is not human is found also in Samuel's speech to Saul in 1 Sam. 15.29. There, however, it is adduced as evidence for God's intractability, his immunity to changes of mind or pity. The remorse or regrets (*nihûmîm*) stirred up in v. 8 are specifically denied him. As we found in discussing 6.6, Hosea is a latter-day Samuel who reverses his message.

The last two verses switch from the immanence of God and the threat of destruction in the land to exile and return. Distance is imposed in v. 10 by a lapse in first-person speech and in v. 11 by the concluding formula, 'says Yhwh'. The return of the exiles is the outer manifestation of God's unification of his desires, since he returns from exile, together with his people. As in previous instances, the vision of hope is unstable and fleeting; God's change of mind is subject to further revolutions. Nevertheless, its prominence at the end of the major sections, as well as its occultation for the previous chapters, contributes a sense of ultimacy and authority despite disappointment. Although every promise of redemption, even ch. 14, must be undercut with scepticism, there is a possibility of an ending, turning back from the terrors and follies of history.

This is indicated by an inversion of imagery. In 5.14, God presents himself as a devouring lion. Now he is a lion whose roars presage deliverance, a symbol of pride and power rather than ferocity. In 7.11-12 Ephraim is a witless dove flying backwards and forwards between Assyria and Egypt. Now it follows Yhwh from those realms. Lion and birds are correlated images. The fearsomeness of the lion does not, apparently, intimidate the birds, whose normal trepidation is intimated by the word 'tremble'. Whether they tremble for fear or awe, or whether the verb simply evokes their flight, is indeterminate; Eidevall (1993) suggests an allusion to the trembling of mountain and people at Sinai. Closer at hand is the conclusion of ch. 3, in which the people 'come fearfully to Yhwh'.

The children come from the west; the metaphor of filiation concludes with the descendants of the single son of v. 1 retracting his steps, joining the beginning to the end of Israel's history. 'From the west' may also mean 'from the sea', recalling the fatal gathering of the fish of the sea in 4.3, at the beginning of the section comprising chs. 4–11. Flocks flying out of the west or the sea are a figure of effortless travel and vast numbers; the context of migration adds to this perhaps the homing instinct, characteristic especially of doves. If the dove in 7.11 has no heart, now it has found one. Yhwh is transformed from a fowler, setting the snare, to a keeper or tender of birds. He causes them to 'dwell' in their houses. With this, 'returning' (*šûb*) merges with 'settle' (*yāšab*). The twists and turns of the chapter come to an end.

Hosea 12*

(1) Ephraim has surrounded me with deceit and the house of Israel with guile; but Judah still rules with God, and is faithful with the holy ones.

(2) Ephraim shepherds the wind and pursues the east wind. All day long he multiplies lies and pillage, and they make a covenant with Assyria, and oil is brought to Egypt.

(3) There is a contention of Yhwh with Judah, to visit upon Jacob his ways, and requite his deeds.

(4) In the womb he gripped his brother, and in his virility he fought with God.

(5) He strove against the angel, and he prevailed; he wept and he begged mercy from him; at Bethel he would find him; there he will speak with us.

(6) And Yhwh, God of Hosts, Yhwh is his remembrance.

(7) And you—return to your God; keep kindness (*ḥesed*) and justice, and hope in your God continually.

(8) Merchandise is in his hand, fraudulent scales; he loves to oppress.

(9) And Ephraim says, 'Indeed, I have become rich, I have found wealth; all my efforts will not find me, wrongdoing which counts as sin'.

(10) And I am Yhwh your God from the land of Egypt; once more I will make you dwell in tents, as in the days of the appointed festival.

(11) And I spoke through the prophets, and I multiplied vision, and through the prophets I would be compared.

(12) If Gilead has become reprehensible, indeed pointless; in Gilgal they sacrifice bulls, and their altars are like cairns on the furrows of the fields.

---

* 12.1 in the Hebrew text is 11.12 in many English versions, so the number of each subsequent verse of ch. 12 in those versions is one less than the corresponding number in the Hebrew text (e.g. 12.3 in the Hebrew Bible is 12.2 in many English Bibles).

(13) And Jacob fled to the country of Aram, and Israel toiled for a wife, and kept watch for a wife.
(14) And through a prophet Yhwh brought Israel up out of Egypt, and through a prophet it was watched over.
(15) Ephraim has provoked wrath flagrantly; his bloodguilt is evident; his lord will requite his disgrace.

Chapter 12 is the most intricate in the book, and has caused the most critical headaches. In particular, Hosea's references to Jacob have exercised critical ingenuity: are they positive or negative? Did he have a different version of the Genesis narrative? Such questions are not accessible to simple or univocal answers, either because we lack the evidence, or because the Genesis narrative itself presents a complex characterization of Jacob. If Jacob has transmitted anything to his descendants, it is this complexity. Undue attention to how the prophet evaluates Jacob detracts from its place within the chapter as a whole, with its interchange of past and present, and its intense structuring.

Everything bustles: a treaty is made with Assyria; oil is delivered to Egypt; all day long lies and violence multiply; Ephraim is busy pursuing the wind. Much of this resonates with previous contexts: making treaties is characteristic of the meaningless language of kings in 10.4; playing off Assyria against Egypt results in death or exile in both; shepherding the wind recalls the deceptive harvest that does not 'shepherd' in 9.2.

Ephraim surrounds God with lies and deceit: whereas in 7.1-2 the Ephraimites' false deeds surround them, concealing them ineffectively from Yhwh's gaze, here Yhwh is at the centre of, perhaps constricted by, their machinations. In 11.9 he is the holy one in their midst; their intrinsic holiness is belied by their mendacity. Yhwh is either the victim of their guile, anticipating Jacob's struggle in v. 4, or, as in v. 8, guile characterizes their interpersonal relations; the two possibilities are not distinct.

While God is entangled, Ephraim 'shepherds the wind and pursues the east wind'. As in 8.7, cultivation of the wind is supremely foolish and evidence of self-deception. The wind, uncontrollable and empty, is fissiparous, apt to disperse Ephraim; its specification as the east wind not only associates it with dust and drought, but with the Assyrians. In 13.15, however, the east wind comes from Yhwh; Yhwh then is internal to Ephraim, at the centre of its nexus of frauds and conspiracies, and an external malice, of which Assyria is a vehicle.

One who pursues the wind will not catch it. The elusiveness of the wind is suggested by the open syllables and initial 'r's of *rōʻeh rûaḥ wᵉrōdēp*, 'shepherds the wind and pursues...' The courtship of the wind is paralleled by the yield of lies and pillage: speech is empty of substance; the desire for increase, presumably through malpractice, produces destruction, either because cheating and violence are kindred, or because their daily mendacity will magnify the 'pillage' predicted in 7.13 and 9.6.

The first two verses, seemingly extraneous to the main concerns of the chapter, are closely linked with it lexically and thematically. Ephraim's deception corresponds to its shame in v. 15; as Wolff (1974: 207-208) has pointed out, the word for 'guile' (*mirmâ*) is reconstituted in that for 'bitterly' (*tamrûrîm*). The poles of Ephraim's diplomatic endeavours—Egypt and Assyria—are reproduced in the juxtaposition of Jacob's flight to Aram and God's deliverance from Egypt in vv. 13-14. If Ephraim shepherds wind, Jacob was a faithful shepherd (v. 13; Gen. 31.38-41). The word for God (*ʼēl*) in v. 1 recurs in the name Bethel in v. 5; likewise, the word for 'still' (*ʻōd*) echoes in God's promise or threat to return Israel 'once again' (*ʻōd*) to tents in v. 10.

The last half of v. 1, from which these two words are drawn, is very obscure. It is not clear whether Judah is praised or blamed, what it does with 'God' (*ʼēl*), or whether the 'holy ones' to whom it is faithful are Canaanite deities or members of Yhwh's court (another possibility is 'holy things'). 'God' (*ʼēl*) is parallel to the 'holy ones', but they could be opposites or synonymous. El may be distinguished from Yhwh as the head of the Canaanite pantheon. The verb of which Judah is the subject is particularly puzzling, since it could either mean 'rules' or 'rebels', 'is restive'.

Verse 3, with its announcement of a disputation of Yhwh against Judah, would support a pejorative interpretation, but this has its own problems. A disputation against Judah echoes, but is far removed from, Yhwh's disputation against the inhabitants of the earth in 4.1. Why does the climactic last section begin so parochially? And, even if Yhwh does have a particular quarrel with Judah, why do we hear nothing more of it? For such reasons, most commentators regard the indictment of Judah here as a Judean substitution for Ephraim or Israel. Be that as it may, it functions, in our present text, as a momentary distraction from the polemic against Ephraim. Judah is the 'other', equally culpable perhaps, but also a possible exception, as in 6.11–7.1. For the Judaean readers and editors of the book, the disputation remains open; they cannot know, for instance, whether it is identical to the charge against Ephraim.

Judah is paired, in the second half of the verse, with Jacob. The same collocation occurs in 10.11, where, as in our passage, Judah is preceded by Ephraim, and the two together constitute Jacob's plough-team. Judah and Ephraim, as the principal heirs of Jacob, are equally implicated in his story; the citation of Judah at least notionally, communicates a sense of totality (cf. Ben Zvi 2005: 247-48).

Yhwh threatens, in a formula very similar to 4.9, to visit Jacob according to his ways and requite his deeds. 'Jacob' refers both to contemporary Israel and to its common ancestor. As a collective term, it is complemented by the threat to requite Ephraim's sin in v. 15, which, as Jeremias (1983: 152) says, frames the chapter. Whereas in 4.9 the announcement of retribution encounters the problems of the people's ignorance, their inability to return to God, and the possibility of immunity suggested in 4.14, here it introduces a dialectic between present and past, and a minute focus on Jacob's deeds as a prototype for Israel. The question is not only how those deeds are evaluated, but whether they exculpate Israel. If Israel has inherited Jacob's deceitful genes, they cannot be blamed for acting according to their nature. On the other hand, if Jacob is an ideal portrait, then he may serve as a foil to his descendants.

Two conflicts are decisive for Jacob's life, according to Hosea: that with his brother and that with God, and both are perpetuated in his double name Jacob/Israel. In v. 4 the two are precisely parallel: 'In the womb he gripped (*'āqab*) his brother, and in his virility he fought (*śārâ*) with God'. The parallelism generates a transfer, from female to male, from infancy to maturity, from human to divine antagonist. Jacob graduates from human rivalry to contention with God, and he may thus exemplify hubris. But the exact parallelism also suggests equivalence: brother and God are in the same positions; gripping and wrestling are comparable actions; while 'in the womb' and 'in his virility' interchange sexual and generative domains.

If there was no original safe place, then there is nowhere to return. Elsewhere the matrix is the desert or Egypt, and combines attributes of desolation and satisfaction, death and life. Here we go further back, to Rebekah, and to the divine speech unfolded in Israel's fractious history. The pervasive vision of return, to an ideal world, as in 2.16-25 and ch. 14, and to God, is thwarted and rendered more compelling by this initial experience of rivalry. Elsewhere the problem of the book is that birth simultaneously produces death. Here the antagonists confront each other directly. According to Winnicott, an infant needs a play space between itself and its mother in which it can develop its sense of reality, but the play space, for Jacob, is already intruded upon, divided. His relationship to his brother is haunted by secondariness, since he supplants his brother and is thus a usurper.

Esau/Edom does not figure elsewhere in Hosea, which is remarkable for its total lack of a polemic against the nations. Fraternal conflict is an evil perhaps–but not explicitly–exemplified by the strife of Israel and Judah. In contrast, the vision of restoration in ch. 2 is one of familial reconciliation. Jacob's wiliness, however, which gives rise to a second meaning of his name (Gen. 27.36), is hardly in evidence; Esau's grudge is only hinted at by the detail that Jacob fled to Aram in v. 13. As always, biblical poetry focuses on the essential moments; it intensifies the heroic, Promethean aspects of Jacob's struggle and omits the details of daily life and character development.

The womb is Rebekah's, but through the oracle in Gen. 25.23 it acquires a cosmic dimension, as the womb from which the peoples diverge and history unfolds. As the source of the oracle, Yhwh is cognizant of and determines human destinies; the divided womb is that of creation. In the oracle, Yhwh becomes Jacob's patron, siding with Rebekah in her opposition to patriarchal preference and primogeniture.

But he is also Jacob's antagonist, aligned with Esau and patriarchy. The parallelism couples together the two decisive moments, just as in the Genesis narrative Jacob's transformative encounter with the divine being is intertwined with the reunion with his brother. The verb for 'fight' ($śārâ$) only occurs here and in Gen. 32.29, where it is the etymological basis for the change of Jacob's name to Israel. The allusion is thus very direct; however, it recalls other words repeatedly associated with the name Israel in Hosea: $śar$, 'prince', and $sûr$, 'turn aside', in other words, Israel's history of misrule and deviation from God. These alternatives are convoked by the very recondite beginning of v. 5, which with a slight change of vocalization may reproduce the second clause of v. 4, or with another change of vocalization mean 'and God proved himself lord' (Wolff 1974: 206). A meaning derived from 'turn aside' is also possible, though less pertinent; turning aside to an angel would recollect Judah's being faithful to the holy ones in v. 1. The 'angel' is the counterpart of the 'man' who encounters Jacob in Gen. 27.25. God can take many forms; emissaries are constantly crossing between God and humanity, mediating between the extremes of incommensurable difference and immanence supposed in 11.9. Of these emissaries, the prophet is an example, a human analogue.

The problems of the verse are compounded by the uncertainty of subject. Who wept? Who implored? It could be Jacob, referring somewhat dramatically to his plea for a blessing and perhaps to the wound to his thigh, or it could be the angel/God, who begged to be released before dawn broke (Gen. 32.27). Some critics regard the angel as subject of 'and he prevailed', corresponding to 'and God proved himself lord'. This would contradict Gen. 32.26 and 29, in which the divine being sees that 'he could not prevail' and acknowledges that Jacob had prevailed. Eslinger (1980) sees this as a case of inner biblical exegesis, Hosea's rejection of the officially accepted etymology of Israel. However, this interpretation would render the story uninteresting and pointless, especially if it is a prelude to the meeting with Esau. Only if Jacob is the equal opponent of God is the reciprocity of weeping and seeking a boon intelligible, corresponding to the paradox in the Genesis story whereby the victor seeks blessing, and the sign of the divine's concession is the revelation of its power.

Israel's contention with God is then validated by God through the change of name. A divinely given name, as always, is a sign of initiation, of adoption into the divine order. Israel becomes Israel, precisely through its contrariness. The dialogue between God and Israel, as maintained, for instance, by the prophets, is constitutive of their relationship. The verbal plays on the word Israel that we found in the book—the contentions of the 'princes', their habitual 'straying'—are both travesties of that dialogue and compose it, since their history is one of alienation and reconciliation. With all its stubbornness, Jacob/Israel still will not release the deity until it has acquired a blessing. This remains a hope for us, one confirmed in the last part of the verse: 'In Bethel he would find him, and there he would/will speak with us'. Bethel, the house of God, is still the place of the divine–human encounter, despite the perversity that has turned it into Beth Awen, the house of Folly. The previous time that Bethel has been accorded its proper name has been to announce its destruction (10.15); the name now suggests the possibility of continuity.

The doxology that follows, 'Yhwh, God of Hosts, Yhwh is his remembrance', juxtaposes the cosmological expansiveness of 'hosts' with the temporal depth of memory. The word for 'remembrance' is a liturgical expression, used in parallel with the word for 'name' in Exod. 3.15. It calls Yhwh to mind and recalls him to his commitment to the long chain of events that binds him to Israel. The assertion that Yhwh is God of Hosts and hence of celestial order counteracts the threatened fate of Israel in 11.8, with its reference to Zeboiim (for the wordplay linking Zeboiim with $ṣ^eḇā'ôṯ'$, 'hosts', see above, p. 164). One can imagine the formula would be recited in Bethel. However, it only acquires point from its application to the future in v. 7, and its immediate and personal address.

The summons is to 'return'; the bourn is uncertain, since the Hebrew may mean 'with the help of your God' as well as 'to your God' (for a discussion, see Macintosh 1997: 491). It is, however, paralleled by 'keep kindness (ḥesed) and justice'. These are attributes wherewith Yhwh betroths Israel in 2.21; the word 'keep' has occurred also in 4.10, where it refers to the priests' (or people's) abandonment of their responsibility to 'keep' or 'guard' Yhwh. For this they are punished by exact retribution, according to the formula of 4.9. The same formula in 12.3 now finds its correlate; the dereliction of responsibility will be illustrated in vv. 8-9. 'Keeping' or 'guarding' Yhwh is equivalent to keeping or guarding ḥesed and justice. Return, however, is always fraught; Jacob is characterized by his secondariness, his attempt to supplant his brother, and his struggle with a deity with whom he can claim equal status—to be 'a prince with God'—and who is associated with that which he displaces, his brother and the womb. To return is accompanied by maintaining the bounds and bonds of society, as well as those between human beings and God. Closure is deferred; one has to 'hope in' (or 'wait for') Yhwh. If Jacob is a latecomer, his metaphorical fusion with the deity hindered by the intensity of the struggle between them, he is also characterized by his patience.

Verse 7 is a twin of 10.12, in which the collectivity of Israel, personified as Jacob, is urged to cultivate ḥesed and righteousness and wait for Yhwh's advent. There, the cultivation of social and sacred relations is superimposed on the agricultural cycle. Here, as many commentators remark, it is aligned with God's promise at Bethel to restore Jacob to his land and guard him wherever he goes (Gen. 28.15).

In vv. 8-9 we return to Ephraim and contemporary reality. As Utzschneider (1980: 212-16) remarks, there is very little consciousness in Hosea of oppression or exploitation; unlike Amos, he is not primarily a social critic. Here the sketch of Ephraim's malpractice illustrates its lack of good faith, benevolence and justice, its failure to fulfil the injunctions of v. 7, as well as specifying the guile of which it is accused in v. 1. If in v. 2, Ephraim pursues the east wind, accumulating devastation and lies, and engaging in insubstantial diplomatic entanglements, here all its efforts will, it hopes, 'not find me'. One's life's work will normally 'find' one, amounting to the meaning of one's life. The careful disassociation from the consequences of these labours renders them pointless. In v. 5 Jacob finds God or vice versa at Bethel; now the rewards for misdeeds will, Ephraim thinks, not be forthcoming, suggesting laxity or unconcern on the part of the divine guarantor. Instead, Ephraim has found 'wealth'; the word for 'wealth' ('ōn) is the same as that for 'virility' in v. 4, and consonantally identical with that for 'folly' or 'evil' ('āwen) in v. 12. In 9.4 the same word signifies 'mourning' (cf. p. 130 above).

In v. 4 Jacob's virility is in apposition to the womb from which he came; his masculinity proves itself against the dominant powers—his brother, God, father and father-in-law. The aspiring male has to win a place in the sodality of men. The struggle has two aspects, however, since God imparts the oracle in the womb, and since Laban, as the mother's brother, is the guardian of the matrix. The God against whom he fights represents maternal attachment as well as fraternal antagonism. Violence is transmuted into tears and thence into speech, perpetuated through the bonds of *ḥesed* and justice. Phallic rivalry becomes patriarchal communion, protective of women and children. In v. 9, however, phallic power is identified with wealth; the phrase 'I have found virility/wealth' is prefaced by 'I have become rich'. The love that should be the medium of social as well as sexual relations is the instrument of narcissistic aggrandizement and sadistic humiliation, since Ephraim 'loves to oppress' (v. 8). Sexuality is converted into the currency of deferred pleasure and anxious self-protection; finding wealth and power is the antidote that ensures that 'my efforts will not find me'. Rudolph (1966: 234) imagines Ephraim arguing that prosperity is proof of divine favour and forgiveness of minor sharp practice. Davies (1992: 279) notes a word play between 'I have found wealth' (*māṣā'tî'ôn*) and its complement 'will not find... iniquity' (*yimṣe'û 'āwôn*).

Ephraim is guilty of oppression, but we hear nothing of the oppressed. Those addressed in the book are elites: conspirators, priests, judges. Possibly the rites on the high places in ch. 4 afford a view of popular religion, but no insight into the status of its participants. The poor simply do not figure in Hosea's thinking; they are subsumed in Israel's collective impurity.

The first word of v. 8, 'merchandise' or 'trader', may also mean Canaan; most commentators remark on the insinuation that Jacob's descendants are indistinguishable from Canaanites. There is a word play between 'merchandise/Canaan' ($k^ena'an$) and 'like a cloud' (ka^anan) in 13.3; the wealth and schemes with which it seeks to substantiate itself are on the verge of dissolution.

From the speech of Ephraim we turn to that of Yhwh in v. 10: 'And I am Yhwh your God from the land of Egypt'. The formula is obviously reminiscent of v. 6, and, as there, juxtaposes the memory of God's association with Israel with Ephraim's delusion that its deeds will be forgotten, that its 'wrongdoing' ($'āwôn$) will not count as 'sin' (v. 9). It may be an abbreviated version of the first commandment (Jeremias 1983: 155; Rudolph 1966: 238), and thus remind Israel of its formative encounter with God, just as v. 6 recalls Yhwh's self-disclosure at the Burning Bush in Exod. 3.15. At any rate, it is accompanied by the determination to make them dwell in tents once more, 'as in the days of appointed festival'. The festival may be a time of pilgrimage, perhaps to Bethel, and hence of participation in sacred time, a recollection of God's initial encounter with Israel. Daniels (1990: 47) suggests that the festival may be Passover, since Tabernacles is celebrated in booths (Lev. 23.42). At any rate, the prospect is of a resumption of nomadic life, whether in exile or as a renewal of the Exodus. In 2.13 festivals are abolished; in 9.5, 'the day of appointed festival' marks the return to Egypt (9.3, 6) and is celebrated with the bread of mourning. There tents are figures for abandonment, possession by thorns, instead of dwelling. Our verse is then a reversal of 9.4-6; if the mourning ($'ônîm$) of 9.4 proleptically casts a shadow on the wealth ($'ôn$) of v. 9, on the other side of destitution is the possibility of restoration (Sweeney 2000: 124).

The word for 'once again' ($'ōd$) with which the prediction begins comes to rest with the 'meeting' or 'recurrent time' ($mô'ēd$) with which it ends. The reversion to nomadism is enclosed within its cycles of repetition, as the future reflects the past, and the single event, the Exodus, multiplies indefinitely. The nostalgia is overdetermined by the correspondence between the word for 'your God' (*ᵉlōhêkā*) and that for 'tents' (*ᵒhālîm*); God has an affinity for the liminal period of the wilderness. There may be a reminiscence of the 'Tent of Meeting' (*'ōhel môʿēd*) in the wilderness (Andersen and Freedman 1980: 618; Ben Zvi 2005: 264). The flimsiness of tents is guaranteed by the intangible presence of God.

Multiplication continues in the next verse: 'I spoke to the prophets, and I multiplied visions'. It continues God's recital of his deeds: the emphatic pronoun 'I' (*'ānōkî*) of 'I am Yhwh your God from the land of Egypt' is echoed by that of 'I multiplied visions'. 'I spoke' (*dibbartî*) alliterates closely with 'I multiplied' (*hirbêtî*); speech disseminates, word matches vision. Words, like visions, are differentiated; the number of visions testifies to the variety of divine–human experiences, and the incompleteness of any symbolic expression. Human speech imperfectly communicates divine reality; consequently, the prophets find metaphors for God, just as the visions represent the invisible. Metaphors translate, displace and are provisional, since every likeness is a trope for incomparability. Of this speech, the book of Hosea is exemplary.

The word for 'compare' (*dmh*) is the same as that for 'destroy', used in 4.5 and 6 for the doom of the priest's mother and the destruction of the people 'without knowledge'. In 10.7 and 15 the two meanings converge in the figure of the king who is annihilated simultaneously with his comparison to something that vanishes. If the people is destroyed without knowledge because the priests have neglected their responsibility, that task is maintained by the prophets, in indirect, imaginative language, which thus permits its survival.

Prophetic speech, however, is also the agent of death (6.5), it destroys as it creates. In 9.7-8 the prophet is a source of enmity in God's house, afflicted with madness, and a trap on Ephraim's paths. How may the benign image of the prophet in our chapter, culminating in the prophet's bringing up Israel from Egypt in v. 14, be reconciled with his destructiveness? In vv. 4-5 Jacob is the one who contends with God; the prophet sustains that contention, which is transformed into speech and communion. The speech reflects on and survives death; its ambiguity ensures the future as a realm of possibility. Death and silence are transfigured into simile, whereby God is immanent in language, if only in disguise.

Hosea 12

From the speech of the prophets, their visions, the attempt to find a language for divine reality, we go to sacred sites and geography. The transition is abrupt, and has induced commentators to regard it as an extraneous fragment; indeed the whole of the last part of ch. 12 lends itself to interpretation as a collection of apothegms. In fact, however, the juxtaposition intensifies contrast, between the daylit, familiar world of shrines and the perhaps ecstatic and nocturnal hallucinations and the strange words and behaviour of the prophets.

The verse is interconnected by wordplay and correlations with other parts of the book and of the biblical tradition. Gilead is coupled with Gilgal, which in turn resonates with *gallîm*, 'heaps'. The regional shrines correspond to and are complemented by the plethora of local altars, excoriated in 8.11 and 10.1. The pointlessness (*šāw'*) of Gilead's conduct alliterates with the 'bulls' (*šᵉwārîm*) that are sacrificed in Gilgal. The substantiality of the bulls as media of divine–human communication is nullified by God's rejection. As already noted, *'āwen* is akin to *'ôn*, 'wealth', in v. 9; Gilead's prosperity is ill-founded.

The reference to Gilead is an abbreviated citation of 6.8, 'Gilead is a city of evildoers (*pōʿᵃlê'āwen*), tracked with blood'. Their misdeeds are specified as murder, and the word 'tracked' (*ʿᵃqubbâ*) is semantically linked to 'Jacob'. On his heels, his descendants trace his path in blood. Gilead is associated both with Jacob's treaty with Laban and his struggle with God. Gilgal is another liminal site, marking the entrance of Israel into the land; its twelve stones, according to Joshua 4, represent the unity of Israel, near the banks of the Jordan that divides it. Davies (1992: 281) suggests that the Transjordanians had a special devotion to Gilgal; the juxtaposition promotes semantic equivalence. If the Gileadites offer bulls in vain at Gilgal, then the total evil that Yhwh perceives there in 9.15 may be identified with their opprobrium.

The last clause matches 10.4, since both end with 'on the furrows of the field'. In 10.4 justice flowers like poisonous weeds, in the context of empty speech and vain oaths; here the subject is the altars whose sacrality is inverted into sin. The stone heaps are simultaneously an image of impending destruction and agricultural stability; but they may also have a polemical twist, in that the altars are but piles of stones. They contrast with the field which Jacob tends in 10.11, and his faithful service in the field of Aram in v. 13.

Verse 12 is the culmination of the plays on different meanings of the syllables *gil* and *gal* that we have found in chs. 9 and 10. They span a trajectory from joy to grief, entrance to the land to exile from it, the central cult of the calf to the periphery.

Verses 13-14 are syntactically paired: each ends with the verb 'guard' or 'watch', and in each the parallelism between the last two clauses is maintained by the repetition of the prepositional phrase, 'for a woman' in v. 13, 'by a prophet' in v. 14 (in Hebrew, both phrases are introduced by the same preposition, b^e). Most commentators regard the coupling as an animadversion against Jacob; Jacob's service for his wife, they hold, is a humiliation, compared to Yhwh's deliverance of Israel from Egypt. The parallelism, on the contrary, would make Jacob a prototype of Moses and of Yhwh in his deliverance of Israel (Sweeney 2000: 128; Ben Zvi 2005: 261). Moses is evidently modelled on Jacob: both are shepherds, meet their future wives at wells where they perform heroic feats, and both are fugitives. The image of Israel as God's wife, and of the wilderness as the scene of their first romance, is familiar from the first chapters; Jacob's care for the sake of his wife is then analogous to that of God for Israel.

Jacob is presented without guile, without incident; the long years in Aram are informed by the solitude, patience and endurance of the shepherd, reminiscent of his self-vindication in Gen. 31.38-41. The virility manifested in conflict is transformed into erotic desire; the moments of crisis are set against sheer duration and both determine his character. His service as a shepherd corresponds to 'guarding' kindness and justice, and thus to the priestly role as guardians of Yhwh in 4.10. Shepherds are associated with the conventions of pastoral poetry, whose roots are very ancient, and with the responsibility of kings and gods. There is thus a double implicit metaphor for Yhwh: as shepherd and as lover. Both replace, and reverse, the contentiousness of Jacob and Yhwh in v. 4.

These personae also characterize the prophet, through whom Israel came forth from Egypt. The function of the prophets has mostly been combative: they pronounce doom; their words bring death; they are traps in God's house. They perform the role of the emissary or angel in v. 5. Now the prophet is the shepherd and lover of Israel. Hosea replaces Samuel with Moses as the archetypal prophet. If Samuel is the opponent of monarchy and exemplifies God's inflexibility, Moses is the liberator and intercessor, who preserves Israel on its way.

How is Jacob presented in these vignettes? Why are they so widely separated? Jacob is lover, shepherd, indomitable and unyielding. In the Genesis narrative, he strives to reconstitute the matrix that was never secure by being his mother's son, by preferring the women's domestic sphere to masculine activity, and finally, by going to the maternal home in Haran. Here, his wooing of a woman, the ancestress of Ephraim, preserves the matrix and thus continuity. It is achieved, however, across the span of the chapter, which moves from conflict to the possibility of reconciliation.

The last verse returns to the present, to divine retribution and the natural consequences of bloodshed. It is, as we have seen, a reiteration of v. 3, which gives the chapter a disagreeable circularity. The condemnation is supported by the descriptions in vv. 8-9 and 12. The conflict between reality, desire and memory is, however, inescapable; the voices of vv. 13-14 are not silenced, especially since, according to a possible reading of v. 6, Yhwh is his memory.

Hosea 13.1–14.1*

(1) When Ephraim spoke terror, he became dominant in Israel, and he incurred guilt through Baal, and he died.
(2) And now they continue to sin, and they make themselves molten images from their silver, idols according to their understanding; all of it is the work of craftsmen; of them they say, 'Those who sacrifice humans kiss calves'.
(3) Therefore they shall be like the cloud of morning, like the dew that speedily passes away; like chaff swirling away from the threshing floor, and like smoke from a window.
(4) And I am Yhwh your God from the land of Egypt; a god besides me you do not know, and a saviour there is none but I.
(5) I knew you in the wilderness, in the land of drought.
(6) According to their pasture, they were satisfied; they were satisfied and lifted up their hearts; therefore they forgot me.
(7) And I became for them like a lion; like a leopard on the way I would lurk.
(8) I would encounter them like a bereaved bear; I would rip open the enclosure of the heart; and I would eat them there like a lion, a wild beast would cleave them.
(9) Your destruction, O Israel, for it is against me, against your help.
(10) Where, where is your king, that he might save you, in all your cities; and your officials, of whom you said, 'Give me king and princes'?
(11) I gave you a king in my anger, and I took him in my wrath.
(12) The iniquity of Ephraim is bound up, its sin is stored away.
(13) The pangs of childbirth come upon him; he is an unwise child; for the time will not stand still in the breaking of children.
(14) From the hand of Sheol I would deliver them; from Death I would redeem them. Where are your plagues, O Death? Where is your sting, O Sheol? Pity is hidden from my eyes.

* 13.16 in many English versions.

(15) For he flourishes/grows wild among brothers/reeds. The east wind comes, the wind of Yhwh from the desert rises up, so that his spring is confounded, his source dries up. He will despoil the treasure, every precious vessel.
(14.1) Samaria is guilty, for she has rebelled against her God. They will fall by the sword; their infants will be dashed to pieces; their pregnant women ripped open.

Verse 1 introduces the major theme of the chapter: death. Another historical reprise is suddenly cut short: Ephraim speaks, exalts himself, sins, and dies. The predicate of 'when Ephraim spoke', $r^etēt$, 'terror', only occurs here in the Hebrew Bible (though it occurs in the Dead Sea Scrolls and is well attested in rabbinic Hebrew; cf. Ben Zvi 2005: 283), and has received a variety of interpretations: Ephraim's speech induces terror (Davies 1992: 286), or his cries are a sign of piety (Jeremias 1983: 161. Andersen and Freedman 1980: 629 and Yee 1987: 250 take Yhwh as the subject of the terrifying speech, while Rudolph 1966: 237 renders 'stutteringly'. See the extensive discussion in Macintosh 1997: 518-19). More important than its exact meaning is its extreme compression and its introduction of a tone of anxiety to the chapter. The inarticulacy, supported by the sharpness of the double 't's and the 'r', echoes in the climactic verse of this section, in which Samaria 'rebels'($māRtâ$) and its infants are shattered ($y^eRuTTāšû$), which likewise alliterates with Ephraim's bitter vexation ($TaMRûRîM$) of God in 12.15. Under the pressure to express horror, the chapter will oscillate between elliptical, ambiguous language, seemingly on the verge of breakdown, and a relaxation of tension, as in the chains of similes or God's formulaic self-definition. Poetic pleasure will interact ironically with the catastrophe it represents.

Ephraim's preeminence in Israel recalls the condemnation of Ephraim in a tribal assembly in 5.9, with which it shares a premonarchic setting. No specific incident corresponds to the narrative here; it refers back to the primordial apostasy in 9.10 and 11.2, and prospectively to Israel's impending destruction. The history of Ephraim is encapsulated in a moment, as if from a great distance. But it is also rendered remote by the interposition of death, the other side of which is marked by the 'Now' of v. 2. Contemporary Ephraim is composed of survivors and has a shadowy afterlife, perhaps associated with the founding of the monarchy (vv. 10-11), which, at least according to the biblical historian, was responsible for the establishment of the state cult. The transition from apostacy to idolatry, from first to second commandments, implies either continuity or augmentation of sin (both possibilities are suggested by the Hebrew). The guilt of Ephraim is reflected in that of Samaria in 14.1, which rebels against its God, to enclose the chapter in a frame. Allegiance to other deities, like negotiations with foreign powers (12.3), is internalized as social and sacred entropy, an absence of the knowledge of God (vv. 4, 6) filled with the works of the imagination.

The circularity of ch. 13 suggests that the guilt of Ephraim is inescapable. Nevertheless, the word 'guilt' occurs also in 5.15, in a context closely linked to our chapter. There it signifies the possibility of repentance and a new beginning, which transfers itself to ch. 14. On the one hand, the hopes of ch. 5 are aborted in ch. 13; on the other hand, the closure is not absolute.

Verse 2 is remarkable for its accumulation of synonyms for idolatry: 'molten images', 'from their silver', 'idols', 'the work of craftsmen'. Appropriately, the words for 'molten images' and 'from their silver' interfuse: *massēkâ mikkaspām*. The central expression, 'according to their understanding' unifies the sequence; it is their conception of divinity, as it is their wealth, that solidifies in these forms. The attempt to capture divinity, to make it a cultural artifact, contrasts with Yhwh's repeated self-reflections. (Others read the anomalous *kit^{e}bûnām* as 'according to their likeness'; cf., e.g. Borbone 1990: 177.)

In the midst of the judgment, other voices are heard: 'Concerning them, they say, "Those who sacrifice humans kiss calves"'. (This may also mean 'human sacrificers'. For the ambiguity, see Ben Zvi 2005: 282.) The citation allies the prophet/God with a popular perception of the inversion of values. As in 8.7, its epigrammatic neatness gives it the authority of the wisdom tradition. The prophet/God are not alone in their critique. The inverted world, in which humans are sacrificed and calves kissed, is encapsulated by anxious laughter, whose aphoristic control belies terror. The state cult would conform to the conventions of the Bakhtinian carnival, as a licensed release of illicit drives, such as bestiality and homicide, except that it is the official order. The reversal culminates in v. 11, where the monarchy itself is a burlesque, given and taken in a fit of divine temper.

The inset speech is linked to two others: the people's self-exhortation to return to Yhwh in 6.1-3, whose dismissal in 6.4 is echoed in v. 3; and the anticipated contrition of 14.3-4, which likewise transforms bovine sacrifice. Here the substitution of a human for an animal, a reversal of the usual sacrificial displacement, may be either literal and/or metaphorical; it may refer to the murderous priests of 6.9 or their exploitativeness in 4.7-8. Whether or not it was actually practised, human sacrifice is a pervasive motif in the prophetic writings, and in particular child sacrifice. With it the motif of 'humanity' or 'Adam' that began in 6.7 comes to an end. To be human is to betray the covenant; God cares for the child Ephraim with human love; parents are bereaved of their children. Here they sacrifice their children, and with it their humanity. In 11.8 God refuses to destroy Israel like Admah, like the earth or humanity. The ultimate desolation is practised by parents who offer their children to God.

The same people kiss calves. The calf may be a symbol of state power; kissing it is a sign of submission (1 Kgs; 19.18; cf. Gen. 41.40), adoration or love, which recalls the association of promiscuity with Baal, evoked in v. 1. The interfusion of sexuality by death, the coincidence of progenitor and sacrificer, anticipates the ambiguities of v. 14.

Verse 3 replicates the similes of 6.4; the transitoriness of the people's affections which occasions God's despair in 6.4 is transferred to their own evanescence. As in 6.4, the figures morbidly reverse their normal association with fertility. The parallelism is complemented by two matching similes: chaff from a threshing floor, smoke from a window. If the similes in 6.4 conform to the diurnal and seasonal imagery of that passage, these extend the range of reference to different semantic realms. Likewise, however, there is a reversal of expectations; chaff leads us to await the harvest, smoke is an index of domestic comfort. The word for 'swirl', nevertheless, comes from the same root as that for 'stormwind'; the underlying metaphor is that of Yhwh as the storm. Similarly, the fire without which there is no smoke may be a conflagration, as in 8.14.

The finding of beautiful and apt similes evokes a poetic eroticism, a love of the everyday world and of language, that both defers the moment of destruction and ironically is pervaded by it. The lingering lyricism, the vanishing of the smoke, is interrupted by the starkness of the divine declaration in vv. 4-5. The refrain, repeated from 12.10, is a touchstone of identity for the two chapters. God's self-awareness is expressed through the continuity of his relationship with Israel and his role as deliverer.

But the development of the two passages is entirely different. In ch. 12, God's care is mediated through prophets, who find similes for God. Here nothing intervenes between God and Israel. They know no other gods; he knows them in a wilderness where there is nothing else. The passage lacks all trace of the sensual delight and excitement of discovery of 9.10. What God knows is indeterminable; the verb suggests an intimacy without impediment or illusion. It may be compared with 5.3, in which God's knowledge of Ephraim allows no concealment. For its part, Israel's non-cognition of other gods renders its subsequent history a pursuit of ignorance.

The setting is the same as the evocation of the wilderness idyll in 2.16, but without the amorous metaphor. Perhaps Israel's feminine persona was a guise that allowed God his initiatory romance. Without that guise, Israel cannot but be known as bad and perfidious. Its nursery, to borrow the image from 11.1-4, is then insecure, crossed from the beginning, a land of thirst.

Yhwh's grammatical masculinity is aligned with the adoptive or natural paternity we have discerned in chs. 11 and 12. As father, he demands obedience to a transcendent order, communicated through his infallible knowledge. In our chapter, the normative constructions of both Yhwh and Israel as masculine are unchallenged, until they are dramatically overturned in the last verses.

The proclamation, 'A god besides me you do not know, and a saviour there is none but I', like 12.6, has the ring of a liturgical formula, and is echoed many times in the Hebrew Bible (Exod. 15.11; 2 Sam. 7.22; Isa. 45.5; etc.). The matched pair, 'god' and 'saviour', is isolated in its majesty by the vacuity that surrounds it: the people's not-knowing corresponds to the non-existence of the other deities. The gap is filled by words, whose solemnity, as part of a protracted formal parallelism, is proportional to their lack of any particular meaning. The formula is a foil to the inversion of values and the concentration on God's identity in the succeeding verses. God's transcendence is immediately juxtaposed with the intimacy of his knowledge, which in the context of the wilderness journey must also allude to his care. The persecutory and benevolent aspects of God's knowledge are mutually reinforcing as well as contradictory. As the next verse will show, Israel's guilt is compounded by ingratitude.

Verse 6 summarizes the plot of the first part of ch. 2, in which Israel's prosperity leads to forgetfulness. Oblivion corresponds to the evanescence of v. 3. God's knowledge is matched by Israel's aphasia; the fuller and more exalted the heart, which in Hebrew is an intellectual as well as affective organ, the less it remembers.

At the centre of the first part of the verse is a repeated verb, 'to be satisfied'. On either side of it is an alliterating spatial figure: their pasture ($k^emar'îtām$) and the uplifting heart ($wayyārom\ libbām$). As in 4.18, doubling is a form of intensification; the super-satiation weighs them down and contrasts with the lightness of their memory, which is appended as an afterthought to the verse. In 4.10, which corresponds to 4.18, eating does not grant satisfaction. Here the repetition may indicate similarly an anxiety of gratification, a consumer ambition, suggested also by the overweening heart that inevitably is frustrated.

Verses 7-8 consist of a chain of similes that corresponds to those in v. 3. Verses 1-3 and 4-8 have identical structures:

Verses 1-3	*Verses 4-8*
vv. 1-2: The narrative from the point of view of Ephraim	vv. 4-6a: From the point of view of God
v. 3a: Consequence: evanescence	v. 6b: Consequence: forgetfulness
v. 3b: Chain of similes	vv. 7-8: Chain of similes

In v. 2 Ephraimites kiss calves, while in v. 6 the image of pasture conventionally likens them to domestic beasts. The transformation of God into predator is thus metaphorically apt. As Fisch says (1988: 151-52), 'the shepherd suddenly turns round to attack the flock'. The sequence begins with a key word, $^eh\hat{i}$, 'I am', which keeps on recurring with different meanings, and hence is both structurally determinative and destabilizing. God's comparison of himself to a lion contradicts the certainty of his self-perception as 'Yhwh your God' and his role as sole deliverer. He runs through a zoological inventory before settling on the global category, 'beast of the field'. The similes interchange, to create an impression of a composite creature, but also to suggest their inadequacy. God becomes a destructive agency, from whom, if v. 4 is correct, there is no deliverance.

The passage echoes 5.14 and the rapacious fantasy of 2.14. Both are preludes to God's change of mind: the covenant with the beasts of the field in 2.20; the return to his lair in 5.15. In 11.10

the lion is a redemptive figure, adumbrating the motif of repentance. The apparent fulfilment of the lion's destructive intent here has a double modality. On the one hand, it exposes the falsity of the hopes raised by 5.15 and 11.10; on the other, it too is subject to suspicion. We have become accustomed to the final straw proving inconclusive. As in 5.14, moreover, the beasts are representations of the actual enemy, the Assyrians; the identification is enhanced by the pun between 'I will lurk' (*'āšûr*) and 'Assyria' (*'aššûr*). If deliverance from Egypt is the prototype of salvation from the nations, God is on the sides of both Israel and its adversaries.

The sequence passes from lion to leopard to bear and thence again to lion, using a different word for lion, *lābî*'. It is thus enclosed by references to the fiercest of beasts. The leopard is a feline parallel to lion, as in the Song 4.8, noteworthy perhaps for its camouflage and its skill in ambush (Feliks 1981: 88). The image evokes the way to the woman's lovers that Yhwh hedges about in 2.8. The bear is associated with bereavement (2 Sam. 17.8, Prov. 17.12); the slippage from female to male reminds us that it is Yhwh who is bereaved, that he is destroying his own children (Eidevall 1996: 207). Yhwh then is in the position of the sacrificing parents of v. 2.

The leopard 'lurks' or 'watches' on the way, seeing the prey approach unsuspecting, just as the journey to Assyria for healing in 5.13 is the occasion for injury. Verse 7 anticipates v. 8, in which the victims are caught and consumed; feral violence is actualized in the evisceration of mothers and children in 14.1. With the wildlife at the end of v. 8 the distance imposed by the simile vanishes, since God is no longer the subject, but an indiscriminate voracity. Correspondingly, the dismembered inhabitants are figures for decomposition. In contrast, God/the bear tears open the enclosure of their heart, the latter image suggesting a peculiarly intimate violation, as if, after ravaging the rest of the body, only the heart remains intact. The climactic phrase is the penultimate one: 'and I will consume them there like a lion'. Incorporation in God is the contrary of the dispersed disiecta. At either extreme, the integrity of Israel is broken. 'There' (*šām*) is a useful filler word in Hosea (cf. 6.10), which echoes the last syllable of 'I will encounter them' (*'epgᵉšēm*). Where God, as bear, meets Israel, there he will dispatch them. 'There' serves to place Israel, before its disappearance.

The ruptured heart is, evidently, the same as that which, in its satisfaction and pride, forgot God in v. 6. The word for 'heart' (*lēb*) is, in each case, in apposition to a hostile environment or agent: the land of drought—the exact meaning of the word, only occurring here, is uncertain—in v. 5 and the lion in v. 8. Both of these are characterized by an identical word play: 'drought' (*tal'ubôt*)shares its core consonants with 'lion' (*lābî*). The heart (*lēb*) is framed by two entities that alliterate with it and threaten to destroy it.

Verse 9 is extremely elliptical and lends itself to scholarly reconstruction and emendation in the interests of smoothness. It is, however, interjectory; the discontinuity of the language, in which each word is syntactically isolated, communicates emotional intensity and a resistance to coherence. Israel is addressed as it autodestructs; the repeated 'against me, against your helper' suggests Yhwh's grievance and the irony that Israel turns against its one ally. The compression of the verse contrasts with the expansiveness of the chain of similes that preceded it.

The words, moreover, compound alternative meanings. Israel's self-destruction is also its corruption; both meanings coincide in the word *šiḥēt*. In 9.9 their corruption is compared to the days of Gibeah, inducing the madness of prophetic speech and divine animosity; in 11.8, in contrast, Yhwh refuses to 'destroy' Ephraim, using the same word. Here he disclaims responsibility. It is not that Yhwh, through metaphorical and imperial guises, destroys Israel, but that Israel has arranged its own demise. We have found a similar collaboration of inner disintegration and external danger in 5.12-14. *Bî* 'against me' may also mean 'by me', and is a familiar self-adjuration by God (for example, Gen. 22.16); the covenantal language of confirmation becomes the mode of destruction. Similarly, it could mean 'through me', in other words that God is the instrument of destruction. 'Your helper' evokes liturgical rhythms, such as those of ancestral blessings (Gen. 49.25); the dislocation of the verse, as a figuration of chaos, is emphasized by distorted echoes of benediction. In the centre is Israel, isolated in its promise, its stance as covenant auditor, surrounded by the shards of divine–human discourse.

Fisch (1988: 152) suggests that the language is 'out of control', symptomatic of a relationship that has gone 'wildly wrong'. The pressure on the words, the fragmentation, however, suggests not loss of control, but an attempt to represent the inarticulacy of rage. The similes in the previous verses are traditional poetic tropes that conceal the violence against language. Their elaboration defers attention from the conflicts within God between the desire to help and mortification; from the danger to himself, implicit in 'against me'; and from the experience of dissolution comprised in Israel's corruption.

Verse 10 reintroduces the keyword *'ehî*, 'I am' or 'Where is?' Sweeney (2000: 132) points out that, as in 1.9, this recollects Yhwh's self-identification as 'I am' in Exod. 3.14. Israel's corruption and rebellion against Yhwh is paradigmatically represented by its desire for a king, who is also a usurper. Yhwh's claim to be king—reading the beginning of the verse as 'I am your king'—can only be realized by the destruction of the kingdom. Verses 10-11 are a summarizing statement of the effeteness of Israel's kings, corresponding to the epigram with which the topic of the calf closes in v. 2. Calf and king are in consort in ch. 8, which has close lexical links with our chapter. Likewise, the making of kings and princes in 8.4 parallels the desire to acquire kings and princes in our verse. Here, however, we pass from the immediacy of preceding discussions to an overview of the entire institution of the monarchy, and, in particular, a citation of its inception.

The inset quotation at the end of v. 10 matches that at the end of v. 2, providing a further structural link between the sections. Here, in contrast to v. 2, popular demand is for a king and princes; the summoning up of voices inserts us into the drama of 1 Samuel 8–12, when the monarchy was established. Hosea, and God through him, unambiguously endorses Yhwh's view there that the request is a rejection of himself (1 Sam. 8.7). God's gift of a king, then, is poisoned. David Gunn's argument, in *The Fate of King Saul*, that King Saul was a scapegoat for the sacrilege of establishing monarchy can be extended to the entire history of the kingdom.

This history is an epoch of divine wrath, a malicious concession to the people's whim, just as, according to Psalm 90, our lives are passed in the face of God's fury. Even God's indulgence is a trap, and the prophet, we know from 9.8, is the one who sets the trap. Hosea puts himself into the position of Samuel listening to the people's demands, as well as, at the other end of the sequence, that of a counter-Samuel, announcing Yhwh's reclamation of his gift. The people's plea, 'Give me king and princes', contrasts with Hosea's inability to petition, in 9.14: 'Give, what can you give?' If Hosea is a Samuel with qualms, as 6.6 suggests, and a would-be intercessor and shepherd, like Moses, there is no trace here of mollification, no room for interruption.

What do the people want? In 1 Sam. 8.5, they wish to be like the other nations. In Hosea, the combination of king and princes is associated with the burden of the Assyrians (8.10), with assassination (7.3-7), with power politics and with exploitation. To ask for a king displaces Yhwh and claims an autonomy that is at the same time an enslavement. It is apparently a free gift, so that the king, as in standard royal theory, is God's representative, standing in for the absent deity, but in 8.4 God disassociates himself from knowledge of the succession of kings and princes, and in 10.3 the impotence of the king fosters the lack of fear of God, a theocratic vacuum. From the exclusive knowledge in the wilderness, shared by God and Israel, kingship implants a zone of ignorance and indifference.

The request for a king is preceded in our chapter by the rise and fall of Ephraim in v. 1, and the narrative of the entrance into the land and collective aphasia in vv. 4-6. The narrative of the sin of Gibeah is the culmination of the age of the Judges, punctuated by the refrain, 'In those days there was no king in Israel'. It is not clear whether the word 'judges' in v. 10 refers to royal officials, as in 7.7, or to the premonarchic age. Consequently, there was no age of innocence and of untroubled divine rule, unless the period of Samuel, between the horrors of Gibeah and the anointing of Saul, was such an interval. One may note that Andersen and Freedman (1980: 621) suggest that Samuel was the second prophet through whom Israel was 'kept' in 12.14. In that case, Samuel, as a prophetic model, is not simply critical. This, however, is to argue from silence. On the other side of the voices demanding a king is an alleged ideal that is nevertheless suspect.

Like the previous verse, this section is characterized by syntactic disjunction and incompleteness. Its restlessness is indicative of that of its search: the initial question, 'Where, where is your king?' is repeated, through the matching of two words for 'where' ($^{e}h\hat{\imath}...'\bar{e}p\hat{o}h$); the search is pursued to 'all your cities'—the word possibly a pun on 'your enemies'—before breaking off at the word 'judges'.

We have progressed from the images of God created by human beings, to similes for God, whose multiplicity suggests their inadequacy, to human representatives for God, and finally to the disjunction between God's 'I am' and its predicates. 'I am' will interact complexly with 'Where are?': God's 'I am' exposes the vacuity of kings and officials, but raises also the question, 'Where (or who) am I?' In 11.9 God's holiness, or transcendence, is defined as his immanence. His anger, however, threatens to remove all his objects of desire, anything in which he might be invested. The relationship between God's 'I am' and his anger, that primal destructiveness, is then one of identity and opposition, since the 'I' tries to preserve its objects.

Verse 11, with its tight matching of beginning and end, all pervaded by God's wrath, seems to be Hosea's last word on Israel's experience of God, as well as his final judgment on the monarchy. Verse 12 corresponds to it, as an equally brief, conclusive parallelism on Israel's sin. The iniquity is 'bound up'; the image of the bundle could refer to a special treasure, like the bundle of myrrh in the Song 1.13, or to a document (Macintosh 1997: 542; cf. Isa. 8.16). It may also imply inextricability. Jeremias (1983: 166) suggests that it indicates both closure and explosiveness: Ephraim's sin is a timebomb.

Death and birth converge in the last section; Ephraim is mother and child. The birthpangs of the beginning of v. 13 are evidently those of death, corresponding, most commentators assume, to the final siege of Samaria. They cannot be dissociated from the parody of birth practised on the pregnant women of 14.1. The pains (*heblê*) of birth resonate with the cords (*hablê*) of love with which Yhwh drew Israel from the matrix of Egypt in 11.4. The birth is usually understood as a stillbirth; the child does not appear, or cannot withstand the stress of parturition. If so, what is born at the 'breaking of children', another allusion to the shattering of infants in 14.1, is death itself. 'Time' may be the subject of the second half of the verse, introducing the abstractions of v. 14; nothing can prevent the baby from being born. It contrasts with the propitious 'time' of 10.12, when the rhythms of the seasons and of proper human relationships are attuned to the timeliness of seeking Yhwh.

The 'unwise son' does not know the proper time to be born, but cannot be dissociated from the folly of Ephraim throughout the book. The child gives birth to its own perdition. The king is swept away on the surge of waters in 10.7. The metaphor of son giving birth to itself allows a transfer from male to female personae. As well as son, Ephraim is travailing mother, who is either monstrous, since she destroys her children, or unappeased, since she suffers or dies for them. The conventional male persona of Ephraim, maintained throughout by grammatical suffixes, masculine pronouns and so on, gives way to the maternal body, as the repository of identification and pity as well as condemnation. The womb image attaches itself to the other entities in the passage: death, Sheol, and even Yhwh. At the same time, it splits prophetic and divine voices. If, according to v. 14, Yhwh is the instrument of death, from whose eyes pity is hidden, the prophet is the child of Ephraim, and his poetry cannot but communicate empathy as well as alienation.

The 'breaking of children' multiplies the unwise son; the matrix has more than one occupant. The final spasm thus recollects the initial one, in which Jacob fought against his brother, as a foreshadowing of his struggle with God. The unwise child, who does not know it is time to leave the womb, is the antithesis of the determined Jacob who fought for priority. The insecurity of the womb, as a place to which one cannot return, makes Yhwh the object of sole return in ch. 14. The womb of Rebekah, encoded by divine speech, and preserved by Jacob and his prophetic successors, is the site of devastation. One is reminded also of the death of Rachel in childbirth.

In v. 14 Death and Sheol appear as characters for the first time; they are the presences behind the destructive similes and forces in the book. Personification gives them a voice, or at least an ear, inserting them into the imaginative space of the poem, from which, however, they are inherently excluded, since death defines the limits of the human world, and, as non-being—or unbeing, as Lacan puts it—is beyond representation. Death is the contrary of God, whose affirmation as 'I am' it constantly negates. Verse 14 confronts the two antagonists, in the context of a birth that is also death. Only in extremity can God's power over death be tested, and whether God is ultimately an agent of death or life.

God 'would' or 'will' ransom them from Death and Sheol. This conforms to the expectation of the divine 'turn' which arises from 11.8-9 and which is connected through the root $nḥm$, 'pity, change one's mind', to our verse. Yhwh would act as midwife, rescuing the child either from the womb of Sheol or delivery into a deadly world. Time, hurrying on to a climax, is thwarted by divine intervention, whose suddenness is communicated by the lack of transition. Redemption from Death and Sheol may most naturally mean last-minute reprieve. The siege of Samaria, for instance, would be miraculously lifted, like that of Jerusalem, according to 2 Kgs 19.35 and Isa. 37.36, some years later. Such hopes or intentions are foreclosed by the destruction of Samaria in 14.1.

Alternatively, the verse may portend survival after death as a metaphor for the continuity and restoration of Israel after the destruction of its political institutions, as in 3.4-5. But this, though in accord with Hosea's general future scenario, is ancillary to the mythological connotations of the promise. Death was an ancient deity; the grand personification suggests a universal significance. God's defeat of death would be a release from mortality, whether as resurrection or eternal terrestrial life. Immortality is a rare hope in the Hebrew Bible; the nearest parallel is Isa. 25.7-8, usually regarded as very late. It corresponds to the people's confidence in being revived in 6.2, and may evoke, if only by contrast, the cosmic covenant of 2.20. The world without violence would be matched by a life without death.

The statement of intent or desire, perhaps aborted by the people's sinfulness, is immediately complicated by the multiple ambiguities of the following phrases. The word $'^eh\hat{i}$, 'I am/where are', returns; in addition, the following word, $d^eb\bar{a}r\hat{e}k\bar{a}$, may mean both 'your words' and 'your plagues'. Hence 'I am/where are your words/plagues, O Death; I am/where is your sting, O Sheol' (the pun is noted by Ben Zvi 2005: 275). Continuity with the promise of redemption from death would clearly support the second reading, 'where are?', for $'^eh\hat{i}$: death would be evoked merely to be dismissed, its language and its diseases no longer available. Similarly, the parallel with 'sting' would foreground the meaning, 'plagues', for $d^eb\bar{a}r\hat{e}k\bar{a}$. But one should not therefore exclude the other possibilities. $'^eh\hat{i}$ as 'I am' or 'I will be'—Hebrew does not distinguish clearly between the present and the future—impresses itself on our attention from v. 7 and v. 10, where God identifies himself as a devouring lion and as a king who destroys his kingdom. On that reading, God would be the plagues/words of death and the sting of Sheol. Likewise, 'plagues' are the visible signs or words of death. Throughout the book God puts death into words, as, in 6.5, the prophetic word is the instrument of death.

The two possibilities are mutually exclusive. According to the one, death is abolished, its words and signs subsumed in the divine triumph; Yhwh vindicates himself over his ultimate adversary. According to the other, Yhwh is an agent or emissary of death, the presence behind the plagues—Assyrians. etc.—and words of the book. On this model, death is the ultimate reality, which Yhwh transforms into words and life. Our world is unstable, always threatening to revert to chaos, to the surrounding nothingness. Of this the corruption of Israel in v. 9 is emblematic.

The last phrase in the verse is also ambiguous: 'pity/change of mind is hidden from my eyes'. It contradicts 11.8, where Yhwh's 'compassions' or 'changes of mind' are stirred up altogether. Either his destructive resolve is inflexible, by dint of setting aside pity, or else his triumph over death will never be revoked; for death there is no pity. In that case, the following verses, in which the destruction of Samaria is finally consummated, are immediately disillusioning. The concealment of pity or regret suggests a willed constancy, always open to subversion, to the insidious return of the repressed. In 11.8 Yhwh unifies himself momentarily through the fusion of his 'compassions'; here their removal performs the same task.

God's personality, his assertion as 'I am' (*'ehi*), is imperiled from the beginning of the book by the possibility of reneging on his commitment to Israel and thus his contact with the world. *'ehî*, as 'I am', vanishes into *'ehî* as 'where?' He is both an immanent holiness and utterly different, wrathful and compassionate, metaphorically related to humanity and unknowable by them. Amidst his various personae, his different moods, there is no consistency. The search for a unitary self constitutes the metaphorical work of the poem, which is thus never complete.

If God redeems from death, he cannot at the same time be subordinate to death, and the negative interpretation of the verse would consequently be eliminated. God's self-identification as the words of death, however, opposes language to silence, meaning to non-meaning. God transforms death into life, uncreation into creation. But there is another possibility: redemption from death, as in Amos 9.2, is from an ultimate refuge. Even the grave provides no safety.

Verse 15 returns to the imagery of birth: the east wind of Yhwh comes up from the desert and blasts Ephraim's spring and source. The east is the direction from which Yhwh is imagined as rising like the dawn to revive Israel in 6.3, a simile transformed into one for retributive justice in 6.5. In 12.2, Ephraim shepherds the east wind; it now reaps what it sows. In 12.2, the east wind may be identified with Assyria, which accordingly is correlated with Yhwh. 12.2 and 13.15 enclose chs. 12 and 13; Ephraim's striving after emptiness and cultivation of foreign powers rebounds.

The wind comes from the wilderness, the place of theophany; the east wind is frequently associated with divine power (e.g. Exod. 14.21). The spring of Ephraim, the source of its vitality, may be identified with Samaria, the capital city and subject of the next verse; the association of femininity with springs is established both intertextually, as a euphemism or metaphor for a woman's genitals (Lev. 12.7; 20.18; Jer. 51.36; Prov. 5.18; Song 4.12), and through the context of birth. One of the words for 'parched' or 'dried' may also mean 'to be ashamed'—translated here as 'confounded'—and thus confirms a linkage with the 'shame' of 4.18-19. The desiccation of the spring recalls the withering breasts as well as the bereaving womb of 9.14, since it is the source of life-giving water as well as fertility.

Samaria, at the centre of the sacred and political system, represents Ephraim's rootedness in the land and dependence on its indigenous maternity. The antithesis of Samaria is the wilderness, as the matrix of the relationship of God and Israel. The two matrices finally are in conjunction. The wind/spirit from the wilderness destroys Samaria just as the wind/spirit of promiscuity caused Israel to stray from God in 4.11. The wilderness and Samaria are, nevertheless, equivalent; the wind turns Samaria into a wilderness. Conversely, in 2.16-17 Yhwh promises to transform the wilderness into fruitful land.

The beginning of the verse is interpreted in two main fashions. The word for 'reeds' or 'rushes' may be 'brothers', while 'flourish' may signify 'grow wild'. The word for 'flourish' (*yaprî*) is yet another word play on 'Ephraim'. (In addition, the word for 'between' [*bên*] may be read as 'son' [*bēn*] in some manuscripts, reinforcing the familial imagery and the association with Ephraim.) The following permutations would result: 'For he would flourish/grow wild (*yaprî*) among the reeds/his brothers'. At the beginning of ch. 13, Ephraim is exalted in Israel. Here he either flourishes among brothers or is the wild one among them. In Genesis, the wild ass among brothers is Ishmael (Gen. 16.12), the desert-dweller. Desert and fertile land, the marsh where the reeds grow, perhaps as a figure for fraternal solidarity, and their vulnerability to the wind and drought are perceived simultaneously.

The wind despoils treasures, and every delightful vessel; the treasure, like the vessels, is metonymous with Samaria's wealth and the silver devoted to idols. In parallel with the spring and source, the metaphor of rape is evident; the Assyrian destruction of the city is sexual violation. The military cliché becomes horribly literal in the next verse, in which the prediction that the fate of Beth Arbel in 10.14 will be Samaria's is fully realized. The sadism of the conqueror enacts the violence of the wild beasts in v. 8, with which it shares a common verb, *bq'*, 'rip, tear apart'.

Why is there the focus on women and infants, while the men are briefly passed over? Perhaps it arouses compassion; perhaps it revokes the immunity granted to groups of women in 4.14, so as to raise the question of responsibility. Once again there is a switch from masculine to feminine personae. The opening of the womb is a cleavage, filled with pain and shock, that would apparently render divine-human discourse impossible. Yhwh's fantasies of infanticide and matricide in ch. 2 are accomplished. But it is also Yhwh's child, and Yhwh's matrix, from which he receives life-giving sustenance in the desert, where it was the repository of his care and knowledge. The object of desire is invested with terror and rage; Yhwh's destruction is also self-destruction.

From the enemy's point of view, it is perhaps quite simple: atrocities will discourage other rebellions; dehumanizing the subject people will assert the superiority of the conqueror, release repressed murderousness, and so on. The horror is justified, however, not by rebellion against Assyria, but against God. Dissonance between God and the Assyrians, suggested by the ambiguities of v. 15, the conflict of wills, the desire to redeem, might lead us to wonder to what extent the Assyrians are the instruments of God, or whether God, as the word or plague of death, is its emissary, just as the wind/spirit of Yhwh carries the destructive and germinal potency of the wilderness.

Hosea 14.2–10[*]

(2) Return, O Israel, to Yhwh your God, for you have stumbled in your iniquity.

(3) Take with you words, and return to Yhwh; say to him, 'Forgive all iniquity, and take goodness, and we will offer up the bulls of our lips.

(4) Assyria will not save us; we will not ride on horses; no more shall we call the work of our hands our gods; for in you the orphan shall be comforted.'

(5) I will heal their backsliding; I will love them freely, for my anger has turned back from them.

(6) I will be like the dew to Israel; it will flourish like the lily; and it will put down its roots like Lebanon.

(7) Its shoots will spread; its splendour will be like the olive tree; and its fragrance will be like Lebanon.

(8) Those who dwell in its shade will return; they will bring to life new grain; they will blossom like the vine; its remembrance will be like the wine of Lebanon.

(9) Ephraim—What have I still to do with idols? I answer and I will watch over him. I am like a leafy cypress tree; from me your fruit is found.

(10) Who is wise and will understand these things, capacious and will know them? For straight are the ways of Yhwh, and the righteous walk in them, and the transgressors stumble in them.

Chapter 14 is, apparently, a poetic wish-fulfilment; the corpse rises and lives happily ever after. The poetic texture, too, is clear, untroubled by the tensions, compressions, and reversals of the rest. It conforms to the agenda of return following catastrophe that we have found at various points, and shares in their subversion, but its finality—disregarding the last verse—makes it conclusive; this is the book's culminating statement of the relationship of God and Israel. Following the fulfilment of the

---

[*] 14.1-9 in many English versions.

sadistic fantasy of 2.4-15 in 14.1, its closest parallel as a sustained vision of reconciliation is 2.16-25. However, direct correspondences are surprisingly elusive; the book avoids simple circularity. Similarly, the permutation of various forms of the words *šûb*, 'return', and *yāšab*, 'dwell', connects our chapter with the climactic turn in chs. 3 and 11, so that the conclusions of the three main sections of the book share the same leitmotiv. Nevertheless, ch. 14 lacks the specifics of the return from exile of chs. 3 and 11, and the marital imagery and cosmic covenant of ch. 2. There is a trace of the reversal of names; the gifts of corn, wine and oil are reflected in the description of Israel's prosperity in vv. 6-8. The recognition that Assyria and military power are powerless to save adduces the perspective of a world, at least a people, not dependent on war in 1.7 and 2.20. The wordplays on the name Ephraim converge, and become entirely positive. Words and images carry with them the associations acquired in the rest of the book; what is important, however, is the transformation, the newness of vision. This may be illustrated by a comparison with ch. 2:

2.16-25	14.2-9
vv. 16-17: Return to the wilderness; the bride's answer	v. 2: Return to God
vv. 18-19: Removal of the names of Baalim; transformation of God's name	vv. 3-4: Israel's prayer. No longer calling the work of their hands 'our God'
v. 20: Cosmic covenant	vv. 5-8: Lebanon and tree
vv. 21-22: Betrothal	–
vv. 23-25: God's answering heavens; reversal of names	v. 9: God's answer

Within the same frame, the difference is evident: a transfer from the historical and geographical contingencies of ch. 2—the Exodus, the land of Israel, Jezreel—to the mythological, politically unconditioned realm of Lebanon and shelter under a divine tree.

The chapter consists of two sections: Israel's/the prophet's prayer in vv. 2-4 and God's response in vv. 5-9. They may illustrate the dialogue of God and Israel in 2.16-17, in contrast to the inability to hear, the twisting of words that characterize the rest of the book. Like any true dialogue, moreover, it is not simply sequential—Israel's prayer followed by God's accession. God's intent to love Israel freely in v. 5 is apparently an independent decision. Instead, the voices interfuse; Israel's turning to God and God's turning to Israel are simultaneous processes. The panels match each other syntactically and lexically, especially at their beginning and end. Verses 2 and 5 have the same syntactic structure and emphasize the same word, 'return'. Both end with a statement of dependence, allude to Assyria and Ephraim, and reflect on the renunciation of idols, from opposite points of view.

How convincing is the dialogue? Nothing in it mitigates the reality of the conquest and the impossibility of integrating the split personalities of God and Israel in the previous chapters. It is, moreover, constructed by the prophet, or by God through the prophet; Israel's speech, in particular, is framed as part of the prophetic exhortation. With the transfer to God in v. 5, the distance between divine and human voices closes, culminating in the last phrase of God's speech in v. 9, which may be taken to be a true statement of relationship. The inset vision of a restored Israel, distanced by simile and the paradisal setting, detaches this closure from time and space. We do not know whether it is purely fabulous. Thus the book ends, disregarding v. 10 for the moment, in an indeterminacy, striving, however, to be determinate.

The repeated summons to return leads us to expect poetic as well as psychic recapitulation, as in Song 7.1 (6.12 in most English translations). Return has been postponed throughout the book, from the woman's first grudging expression of a willingness to return in 2.9 to the people's incapacity or refusal in 5.4 and 11.5 and their inadequate overture in 6.1-3. In 5.5-6, the people seek Yhwh with their flocks and herds, but stumble in their sin; here stumbling in sin is redressed with words. The admonition to return has previously occurred in 12.7. In contrast to this and its parallel in 10.12, return now is not a matter of acting kindly and justly and waiting for Yhwh's advent, but an urgent solicitation. It lacks, however, the pilgrimage setting of 5.6, where the flocks and herds sensually communicate motion; the return cannot be located topographically. It consists of an acknowledgment of sin and a renunciation of action. The first half of the speech (vv. 2-3), with its intense imperatives and injunctions, gives way to a second half (v. 4) governed by negation, of Assyria, horses, and the work of our hands. Movement then is to an awareness of dependence, summarized by 'in you the orphan will find compassion'. The passage subverts the language of sacrifice: they bring words, Yhwh takes 'goodness'; they offer up the bulls of the lips. (Many commentators follow the Septuagint in reading *pārîm* as *p^{e}rî*, 'fruit'. For a defence of the MT, see Macintosh 1997: 562-64; Sweeney 2000: 138; Ben Zvi 2005: 293-95, 306-307, and the very ingenious interpretation of Morris, involving multiple puns [1996: 92].) Much of Hosea has been preoccupied with cultic sites and practices. Here we cross the threshold to a pilgrimage not attached to land and history and a ritual without action.

The beginning of the speech is linked to its centre, through its repetition of the motif, 'return to Yhwh'. On either side of the call are intimations of speech ('take words...say'), acknowledgement of sin and its forgiveness, taking words and offering goodness ('take...take'). The midpoint divides the prophet's call from his audience's hypothetical response. The symmetry breaks down: 'take words' bifurcates into '*take* goodness, and we will offer up the bulls *of our lips*', while v. 4 expands into a list of renunciations. The echoes of the first half of the speech are hollow, contrasting the God to whom they return in v. 2 with the manufactured 'god(s)' of v. 4, their actual speech with that they will no longer utter.

'You forgive all iniquity' literally reads, 'all you bear iniquity'. The intrusion of a verb between two dependent nouns in also found in 6.9, which may be rendered, 'the way they murder to Shechem'. As there, it introduces a certain hesitation before specifying direction or category. Everything is borne by God; as a metaphor for forgiveness it suggests that God takes on himself the weight of sin. It is balanced, however, by 'take goodness', which may refer to God's disposition or to human deeds; if the latter, human beings have something to contribute to the moral economy, to God's well being, either as a result of penitence or because the conventional prophetic denunciation of their unrelieved evil is overstated. A reality sense may supervene momentarily on the polarities the book presupposes. As a result of divine forgiveness and acceptance, they will 'pay (or offer) the bulls of their lips'. The word for 'pay' (*n^{e}šall^{e}mâ*) is associated with the peace or communion offerings (*š^{e}lāmîm*) that are the sign of the re-establishment of harmony between God and humanity, following rituals of purgation. The metaphor 'bulls of the lips' abruptly juxtaposes the expected currency of sacrifice with the verbal currency that God prefers.

In 8.3 Israel spurns the 'good'; in 8.5 this rejection is identified with that of the calf, whose divinity exemplifies worshipping the work of one's hands and defiance of God. Here their gift of goodness is coupled with their disavowal of all other supports. They progress inwards, from diplomacy to belief; that Assyria will not save validates Yhwh's status as sole saviour in 13.4 and the impotence of the king in 13.10. According to 11.5, Assyria is their king; ironically, it is both the repository of their hopes and the destroyer.

'On horses we will not ride': in 10.13, trust in military power results in eating the fruit of deceit and provokes Assyrian retaliation. Here the substitution of words for bulls corresponds to the disapprobation of horses. In 1.7 Judah will not be saved by horses or arms, only by Yhwh; the cross-reference is strengthened by the use of the idiom 'bear, carry'($nś$) for 'forgive' in 1.6. There, however, it is Judah that is forgiven and miraculously saved on the other side of the threshold of destruction, while Israel is the Uncompassioned, Lo-Ruhama. Here the orphan receives compassion (y^eruham); the orphan is the inverse of Lo-Ammi, the child disowned by God. If the imagery of bereavement reaches its climax in 14.1, the source in which the orphan finds care is Yhwh. The word for compassion has the same semantic root as that for the womb ($rehem$) which bereaves in 9.14. The return to Yhwh in v. 2 is complemented then by restitution of the matrix.

Yhwh's speech (vv. 5-9) is circular, a complex interplay of efflux and influx. It begins and ends with plays on the word Ephraim: Yhwh heals ($'erpā'$) Ephraim in v. 5, and in him its fruit ($pery^ekā$) is found in v. 9. Yhwh heals their 'backsliding', a continuous movement away from him that he unfailingly repairs; at the same time, his anger turns ($šāb$) from Ephraim, returning to its source in God. He is able to love Israel 'freely', without the anger that accompanies his love in 3.1 and 11.3. The word for 'freely' ($n^edābâ$) is used also for a freewill offering, and thus matches the association with the peace offerings in v. 3. The retraction of God's anger ($'ap$) in v. 5 is reversed in the emanation of Ephraim from him at the end of v. 9 and the free expression of love; thus return is complemented by effusion.

The middle three verses (vv. 6-8) are close to the language of the Song of Songs, and thus a fitting erotic coda to the book: this is how God's love manifests itself. Whereas in the Song of Songs the lovers, especially the woman, are compared to the land of Israel, here the simile ironically reverses the direction of the comparison, since it is in fact a description of Israel's future bounty. The succession of similes turns natural processes into metaphoric ones: the dew is a sign of God's care, the lily of Israel's efflorescence. The language of love poetry reverts to the amorous imagery of the first part of the book. One would expect Israel to be the female partner; grammatically, however, it remains obstinately masculine, as do most of the images. The masculinity is presumably inclusive, comprising Israel as male and female subject. Nevertheless, the elimination of the feminine persona has the effect of desexing the Song; Israel is as much orphan/child as lover. In 13.13–14.1, the grammatical masculinity of Ephraim maintains a semblance of social normality, reducing the figure of travailing mother to metaphor and enabling it to be mother and son at the same time. Here the sexual tensions of the poem are neutralized in part through projection onto the fantasy realm of Lebanon, and in part through making them as ethereal, and as carefully disguised, as possible.

The passage is structured round the threefold mention of Lebanon at the end of the verses, and the repetition of the verb 'flower' in the second and penultimate positions. The parallelism, whereby each verse consists of three matching clauses, and the distance imposed by simile, is broken by 'They shall bring to life new grain' in v. 8. The passage, like the chapter as a whole, is based on a rhythm of expansion and contraction: the tree/Israel strikes roots and sends forth shoots, its fragrance and fame diffuse, while those who sit in its shade return to it.

Lebanon has a dual significance, as a mountain range to the north of Israel, and as a metonym for the cedars of Lebanon; its roots may refer to the embedding of the mountains in the earth (cf. Job 28.9), as well as to the trees. An evocation of depth, as in a mirror, communicates height, and contributes further to the impression of symmetry in the passage. In the Song 4.11 the fragrance of Lebanon is compared to that of the woman's skirts; analogously, it suggests the herbs and wild flowers as well as the coniferous forests with which it is covered. The wine of Lebanon was perhaps especially famous (Davies 1992: 308; Wolff 1974: 232-33), but serves also to include wine in the register of sensations (conversely, in Ps. 80.11, the vine of Israel has divine cedars as its branches). In the Song 1.4, the man's caresses are remembered more than wine; wine is to be savoured, thought about, and recalled. In 12.6 the same word, *zikrô*, 'his remembrance', occurs in the context of Yhwh's liturgical celebration.

Israel's recollection, presumably by others, is as intoxicating as that of wine, and interfuses with the name of God.

In Ezek. 31.2-9 the cedar of Lebanon is the greatest of trees in the garden of God, an association supported by such idioms as 'the cedars of God' (Ps.80.11; cf. 104.16). The paradisal connotations of our passage are clear from the attraction of all the products of the land into the ambit of Lebanon, and by its function of shelter. Lebanon is a representative tree, whose shoots comprise, at least metaphorically, olive and vine. Since it is a designation for Israel, those who sit in its shade are the inhabitants of the land. Their return conforms to the motif of the restoration of the exiles that we found at the end of chs. 3 and 11, and the confluence in both cases of the verbs *yašab*, 'dwell', and *šûb*, 'return'. The cedar/Lebanon protects the land; its immensity is emphasized by the following lapse in the sequence of similes, since the new grain is cultivated by, instead of being comparable to, those who dwell in its shade. In Ezekiel the tree ensconces all nations, beasts, and birds, and thus becomes a cosmic tree; of this fulfilment of the cosmic covenant, the tree in Hosea is an intimation.

The lily in the Song of Songs is a feminine symbol; it is the one instance in the passage where the feminine subject emerges unambiguously. Correlatively, the droplets of dew which initiate the process of fertility suggest male sexuality; God's action as dew corresponds to his answering the heavens in 2.23. The image, however, is entirely incorporeal; the dew is a celestial deliquescence which lacks the phallic overtones of Yhwh's insemination in 2.23-25. Like the rain in 6.3, it is all-encompassing, a life-giving presence in everything. Yhwh's self-affirmation as 'I am' reverses the threat of its negation in 1.9, but is almost intangible, on the verge of disappearing.

The image of dew has previously appeared in 6.4 and 13.5 as a symbol for evanescence. If Israel's *ḥesed* is transitory, Yhwh's is unfailing. The combination of opposites in the one term effects a transposition: God gives permanence to ephemeral Israel.

Verse 9 is as puzzling as any in the book: Yhwh addresses Ephraim, but also speaks of it in the third person; it is a dialogue with himself, into which Ephraim is drawn. It begins with a question, in line with the other questions God asks himself, expressive of God's dilemma. The context, in which God compares himself to dew, links it most closely to God's question in 6.4: 'What shall I do with you, Ephraim?' But here it turns back to

God: 'What have I still to do with idols?' The subject may be either Ephraim or God. If the latter, then God's being concerned with idols is no longer of any importance; much of the occasion for anger in the book disappears. The renunciation seems to be without irony, because it is reciprocal. Idols, substitute objects, will no longer intervene between God and Ephraim. In 4.17 the word for 'idols' (*ᵃṣabbîm*) is paired with that for the 'wood' (*'ēṣ*) of which the people inquire in 4.12; here the dead wood is contrasted with the living tree.

God answers, just as he does in 2.23-25; it may be a response to Israel's prayer in vv. 3-4. The word for 'answer' (*'ānâ*) is close to that for 'afflict' (*'innâ*); God's response to Israel's waywardness has generally been the infliction of pain (*ᵃṣābîm*), a pun on the word for idols. Yhwh's responsiveness is maintained and illustrated by his watchfulness. 'I will watch over him' (*'ᵃšûrennû*) uses the same verb as 'I will lurk' (*'āšûr*) in 13.7. This is the last of the many echoes linking chs. 13 and 14: the dew turns from a symbol of transitoriness in 13.3 to one of persistence in v. 6 ; the idols of which Ephraim is guilty in 13.2 are abjured in v. 5; the anger with which God gives and takes the king in 13.10 is removed. We have seen correlations of bovine cultic imagery; both chapters have matching but opposed sets of similes. Nevertheless, the fastening together of the two chapters establishes points of separation: ch. 14 has no equivalent of the historical reflection of ch. 13, while ch. 13 lacks its vision of the future.

In 13.7 'I will lurk' (*'āšûr*) is a wordplay on the name of Assyria. If, according to v. 4, Assyria cannot save, God will be Ephraim's Assyria; from being the instrument of affliction, God's principal response to Ephraim's sedition, Assyria becomes a symbol for his sovereignty and providence. Assyria and Ephraim are coupled together in this final verse, both endorsed by God.

There may be other connotations: 'I will watch over him' (*'ᵃšûrennu*) is very similar to the verb 'to make straight' (*'aššēr*) and the word for 'happy' (*'ašrê*) which introduces many Psalms. Some critics have perceived in the words 'I answer' (*'ānîtî*) and 'I will watch over him' (*'ᵃšûrennu*) an oblique reference to the names of the goddesses Anat and Asherah, and thus another recollection of 4.13-14 (Loretz 1989 and Emmerson 1984: 49-52; the suggestion goes back to Wellhausen). Yhwh, in the context of arboreal imagery, adopts the persona of the goddess whose worship recalls the prostitution under sacred trees in 4.12-14. The transfer of gender would then be complete.

At the end of the verse, God compares himself to a 'leafy cypress tree'. The two images for God obviously complement each other: the pervasive, unremarked dew and the ever-flourishing tree. It coincides with the image of Israel as a tree. If God is a tree from which Ephraim finds its fruit, and thus is associated with the Tree of Life, Israel is the universal tree under which all find shelter. Cypresses are a typical tree of Lebanon, almost always coupled with cedars. The metaphors for God and Israel converge.

From that tree Ephraim finds its fruit. Everything Ephraim does, all the work of its hands, comes from God, which makes its disassociation from idols paradoxical. Equally, all Ephraim's fruit is found in God and is part of its prophetic task of constituting and reflecting God's image. In 9.10 God found Israel like grapes in the wilderness; Israel formed a matrix for God. Now its fruit, the fruit of the vine in 10.1, the wine that they share in v. 8, is discovered in God, who is thus a matrix for Israel. The two images are reversible throughout the book, in which God and Israel nurture and destroy each other.

The very last verse of the book is generally regarded as an addendum, in which its composers, editors or shapers provided a key to its interpretation. According to them, it is very simple: the righteous walk untroubled in the ways of Yhwh and the rebels stumble in them. Gerald Sheppard (1980: 129-36; cf. 1993) has shown how the message is adapted to the terminology of the book; for instance, the conventional antonym of the righteous, namely 'the wicked', is replaced by 'rebels'. This is the knowledge that the wise son, in contrast to the unwise son of 13.13, would acquire. However, in the book, the ways of Yhwh are by no means straight, just or easy to comprehend; they are characterized by twists and turns, vacillation, and anguish. The ways of the prophet too, the person of understanding who communicates the knowledge of God, are hardly clear; he is a trap, or there is a trap laid for him, across all his paths. His speech verges on madness, according to 9.7; the abrupt shifts in tone, imagery and rhetoric of the book cannot be reduced to rational dichotomies. Finally, the codicil smugly concludes that the rebels stumble in Yhwh's ways. However, at the beginning of our chapter, it is Israel itself that has stumbled in its iniquity. There is no evidence for a distinction between the righteous and the wicked, that for example the pregnant women and shattered babies were morally culpable and deserving of their fate.

Moreover, though Israel stumbles, it has the chance to return. The rebels can pick themselves up and continue on the way of Yhwh, pursuing *ḥesed* and justice They can turn into the righteous, or at least God can remove the tripwire, and they can read the book without ideological blinkers. And theirs, I suspect, will be the more interesting experience.

Select Bibliography

Commentaries

Andersen, F.I., and D.N. Freedman, *Hosea* (Anchor Bible; New York: Doubleday, 1980).
Ben Zvi, E. *Hosea* (The Forms of the Old Testament Literature, XXIA/1; Grand Rapids, MI: Eerdmans, 2005).
Davies, G.I., *Hosea* (New Century Bible Commentary; Grand Rapids, MI: Eerdmans; London: Marshall Pickering, 1992).
Hubbard, D.A., *Hosea* (Tyndale Old Testament Commentaries; Downers Grove, IL: Inter-Varsity Press, 1989).
Jeremias, J., *Der Prophet Hosea* (Das Alte Testament Deutsch, 24/1; Göttingen: Vandenhoeck & Ruprecht, 1983).
Kidner, D., *Hosea* (Tyndale Old Testament Commentaries; Downers Grove, IL: Inter-Varsity Press, 1981).
Macintosh, A.A. *Hosea* (The International Critical Commentary; Edinburgh: T. & T. Clark, 1997).
Mays, J.L., *Hosea* (Old Testament Library; Philadelphia; Westminster Press, 1969).
Rudolph, W., *Hosea* (Kommentar zum Alten Testament, 13/1; Gütersloh: G. Mohn, 1966).
Stuart, D., *Hosea–Jonah* (Word Biblical Commentary, 31; Waco, TX: Word, 1987).
Sweeney, M.A., *The Twelve Prophets*, I (Berit Olam; Collegeville, MI: The Liturgical Press, 2000).
Wolff, H.W., *A Commentary on the Book of the Prophet Hosea* (trans. G. Stansell; ed. P. Hanson; Hermeneia; Philadelphia: Fortress Press, 1974).

Special Studies on Hosea

Balz-Cochois, H., *Gomer. Der Höhenkult Israels im Selbstverständnis der Volksfrömmigkeit. Untersuchungen zu Hosea 4, 1–5, 7* (Frankfurt and Berne: Peter Lang, 1982).
Borbone, P.G., *Il libro del profeta Osea: edizione critica del testo ebraico* (Turin: Zamorani, 1990).
Buss, M., *The Prophetic Word of Hosea* (BZAW, 111; Berlin: de Gruyter, 1969).
Daniels, D.R., *Hosea and Salvation History* (BZAW, 191; Berlin: de Gruyter, 1990).
Davies, G.I., *Hosea* (Old Testament Guides; Sheffield: JSOT Press, 1993).
Eidevall, G. *Grapes in the Wilderness: Metaphors, Models, and Themes in Hosea 4–14* (Coniectanea biblica Old Testament series, 43; Stockholm: Almqvist & Wiksell, 1996).
Emmerson, G.I., *Hosea: An Israelite Prophet in Judean Perspective* (JSOTSup, 28; Sheffield: JSOT Press, 1984).

Holt, E.K. *Prophesying the Past: The Use of Israel's History in the Book of Hosea* (JSOTSup, 194; Sheffield: Sheffield Academic Press, 1995).
Keefe, A.A. *Woman's Body and the Social Body in Hosea* (JSOTSup, 338; Sheffield: Sheffield Academic Press, 2001).
Kelle, B.E. *Hosea 2: Metaphor and Rhetoric in Historical Perspective* (Atlanta: Society of Biblical Literature, 2005).
King, P.J., *Amos, Hosea, Micah—An Archaeological Commentary* (Philadelphia: Westminster, 1988).
Kuhnigk, W., *Nordwestsemitische Studien zum Hoseabuch* (Rome: Pontifical Biblical Institute Press, 1974).
Morris, G. *Prophecy, Poetry and Hosea* (JSOTSup, 219; Sheffield: Sheffield Academic Press, 1996).
Neef, H.-D., *Die Heilstraditionen Israels in der Verkündigung des Propheten Hosea* (BZAW, 169; Berlin: de Gruyter, 1987).
Sherwood, Y. *The Prostitute and the Prophet: Hosea's Marriage in Literary-Theoretical Perspective* (JSOTSup, 212; Sheffield: Sheffield Academic Press, 1996).
Utzschneider, H., *Hosea: Prophet vor dem Ende* (Orbis biblicus et orientalis, 31; Freiburg: Universitätsverlag; Göttingen: Vandenhoeck & Ruprecht, 1980).
Willi-Plein, I., *Vorformen der Schriftexegese innerhalb des Alten Testaments: Untersuchungen zum literarischen Werden des auf Amos, Hosea und Micha zurückgehenden Bücher im hebräischen Zwölfprophetenbuch* (BZAW, 123; Berlin: de Gruyter, 1971).
Yee, G.A., *Composition and Tradition in the Book of Hosea: A Redactional Critical Investigation* (Atlanta: Scholars Press, 1987).

Articles on Hosea
Ackroyd, P.R., 'Hosea and Jacob', *VT* 13 (1963), pp. 245-59.
Alt, A., 'Hosea 5:8–6:6. Ein Krieg und seine Folgen in prophetischer Beleuchtung', in *Kleine Schriften zur Geschichte des Volkes Israel,* II (Munich: Beck, 1953), pp. 163-87.
Bird, P., 'To Play the Harlot: An Inquiry into an Old Testament Metaphor', in P. Day (ed.), *Gender and Difference in Ancient Israel* (Philadelphia: Fortress, 1989), pp. 75-94.
Buss, M.J., 'Tragedy and Comedy in Hosea', *Semeia* 32 (1984), pp. 71-82.
Clines, D.J.A., 'Hosea 2: Structure and Interpretation', in E.A. Livingstone (ed.), *Studia biblica 1978.* I. *Papers on Old Testament and Related Themes* (JSOTSup, 11; Sheffield: JSOT Press, 1979), pp. 83-103.
Cohen, C., 'Foam in Hosea 10:7', *JANES* 2 (1969), pp. 25-29.
Cohen, N.G., Hebrew: 'An Enthusiastic Prophetic Formula', *ZAW* 99 (1987), pp. 219-32.
Coote, R.B., 'Hosea xii', *VT* 21 (1971), pp. 389-402.
Day, J., 'Pre-Deuteronomic Allusions to the Covenant in Hosea and Psalm lxxviii', *VT* 36 (1986), pp. 1-12.
DeRoche, M., 'Structure, Rhetoric and Meaning in Hosea iv 4-10', *VT* 33 (1983), pp. 185-98.
—'The Reversal of Creation in Hosea', *VT* 31 (1981), pp. 400-409.
Dijk-Hemmes, F. van, 'The Imagination of Power and the Power of Imagination: An Intertextual Analysis of Two Biblical Love Songs: The Song of Songs and Hosea 2', *JSOT* 44 (1989), pp. 75-88.

Ehrlich, C.S., 'The Text of Hosea 1:9', *JBL* 104 (1985), pp. 12-19.
Eidevall, G., 'Lions and Birds as Literature. Some Notes on Isaiah 31 and Hosea 11', *SJOT* 7 (1993), pp. 78-87.
Emmerson, G.I., 'Fertility Goddess in Hosea iv 17-19?', *VT* 24 (1974), pp. 492-97.
—'The Structure and Meaning of Hosea viii 1-3', *VT* 25 (1975), pp. 700-10.
Eslinger, L.M., 'Hosea 12.4a and Genesis 32.29: A Study in Inner Biblical Exegesis', *JSOT* 18 (1980), pp. 91-99.
Fisch, H., 'Hosea: A Poetics of Violence', in his *Poetry with a Purpose: Biblical Poetics and Interpretation* (Bloomington, IN: Indiana University Press, 1988), pp. 137-58.
Freedman, D.N., 'Problems of Textual Criticism in the Book of Hosea', in W. O'Flaherty (ed.), *The Critical Study of Sacred Texts* (Berkeley: UCLA, 1979), pp. 55-76.
Friedman, M.A., 'Israel's Response in Hosea 2:17b: "You are my husband"', *JBL* 99 (1980), pp. 199-204.
Geller, M.J., 'The Elephantine Papyri and Hosea 2,3: Evidence for the Form of the Early Jewish Divorce Writ', *JSJ* 8 (1977), pp. 139-48.
Gertner, M., 'The Masorah and the Levites: Appendix on Hosea xii', *VT* 10 (1960), pp. 241-84.
Ginsberg, H.L., 'Hosea', in *Encyclopedia judaica* (New York: Macmillan, 1971), VIII, cols. 1010-24.
—'Hosea's Ephraim, More Fool than Knave: A New Interpretation of Hosea 12:1-14', *JBL* 80 (1961), pp. 339-47.
Gnuse, R., 'Calf, Cult, and King: The Unity of Hosea 8:1-13', *BZ* 26 (1982), pp. 83-92.
Good, E.M., 'The Composition of Hosea', *SEÅ* 31 (1966), pp. 21-63.
—'Hosea 5:8–6:6-6: An Alternative to Alt', *JBL* 85 (1966), pp. 273-86.
—'Hosea and the Jacob Tradition', *VT* 16 (1966), pp. 137-51.
Hoffman, Y., 'A North Israelite Typological Myth and a Judaean Historical Tradition: The Exodus in Hosea and Amos', *VT* 39 (1989), pp. 169-82.
Isbell, C.D., 'The Divine Name Hebrew as a Symbol of Presence in Israelite Tradition', *HAR* 2 (1978), pp. 181-18.
Janzen, J.G., 'Metaphor and Reality in Hosea 11', *Semeia* 24 (1982), pp. 7-44.
Krause, D., 'A Blessing Cursed: The Prophet's Prayer for Barren Womb and Dry Breasts', in Danna Nolan Fewell (ed.), *Reading between Texts: Intertextuality and the Hebrew Bible* (Louisville: Westminster/John Knox, 1992), pp. 191-202.
Kreutzer, S., 'Gott als Mutter in Hosea 11?', *TQ* 169 (1989), pp. 123-32.
Kruger, P.A., 'Israel, the Harlot (Hos 2:4-9)', *JNWSL* 11 (1991), pp. 107-16.
—'Prophetic Imagery: On Metaphors and Similes in the Book Hosea', *JNWSL* 4 (1988), pp. 143-51.
Kuan, J.K., 'Hosea 9.13 and Josephus, *Antiquities* IX, 277-287', *PEQ* (1991), pp. 103-107.
Landy, F., 'In the Wilderness of Speech: Problems of Metaphor in Hosea', *Biblical Interpretation* 3 (1995), pp. 35-39.
Leith, M.J.W., 'Verse and Reverse: The Transformation of the Woman, Israel, in Hosea 1–3', in P. Day (ed.), *Gender and Difference in Ancient Israel* (Philadelphia: Fortress, 1989), pp. 95-108.
Lohfink, N., 'Zu Text und Form von Os 4:4-6', *Biblica* 42 (1961), pp. 303-32.
Loretz, O., 'Tod und Leben nach altorientalischer und kanaänisch-biblischer Anschauung in Hos 6, 1-3', *BN* 17 (1982), pp. 37-42.

—'Anat-Aschera (Hos 14:9) und die Inschriften von Kuntillet Ajrud', *Studi epigraphici e linguistici sul vicino oriente antico* 6 (1989), pp. 47-65.
Lundbom, J.R., 'Contentious Priests and Contentious People in Hosea iv 1-10', *VT* 36 (1986), pp. 52-70.
—'Double Duty Subject in Hosea viii 5', *VT* 25 (1975), pp. 228-30.
—'Poetic Structure and Prophetic Rhetoric in Hosea', *VT* 29 (1979), pp. 300-08.
Lust, J., 'Freud, Hosea, and the Murder of Moses: Hosea 12', *ETL* 65 (1989), pp. 81-93.
Lys, D., '"J'ai deux amours, ou l'amant jugé": Exercise zur Osée 2, 4-25', *ETR* 51 (1976), pp. 59-77.
Margalit, B., 'The Meaning and Significance of Asherah', *VT* 40 (1990), pp. 264-97.
Mays, J.L., 'Response to Janzen, "Metaphor and Reality in Hosea 11"', *Semeia* 24 (1982), pp. 44-51.
Mazor, Y., 'Hosea 5.1-3: Between Compositional Rhetoric and Rhetorical Composition', *JSOT* 45 (1989), pp. 115-26.
McKenzie, S.L., 'The Jacob Tradition in Hosea xii 4-5', *VT* 36 (1986), pp. 311-22.
O'Connor, M.P., 'The Pseudosorites: A Type of Paradox in Hebrew Verse', in E.R. Follis (ed.), *New Directions in Biblical Hebrew Poetry* (JSOTSup, 40; Sheffield: JSOT Press, 1987), pp. 161-72.
— 'The Pseudosorites in Hebrew Verse', in E.W. Conrad and E.G. Newing (eds.), *A Ready Scribe: Perspectives on Language and Text. Essays and Poems in Honor of Francis I. Andersen's Sixtieth Birthday* (Winona Lake, IN: Eisenbrauns, 1987), pp. 239-51.
Paul, S.M., 'משא מלך שרים—Hosea 8:8-10 and Ancient Near Eastern Royal Epithets', *Scripta hierosolymita* 31 (1986), pp. 193-204.
— 'The Image of the Oven and Cake in Hosea vii 4-10', *VT* 18 (1968), pp. 114-20.
Renaud, B., 'Le livret d'Osée 1–3: un travail complexe d'édition', *RevScRel* 36 (1982), pp. 159-78.
— 'Osee ii 2: *'lh mn b'rṣ*: essai d'interpretation', *VT* 33 (1983), pp. 495-500.
— 'Fidelité humaine et fidelité de Dieu dans le livre d'Osée 1–3', *Revue de droit canonique* 33 (1983), pp. 184-200.
— 'Genèse et unité redactionnelle de Os 2', *RevScRel* 54 (1980), pp. 1-20.
— 'Osée 1–3: analyse diachronique et lecture synchronique, problèmes de methode', *RevScRel* 57 (1983), pp. 249-60.
Ruppert, L., 'Herkunft und Bedeutung der Jakob-Tradition bei Hosea', *Biblica* 52 (1971), pp. 442-47.
Ruprecht, K., *ᶜlh mn h'rṣ* (Ex 1:10; Hos 2:2): "sich des Landes bemächtigen"?', *ZAW* 82 (1970), pp. 442-47.
Schmitt, J.J., 'The Gender of Ancient Israel', *JSOT* 26 (1983), pp. 115-25.
—'The Wife of God in Hosea 2', *Biblical Research* 34 (1989), pp. 5-18.
Schüngel-Straumann, H., 'Gott als Mutter in Hosea 11', *TQ* 166 (1986), pp. 119-34.
Selms, A. van, 'Hosea and Canticles', *OTWSA* 7/8 (1964–1965), pp. 85-89.
Seow, C.L., 'Hosea and the Foolish People Motif', *CBQ* 44 (1982), pp. 212-24.
Setel, D.T., 'Poets and Pornography: Female Sexual Imagery in Hosea', in L.M. Russell (ed.), *Feminist Interpretation of the Bible* (Philadelphia: Westminster, 1986), pp. 86-95.
Sheppard, G.T., 'The Last Words of Hosea', *RevExp* 90 (1993), pp. 191-204.

Smith, S.H., '"Heel" and "Thigh": The Concept of Sexuality in the Jacob–Esau Narratives', *VT* 40 (1990), pp. 464-73.
Tomes, R., 'The Reason for the Syro-Ephraimite War', *JSOT* 59 (1993), pp. 55-71.
Unterman, J., 'Repentance and Redemption in Hosea', *SBL Seminar Papers* 21 (1982), pp. 541-50.
Weems, R., 'Gomer: Victim of Violence or Victim of Metaphor?', *Semeia* 47 (1989), pp. 87-104.
Whitt, W.D., 'The Divorce of Yahweh and Asherah in Hos 2:4–7.12ff.', *SJOT* 6 (1992), pp. 31-67.
Wijngaards, J., 'Death and Resurrection in Covenant Context (Hos vi 2)', *VT* 17 (1967), pp. 226-39.
Yee, G.A., 'Hosea', in C.A. Newsom and S.H. Ringe (eds.), *The Women's Bible Commentary* (Louisville: Westminster/John Knox, 1992), pp. 85-102.

Other References

Ackerman, S., *Under Every Green Tree: Popular Religion in Sixth-Century Judah (Atlanta: Scholars Press, 1988)*.
Bach, R., 'Der Erwählung Israel in der Wüste' (Dissertation, Univ. of Bonn, 1952).
Batto, B.F., 'The Covenant of Peace: A Neglected Near Eastern Motif', *CBQ* 49 (1987), pp. 187-211.
Buber, M., *On the Bible: Eighteen Studies* (New York: Schocken Books, 1968).
Carroll, R.P., *Jeremiah* (Old Testament Guides; Sheffield: JSOT Press, 1989).
— 'Strange Fire: Abstract of Presence Absent in the Text. Meditations on Exodus 3', *JSOT* 61 (1994), pp. 39-58.
Cixous, H. *Three Steps on the Ladder of Writing* (trans. S, Cornell and S. Sellers; New York: Columbia University Press, 1993).
Cooper, A., and B. Goldstein, 'The Cult of the Dead and the Theme of Entry into the Land', *Biblical Interpretation* 1 (1993), pp. 285-303.
Douglas, M., *In the Wilderness: The Doctrine of Defilement in the Book of Numbers* (Sheffield: JSOT Press, 1993).
Dworkin, A., 'The Lie', in *Letters from a War Zone* (London: Secker & Warburg, 1988), pp. 9-12.
Eilberg-Schwartz, H., *The Savage in Judaism* (Bloomington, IN: Indiana University Press, 1990).
—*God's Phallus and Other Problems for Men and Monotheism* (Boston: Beacon Press, 1994).
Exum, J.C., 'Of Broken Pots, Fluttering Birds, and Visions in the Night: Extended Simile and Poetic Technique in Isaiah', *CBQ* 43 (1981), pp. 331-52.
Feliks, Y., *Nature and Man in the Bible: Chapters in Biblical Ecology* (New York: Soncino, 1981).
Haak, R., *Habakkuk* (Leiden: Brill, 1991).
Jamieson-Drake, D.W., *Scribes and Schools in Monarchic Judah: A Socio-Archeological Approach* (Sheffield: Almond, 1991).
Jay, N., *Throughout your Generations Forever: Sacrifice, Religion, and Paternity* (Chicago: University of Chicago Press, 1992).
Josipovici, G., *The Book of God: A Response to the Bible* (New Haven: Yale University Press, 1989).
Kaufmann, Y., *The Religion of Israel* (trans. M. Greenberg; London: Allen & Unwin, 1961, abridged edn).

Select Bibliography

Keel, O., and C. Uehlinger trans. T.H. Trapp; *Gods and Goddesses, and Images of God in Ancient Israel* (Minneapolis: Fortress, 1998).

Kristeva, J., *Black Sun* (trans. Leon S. Roudiez; New York: Columbia University Press, 1987).

Long, B.O., 'Social Dimensions of Prophetic Conflict', *Semeia* 21 (1981), pp. 31-53.

Milgrom, J., *Leviticus 1–16* (Anchor Bible, 3; New York: Doubleday, 1991).

—*Numbers* (JPS Torah Commentary; Philadelphia: JPS, 1991).

Murray, R., *The Cosmic Covenant* (London: Sheed & Ward, 1992).

Overholt, T.W., *Channels of Prophecy: The Social Dynamics of Prophetic Activity* (Minneapolis: Fortress, 1989).

Paul, S., *Amos* (Minneapolis: Fortress, 1991).

Propp, W., 'That Bloody Bridegroom (Exodus iv 24-26)', *VT* 43 (1993), pp. 495-518.

Read, K., 'Sacred Commoners: The Motion of Cosmic Powers in Mexican Rulership', *HR* 34 (1994), pp. 39-69.

Samuel, G., *Civilized Shamans* (Washington: Smithsonian, 1993).

Sheppard, G.T., *Wisdom as a Hermeneutical Construct* (BZAW, 151; Berlin: de Gruyter, 1980).

Stewart, S., *Nonsense: Aspects of Intertextuality in Folklore and Literature* (Baltimore: Johns Hopkins University Press, 1979).

Turner, Victor, *The Ritual Process: Structure and Anti-Structure* (London: Aldine, 1969).

Verman, M., *The Books of Contemplation: Medieval Jewish Mystical Sources* (Albany: State University of New York Press, 1993).

Vermes, G., *Scripture and Tradition in Judaism* (Leiden: Brill, 1961).

Winnicott, D.W., *Playing and Reality* (London: Routledge, Kegan & Paul, 1991).

Index of Authors

Ackerman, S. 66, 74
Andersen, F.I. 48, 77, 80, 103, 105, 108, 110, 120, 136, 146, 147, 163, 177, 182, 190

Bach, R. 158
Balz-Cochois, H. 33
Batto, B.F. 46
Ben Zvi, E. vii, 1 n. 2, 18, 36, 37, 44, 48, 49, 51, 63, 64, 70, 79, 81, 82, 92, 101, 111, 114, 117, 123, 127, 131, 132, 136, 140, 147, 148, 156, 158, 159, 161, 171, 177, 179, 182, 183, 193, 200
Bird, P. 34
Borbone, P.G. 183
Buber, M. 21
Buss, M. 17

Carroll, R.P. 1 n. 1, 21
Cixous, H. viii
Clines, D.J.A. 35
Cooper, A. 39

Daniels, D.R. 160, 176
Davies, G.I. 139, 145, 175, 178, 182, 202
Day, J. 112
DeRoche, M. 55, 58
Dijk-Hemmes, F. van 31
Douglas, M. 50
Dworkin, A. 16
Eidevall, G. 114, 115, 165, 166, 187

Eilberg-Schwartz, H. 11 n. 18, 42
Emmerson, G.I. 50, 51, 204
Eslinger, L.M. 173
Exum, J.C. 114

Feliks, Y. 187
Fisch, H. 1 n. 2, 3, 3 n. 4, 3 n. 5, 10 n. 17, 33, 73, 87, 165, 186, 188
Freedman, D.N. 48, 77, 80, 103, 105, 108, 110, 120, 136, 146, 147, 163, 177, 182, 190

Ginsberg, H. 3 n. 4
Goldstein, B. 39
Gunn, D. 189

Haak, R. 5 n. 8
Holt, E.K. 115

Jamieson-Drake, D.W. 7 n. 10
Janzen, J.G. 165
Jay, N. 9 n. 15, 159
Jeremias, J. 3 n. 6, 23, 33, 40, 54, 63, 70, 74, 75, 79, 84, 108, 110, 115, 120, 127, 143, 146, 148, 149, 152, 158, 161, 171, 176, 182, 191, 193
Josipovici, G. 15

Kaufmann, Y. 3 n. 4
Keefe, A. 16, 18, 28, 33, 34, 115
Keel, O. 118

Kelle, B.E. 34, 66
Krause, D. 135
Kreutzer, S. 159
Kristeva, J. 50
Kuan, J.K. 137

Leith, M.J.W. 36
Long, B.O. 7 n. 11
Loretz, O. 204
Lundbom, J.R. 56

Macintosh, A.A. vii, 27, 28, 43, 63, 66, 67, 69, 77, 114, 127, 152, 153, 160, 161, 174, 182, 191, 200
Mays, J.L. 23, 101
Milgrom, J. 59, 116
Morris, G. 40, 63, 67, 73, 77, 132, 143, 200
Murray, R. 28

Neef, H.D. 160

O'Connor, M.P. 30, 119, 120, 135, 138, 141
Overholt, T. 4 n. 7

Paul, S. 105, 110, 122
Propp, W. 43

Read, K. 4 n. 7
Rudolph, W. 127, 140, 144, 146, 152, 156, 162, 175, 176, 182

Samuel, G. 4 n. 7
Schüngel-Straumann, H. 159

Selms, A. van 31
Seow, C.L. 63
Sheppard, G. 205
Sherwood, Y. 28, 33, 40
Stewart, S. 8 n. 14
Stuart, D. 28
Sweeney, M. 20, 45, 54, 57, 76, 105, 110, 127, 144, 148, 151, 161, 176, 179, 189, 200
Tomes, R. 78
Turner, V. 66

Uehlinger, C. 118
Utzschneider, H. 50, 114, 117, 147, 175

Verman, M. 9 n. 16
Vermes, G. 5 n. 8

Whitt, W.D. 33
Winnicott, D.W. 29, 172
Wolff, H.W. 23, 28, 33, 114, 129, 144, 162, 170, 172, 202

Yee, G.A. 182

Index of References

Genesis	
1.26-30	42
1.30	41
2.5	16, 18, 46
3	57
3.7	44
3.18	93, 131, 149
4.1	44
6.1-6	44
6.5	89
8.21	89
9.12-17	42
11.9	105
16.12	195
19.25	165
19.29	165
22.16	188
27.36	172
28.15	174
30.11	100
31.38-41	170
31.49	72
32.26	173
32.27	173
32.29	172
34	94
34.7	95
34.25	95
41.40	184
49.5-7	95
49.19	100
49.25	188

Exodus	
2.20	37
3.14	21, 189
3.15	40, 174, 176
4.22	135, 158
14.21	195
15.11	185
15.13	137
15.26	160
19.4	19, 160
28.30	58
28.39	58
31.17	42
34.6-7	19, 20

Leviticus	
2.12	100
10.11	57
12.7	195
18	44
18.17	94
19.17	56
19.18	48
19.29	94
20	44
20.14	94
20.18	195
21.7	61
21.9	61
22.9	61, 94
23.42	176
23.43	127
25.7	42
26.6	42
27.10	60
27.33	60

Numbers	
5	28
12.13	160
17.25	64
32	76

Deuteronomy	
3.18	77
14.1	110
16.11	127
16.13	127
16.14	127
16.15	127
17.14	127
21.4	144
21.20	69
22.21	17
23.18-19	74
32	88, 144
32.2-3	88
32.2	144
32.11	160
32.39	84

Joshua	
3.16	92
4	178
4.13	77
4.20	140
5.3	140
6	39
7	39
18.13	79
18.23	79

Judges	
4-5	73
4	80
5.7	80
5.14	73, 79
9	94
12.1	73
12.6	73

Index of References

19-21	151	15.29	78	1.1	**14**, 20
19	73	15.37	78	1.2	**14-17**, 19, 21,
20-21	73	16.5-9	78		22, 23, 24,
20	80, 151				45, 48, 64
20.6	95	*Isaiah*		1.3	**17**, 62
20.18-26	80	2.2-4	43	1.4-5	**17-18**, 21, 41,
21.3	80	5.18	161		42, 51
		6	133, 138	1.4	2, 23
1 Samuel		7.1-2	78	1.5	22, 23, 37, 42
8-12	189	8.15	133	1.6	**18-20**, 201
8.5	127, 190	11.9	43	1.7	**20-21**, 22,
8.7	189	19.1	153		23, 41, 51,
10.3	80	20	15		198, 201
10.17-27	72	21.6-10	72	1.8-9	**21-22**
10.25	72	25.7-8	193	1.9	22, 23, 33, 49,
11.14	140	28.7	64		189, 203
12	140	28.13	133	2	2, 3, 4, 11, 12,
13.15	140	28.25	15		26, 27, 37, 46,
15	92	31.4	165		47, 49, 50, 54,
15.22	80	31.4-5	114		56, 70, 110,
15.28	84	38.14	108		156, 159, 172,
15.29	166	45.5	185		185, 196, 198
15.33	81			2.1-3	**22-24**, 46, 51
17.45	51	*Jeremiah*		2.3	26
18.10	132	1	138	2.4-15	10, 26, 198
		2.24	121	2.4-5	27
2 Samuel		5.4-5	60	2.4	26, 28, 29, 32,
7.14	161	11.14	138		33, 39, 56, 64
7.22	185	16.5	110	2.5	27, 28, 29, 35,
12.25	17	17.11	108		36, 41, 44
15.25	137-38	20.7	37	2.6	29
17.8	187	28-29	15	2.7-9	27
		50.7	138	2.7	31, 122
I Kings		51.36	195	2.8-9	30
12	18			2.8	30, 37, 187
12.28-30	111	*Ezekiel*		2.9	31, 33, 87, 199
12.32	128	3.17	72	2.10-15	27
16.7	57	4.4	15	2.10-11	128
18.28	110	6	72	2.10	31, 34, 116, 160
19.18	184	7	72	2.11	37
20-22	37	31.2-9	203	2.12	27, 28, 29,
20.31	81	33.2	72		30, 100
21	18	34.25	41	2.13-14	42
21.29	19			2.13	42, 77, 176
22.10	128	*Hosea*		2.14	27, 28, 29,
		1-3	2, 3, 3 n. 4, 20,		40, 41, 128,
2 Kings			62, 67, 98, 128		135, 186
9	18, 19, 94	1-2	57	2.15	31, 34, 35, 37,
10.30	19	1	1, 2, 3, 24,		**40**, 159
14.26	18		26, 47	2.16-25	10, 37, 41, 87,
					171, 198

Index of References 217

2.16-17	16, **35-39**, 41, 122, 195, 198	4.6	**57-59**, 60, 77, 93, 115, 177	8.2	19, 118, 131, 145
2.16	76, 108, 122, 185	4.7-8	**59-60**, 76, 94, 124, 184	8.3	118, 123, 145, 152, 201
2.17	43, 135	4.7	**60**, 70, 76, 123	8.4-6	116, 142
2.18-19	41, 198	4.8	57, 61, 77	8.4	**116-18**, 119, 122, 189, 190
2.18	37, **39**	4.9-10	**60-63**		
2.19	**39-41**	4.9	5, 58, 62, 69, 74, 75, 171, 174	8.5-6	114, **118-19**, 124, 147
2.20	2 n. 3, 37, **41-43**, 45, 51, 55, 186, 193, 198	4.10-11	63	8.5	32, 38, 125, 146, 152, 201
		4.10	59, 60, 66, 69, 120, 123, 174, 179, 186	8.6	114, 117, 125, 153, 162
2.21-22	**43-45**, 198	4.11-14	66, 110, 149	8.7-8	**119-21**, 124, 128, 134
2.21	37, 154, 155, 174	4.11-12	128		
2.22-25	93	4.11	**63-64**, 69, 76, 110, 128, 195, 202	8.7	169, 183
2.22	9, 33			8.8	122
2.23-25	33, **45-46**, 198, 203, 204			8.9-10	119, **121-22**, 128
		4.12-14	34, 68, 74, 204		
2.23	37, 203	4.12	63, **64-65**, 68, 70, 75, 83, 120, 195, 204	8.9	149
2.24-25	26			8.10	131, 190
2.25	11, 12			8.11	**123**, 131, 144, 178
3	1, 2, 3, 7 n. 12, 26, 47, 148, 166, 198, 203	4.13-14	10, 59, 62, 67, 74, 77, 94, 128, 159, 204	8.12-13	**123-24**
		4.13	55, 63, **65-66**	8.13	70, 125, 129, 130, 132, 162
3.1	**48**, 49, 201	4.14	5, 62, **64, 66**, 68, 69, 74, 111, 171, 196	8.14	**124-25**, 155, 184
3.2	8, **49**				
3.3-5	8, **49-52**			9	5, 11, 128, 129, 134, 147, 148, 151, 157, 179
3.4-5	56, 193	4.15-19	76		
3.4	2 n. 3	4.15	**66-67**, 76, 79, 140, 146		
3.5	2, 2 n. 3, 109				
4-11	3, 4, 54, 94, 166	4.16-19	66, 102, 121	9.1-9	126, 129
4-5.7	75	4.16	10, **67-68**, 69, 73, 82, 118, 119, 121, 129	9.1 4	131, 143
4	5, 8, 11, 31, 41, 47, **54**, 62, 63, 71, 75, 176			9.1-2	**127-28**, 141, 148
		4.17	64, **68-69**, 70, 82, 204	9.1	110, 126, 127, 132, 135, 138, 140, 148, 152
4.1-3	2 n. 3, **54-55**, 164	4.18-19	11, 195		
4.1	9, 44, 57, 78, 80, 83, 115, 170	4.18	60, 63, **69-70**, 73, 186	9.2	68, 110, 129, 155, 169
4.2	61, 67, 93, 101, 146	4.19	**70**, 73, 75, 83	9.3-6	158
		8	5, 10, 78, 119, 128, 129, 146, 153, 154, 189	9.3-4	127, **129-30**, 160
4.3	60, 93, 166			9.3	127, 131, 161, 162, 176
4.4-10	134				
4.4-9	66	8.1-9.9	131		
4.4	**55-56**, 60, 62, 67, 78, 83	8.1-4	146	9.4-6	146, 148, 176
		8.1-3	**114-16**, 131	9.4	114, 127, 140, 175, 176
4.5	31, **56-57**, 93, 177	8.1	6, 116, 123, 124, 132, 146	9.5	127, 130, 176
4.6-10	123	8.2-3	78	9.6-9	127

9.6	93, 122, 127, **130-31**, 133, 141, 148, 149, 162, 170	9.10	12, 16, 21, 93, 126, 134, 135-36, 137, 138, 140, 141, 143, 148, 150, 151, 152, 157, 158, 159, 161, 182, 185, 205		127, 135, **138-39**, 156, 158, 164, 189, 195, 201
9.7-9	6, 7, 72, 114, **131-33**, 134			9.15-17	127, 138, 158
9.7-8	177			9.15	114, 138, **139-40**, 148, 178
9.7	6, 8, 64, 131, 205				
		9.11-14	158	9.16	96, 136, **141**
9.8	72, 74, 114, 129, 141, 189	9.11-13	127	9.17	134, 139, **141**
		9.11	60, **136**, 137		
9.9	6, 73, 74, 123, 140, 150, 188	9.12	**136-37**, 138, 140		
9.10-17	57, 114, **134-35**	9.13	**137-38**, 156		
		9.14	7, 11, 123,		

www.ingramcontent.com/pod-product-compliance
Lightning Source LLC
Chambersburg PA
CBHW050143170426
43197CB00011B/1944